BREAKING POINT

A Journey to Self-Awareness
& Finding Purpose in Pain

A Memoir of
Sammy Wongan Kamara
As told to Carol Mills Kamara

ROCK PRESS

Breaking Point: A Journey to Self-Awareness & Finding Purpose in Pain
Copyright 2015 Rock Press
A division of ROCK, Inc. New York
www.RockReachesOut.org

All Rights Reserved

Editors:
Denis Ledoux – The Memoir Network, www.thememoirnetwork.com
Mary Rosenblum – The Writers Interface, www.newwritersinterface.com

Book Cover Design and interior formatting by Tugboat Design
www.tugboatdesign.net

No part of this book may be reproduced, translated, stored in a retrieval system, or transmitted, in any form or by any means, electronic, mechanical, photocopying, microfilming, recording, or otherwise, without written permission from the Publisher.

Printed in the United States of America

In an effort to reduce the possibility of human error and provide information that is respectful and sound, the authors and editors have checked sources believed to be reliable and the memoir checked for accuracy and credits given for work referenced.

I Can't Make You Love Me
Words and Music by Mike Reid and Allen Shamblin
Copyright (c) 1991 ALMO MUSIC CORP, UNIVERSAL MUSIC- MGB SONGS and BRIO BLUES MUSIC
All Rights Reserved
Used by Permission
Reprinted by Permission of Hal Leonard Corporation

Reprinted with the permission of Fireside, a Division of Simon & Schuster, Inc. from YESTERDAY I CRIED by Iyanla Vanzant. Copyright © 1998 Inner Visions Worldwide Network, Inc.

"You can accept or reject the way you are treated by other people, but until you heal the wounds of your past, you will continue to bleed. You can bandage the bleeding with food, with alcohol, with drugs, with work, with cigarettes, with sex, but eventually, it will all ooze through and stain your life. You must find the strength to open the wounds, stick your hands inside, pull out the core of the pain that is holding you in your past, the memories, and make peace with them."

— Iyanla Vanzant, *Yesterday, I Cried*

PRAISE FOR...

Breaking Point:
A Journey to Self-Awareness and Finding Purpose in Pain

Here at The New York Botanical Garden we are immensely proud of our colleague. Sammy Wongan Kamara. Sammy has worked here for 37 years and is a much-respected employee and friend. We know how strong and determined he has been in his own difficult life. We admire his commitment to the orphanage in Monrovia, Liberia, where the lives of children who have lost parents to war or AIDS have been saved through his grit, generosity, and fundraising. We hope Sammy will soon be able to arrange literacy education for the "adoptees", and after reading his memoir, perhaps you will be moved to support his nonprofit, *Reaching Out to Children with Kindness (R.O.C.K.)* at www.RockReachesOut.org.

- Gregory Long, President and CEO
The New York Botanical Garden

As a former vice president of The New York Botanical Garden, where Sam has been employed since his teen years, I have known Sam for over 25 years and learned of the numerous hardships encountered in his life from childhood and throughout his adult years. In the years of associating with Sam, I was not only intrigued with his life experiences, different from many of his peers, but his quest to make his life whole through his religious convictions and the dedication to his family both here and in Liberia is worthy of admiration to the extreme. In his memoir, *Breaking Point*, he takes us through the unique journey of his life.

-Bob Heinisch
(Former) Vice President of Security and Operations
New York Botanical Garden, Bronx, New York

As you will read in this book, Sammy Kamara has achieved something extraordinary. He has significantly improved his difficult medical condition through lifestyle change, faith and strength of spirit. Through the years that I have treated him, he has opened my eyes to this possibility, and I believe that his book stands as a testament to the importance of a holistic approach to meeting life's challenges.

- Sheryl Haut, M.D.
Professor of Clinical Neurology & Director, Adult Epilepsy
Montefiore Medical Center – Albert Einstein College of Medicine
Bronx, New York

As Vice President of Security and Operations at the New York Botanical Garden where Sammy serves as a Maintainer, I have had the pleasure of knowing Sammy for many years. During this time, I have come to know his story and appreciate the hard road he has had to follow. In *Breaking Point*, he has written a memoir that tells the story of overcoming the hardships that plagued him for so many years and creating a life for himself. From the many losses and brokenness in this life, he seeks wholeness. In the end, this is a story about coming to terms with life, forgiving and loving.

- Mark Cupkovic
Vice President of Security and Operations
The New York Botanical Garden
Bronx, New York

Sam Kamara has not had an easy life. In *Breaking Point*, he writes a stirring memoir about his life's beginnings in a bush village in Liberia. Then we see him being taken to Monrovia and New York City—in both cities working in conditions that resemble slavery. A debilitating disease, an unhappy marriage of more than two decades, a civil war in his homeland, a conflict with the church he served generously for many years, all sapped his energy, but through it all, Sam managed to remain hopeful and cheerful. Finally, we see him settled in a happy relationship, being honored for his commitment to the New York Botanical Garden where I first met him and found that he is a brother in Jesus Christ. What a conscientious worker he has been there. I am so glad that he has been reunited to the family he lost in Liberia and returned to the fold of his church. *Breaking Point* is a story of a hero's journey and is a great read.

- Professor Sir Ghillean Prance FRS
Former Director, Royal Botanic Gardens, Kew, UK

The life that Sammy Kamara has lived is so incredibly different form that which most of us have known that the only way to appreciate it is to read his memoir, *Breaking Point*. Sammy is sent by his parents to Monrovia at the age of 7 to live with an uncle so as to receive an education. What ensues is tragic. Sammy is passed on from one callous person to another—always being made to work and treated abusively—until he ends up taken to New York City against his will and without his parents' knowledge or consent, made to work for nothing and finally thrown out on the street. How he salvages his life and makes something of it is the subject of this engrossing memoir. He is a modern day Joseph on a mission to help his people in Liberia.

- Dr. Cosley Buckley
Senior Pastor, Hope for Generation

DEDICATED TO...

My beloved parents Zlahn and Guataye Wongan, and my foster parents Reuben and Edris Johnson, who loved and cared for me as best they could. Their imprints are all over my life. They all died too soon.

My four dear children, words cannot describe the joy you all bring to my life. My love for you lives on.

My darling wife, Carol, who adds laughter and richness to my life every day.

TABLE OF CONTENTS

Foreword	1
Introduction	5

PART ONE: Life in Liberia — 9
1. Life in the Village of Teahplay — 11
2. Misery in Monrovia — 22
3. The Unexpected is Always Happening — 34
4. Crossing the Atlantic Ocean — 47

PART TWO: The Land of Opportunity & Struggles — 59
5. Nightmare — 61
6. Rescued at Sea — 68
7. Beginning to Work — 77
8. Small Successes — 86
9. Lost Family — 91
10. Oh Happy Day! — 98

PART THREE: Bitter-sweet Waters — 107
11. Holy Matrimony Without Sweet Communion — 109
12. Family in Liberia — 120
13. Marriage versus Family — 128
14. Reunion — 132
15. Mama — 141
16. What is a Christian Marriage? — 147

17. Mixed Blessings	154
18. Solace	159
19. Uncoupling	168
20. Dad's Turn	178
21. God Keeps Silence	187

PART FOUR: The Search for New Meaning in Life — 197

22. Looking for Answers	199
23. The Death of a Marriage	210
24. A New Day	219
25. Serious Conversations	228
26. Engagement	237
27. Learning to be Married	247
28. Dreams and Plans	254
29. The Road to Teahplay	263
30. Heartbreaking News	280

Epilogue: An Important Milestone — 303
Appendix: Finding Purpose in Pain – the Mission of — 313
Reaching Out to Children with Kindness (R.O.C.K.) Foundation

FOREWORD

This Book — *Breaking Point: A Journey to Self-Awareness and Finding Purpose in Pain* — is about life. It is the candid, uncensored, and deeply moving account of the life of Sammy Kamara. I want to start my introduction to this poignant memoir with a few quotes about life.

George Bernard Shaw — "Life isn't about finding yourself. Life is to create yourself." *Abraham Lincoln* — "In the end, it's not the years in your life that count. It's the life in your years." *Cesare Pavese* — "We do not remember days, we remember moments." *Eminem* — "The truth is you don't know what is going to happen tomorrow. Life is a crazy ride, and nothing is guaranteed."

Sammy takes us through the seasons of his life. There were times he was completely lost; without anyone on whom he could securely depend, or anyone with whom he felt connected. These are basic to the self-development and personal growth of everyone. Sammy went without this for a good part of his early life. One would think that during this time his focus would have been on taking care of himself but indeed, it was a time when life was creating the Sammy we know today.

Sammy had more experiences in the early years of his life than most adults encounter in a lifetime. But in the end, "it's not the years in your life that count it's the life in your years". So during all this time, what did Sammy learn from his experiences? How did these experiences shape him? How did these experiences contribute to where he is in life today?

You will learn that his early years were tumultuous. But despite the difficulties, was there any life in those years? I would argue that there was life. If Sammy's early years had been void of life, he would not be here today. By the time Sammy reached age 13, in comparison to many adults, he had lived a full, but very difficult life. So it was those years — that short lifespan — that shaped him into who he is today. It was the life in those years that formed him.

I am sure that there are many, many events in his early years that he recalls. You will see a detailed description of many of his early encounters. However, it goes without question that among the masses of memories, there are significant moments that are etched on his mind, spirit, and emotions. These are the life-changing encounters that have played significant roles in shaping Sammy into the man he is today. It is quite possible that, he remembers location of these important experiences, the time of year, who was involved, and other details. But more than anything else, it is the flavor of those moments; the impact of those experiences that really matters. It is the impact of these experiences that he recalls the best.

If anyone knows that life is full of surprises, it's Sammy. He has the right to say that life is one crazy experience after another. But he also has the right to say, "I overcame them".

You will experience the full range of emotions as you read this memoir. Be prepared to feel angry, sad, happy, disappointed, fearful, and even ashamed. When an innocent child suffers gross injustice at the hands of those who should protect him, deep emotional responses are guaranteed.

This memoir is full of life lessons. Sammy teaches us that life can either make or break us, depending on what we make of it. He teaches us that family and relationships are far more important than treasures. He also teaches that we must have something for which we live. We cannot stroll through life from one season to the next without purpose. One thing that kept Sammy from cowering under the pressures of life was purpose. Another very important lesson is the importance of having God in our lives.

Sammy lived his life guided by these principles, and they got him through what one would call hell on earth. If Sammy did it, you can too. Your situation may not be as bad or it may even be worse. Despite the situation, learn from this memoir that life creates *you*, and no matter how dark your life is, there is life in it. Tapping into that life depends solely on you. Sammy came through his dark times and you can, too.

Rosemarie Downer, Ph.D.

Books written by Dr. Downer

The High Call of Forgiveness. It's A Mandate
A divine revelation of the mind of God, filled with spiritual and practical nuggets written for our inspiration, edification, and transformation.

The Self-Scarred Church
Healing for the Seven Most Damaging Self-Inflicted Wounds to the Church

Homelessness and Its Consequences:
The Impact on Children's Psychological Well-being (Children of Poverty)
Children's psychological well-being as a function of housing status and process resources in low-income families

INTRODUCTION

"Let the redeemed of the Lord say so, whom he hath redeemed from the hands of the enemy'"
- Psalm 107:2

This book arises out of my life experience, my painful struggle to discover who I am, and my fierce determination to hold on to the affection and instruction of my biological parents, as well as my faith in God. For many years, I spent most of my time and talents striving to survive instead of thriving. My intellectual abilities and my imagination were stifled. I can only dream of what I could have been. How I survived to cross over into the land of self-awareness, I will never fully know, but I know for sure that, during the first six years of my life, my poor, uneducated parents gave me something that has stayed with me throughout my life.

Some may wonder why I would want to expose my life to the glare of public scrutiny and to intrusive or unkind comments. I've chosen to share my feelings and to tell my story as I've lived it, not because I want to avenge myself on people who treated me poorly, but because I want to bear witness to my parents' dreams, and to my survival. I also want to say that there is a path to healing and restoration for those who have experienced trauma in their lives. It is possible not only to survive but to thrive. My wish is that the telling of my story will bring hope to those who would have otherwise despaired and given up.

In this book, I share lessons that I learned on my journey to self-awareness. I often wish I could go back to my youthful days when my life held so much promise. Retrospection and introspection have provided insights that make me think of so many things that I would do differently or not at all. But I thank God that there are some things that I now can do better. There are so many scars that I cannot erase, but I rejoice that they are mostly scars and not scabs. Scars are reminders of a past hurt but scabs still hurt. Even as recently as the mid-2000s, I have to admit that some memories were still scabs.

Hidden in the recesses of my soul was a giant anger that was stronger than I could imagine. I didn't start understanding the degree of its strength until after my divorce and my rejection by my own church. I'm not fully healed of that anger, but I'm in a better place, a joyful place. I am content. May you find my stories useful on your own journey to greater self-awareness.

Reaching a breaking point affects our mental, physical, spiritual, and emotional health and can lead to two different outcomes. At the breaking point, a person can feel overwhelmed, burnt out, emotionally wounded, resentful, and hopeless. This can manifest itself in irritability, depression, angry outbursts, and suicidal or even homicidal feelings. If the stressors remain constant and unabated, they could result in a break that leads to self-destruction or to the destruction of others. But, a breaking point can result in a positive outcome: an awakening of self-awareness or self-understanding. Self-awareness is indeed a journey.

Soren Kierkegaard, a Danish philosopher and theologian, made an insightful commentary about awareness when he said, *"We live life forward, but we only understand it backward."* It is only in hindsight, after the fact, that we see what we should have done, the stupid mistakes we made, the heartbreaks we could have avoided. As we look back, we begin to understand our experiences. Our values, beliefs, attitudes, and this new understanding all affect our thinking, our behaviors, and our relationships. We also understand better how others perceive us and whether we should let their perception of us affect us in any way.

Self-awareness is born out of a self-reflection that gradually and eventually results in a willingness to accept feedback. We become less guarded and less afraid of being vulnerable. We learn to become more transparent, more honest with ourselves and others. We become authentic and therefore live real, unpretentious lives.

I challenge you to make good use of a *breaking point* in your own life, that point where the tension is greatest. That is the time to turn to self-reflection and self-knowledge, the time when you no longer live solely by the dictates of others. The truth is, we all have one life to live and we should not die with an unlived life. A lack of self-awareness at your *breaking point* can eclipse your potential and steal joy from your life. Your *breaking point* is an opportunity to learn to spend your one life by your own rules. Charles de Lint makes a disturbing observation: *"We're so quick to cut away pieces of ourselves to suit a particular relationship, a job, a circle of friends, incessantly editing who we are until we fit in."* Stop carving yourself to fit other peoples' molds just to fit in. Rather, be your best self because that is who you were meant to be.

That is what a b*reaking point* can teach you, if you make good use of it.

Some people like me learn to be our best selves late in our lives, and we do so after we have been broken, after we have failed, after hurt, after much loss. Chuck Swindoll, the famous expository preacher, on his program *Insight for Living*, asked a very thought-provoking question, *"What does it take to be wise?"* He answered by stating that he had seen many brilliant and talented young people but he had never encountered a wise young person. Swindoll suggested that wisdom comes through lived experiences, through brokenness, through hurt, and through loss.

Not everyone learns from their experiences, but religion and divorce can be powerful teachers of wisdom. They, combined with other experiences, have made me wiser than I otherwise would have been. The Scripture says whoever lacks wisdom should ask God for it. If we choose to ask God for wisdom, how does God give us wisdom? Does he hand it to us on a platter, or do we acquire wisdom through the experiences that God allows?

This book is full of experiences that God allowed in my life. It is an accurate telling of the circumstances of my life. However, I have not used the actual names of some individuals in consideration of their privacy.

PART ONE:
LIFE IN LIBERIA

Chapter 1

Life in the Village of Teahplay

"Birth is the sudden opening of a window, through which you look out upon a stupendous prospect. For what has happened? A miracle! You have exchanged nothing for the possibility of everything."
— William-MacNeile Dixon

Most parents are willing to move heaven and earth to give their children a life better than the one they lived. My poor, illiterate parents were no different. They desired a better life for me and our family so they conceived a grand plan that shaped the course of my life.

I was born Gontor Wongan in the village of Teahplay, Liberia, West Africa, on September 3, 1958. My father's first name *Zlahn* means "the Almighty God", and his surname *Wongan* means "Root" or "the beginning of Judgment". Zlahn and Wongan together make for an ambitious name. Some may even think it's presumptuous to give a child a first name that means "the Almighty God." However, when I was a child, for me, my father had the status of a mighty person. He might not have been almighty but he *was* mighty. His over sixfoot height meant I and others had to look upward when addressing him. He was lean, with a flat belly, but he was muscular and would carry loads of produce from the farm on his shoulders. People say that when I am upset my eyes and nostrils widen. If this is so, then I must have inherited those traits from my father because his eyes and nostrils would always widen whenever he was upset. Papa, or *Dah* as I addressed him in our Gio dialect, was usually serious. If you didn't know him, you would think he wore a constant frown on his face. He didn't laugh much and was a man of few words, but he was friendly, with a deep and commanding bass voice.

Farming was how he and my mother fed the family. There were no handouts or other forms of help from the government. If my parents didn't work, we wouldn't eat. I was amazed at how hard Mama worked, because she was so slender. Her name, *Guataye*, which means "small or flat belly", was a perfect description of her. The opposite of my father, she was an extrovert, with a ready smile and encouraging words. I could always count on her to scold me in private and not in the glare of the public's eye. She was firm but gentle and would only spank me after she had given me three warnings. Papa, on the other hand, spanked me only once and didn't have to spank me again. I learned my lesson quickly. After that spanking, he only needed to look at me. That look was his rod of correction.

Mama and Papa loved each other very much. Her nickname was *Naar*, and I loved to hear Papa call her that. At the time I was born, I had only one sibling, a sister named Tolema. We were the pride and joy of our parents' lives and they were our first teachers in this university of life.

Teahplay is a little-known village in Nimba County. Located in the northeastern part of Liberia, Nimba County is bordered by Guinea on the north and Côte d'Ivoire, or the Ivory Coast, on the east. The county is one of fifteen in Liberia, and its residents belong to the Gio and Mano tribes. Ninety-five percent of Liberia's population is comprised of various ethnic groups and indigenous African tribes: Kpelle, Bassa, Gio Kru, Grebo, Mano, Krahn, Gola, Gbandi, Loma, Kissi, Vai, Dei, Bella, Mandingo, and Mende. These tribes play intricate roles in Liberia's ethnic and linguistic history and culture.

Americo-Liberians make up the other five percent of the population.

They are descendants of former slaves who emigrated from the United States of America or the Caribbean to Liberia.[i] Although English is the official language and is used in schools and universities as well as in government and businesses, Liberia's linguistic composition includes at least sixteen tribal dialects or languages.

The name *Teahplay* means "Steel Town" or "Town of Steel". One would think that steel was manufactured in the village, but it was not. The name derives from our forefathers' reputation for being fierce warriors who demonstrated an iron, or rather steel will in the battles they fought for their survival. After bellowing the war chant, the men were willing and ready to defend their families and the village at any cost. Notwithstanding this history, I didn't experience aggression or war in the village. Instead the villagers displayed their "steel" through strength of will and endurance, especially the men. In fact, the villagers were very peaceful and friendly people who looked out for each other's well-being and whose elders and chiefs provided justice and leadership.

We lived in single-room huts made of wattle and daub construction. Wattle and daub is a process wherein thin branches are woven together and held by a mixture of mud, clay and chalk or limestone dust, then plastered to make the huts waterproof. The roofs were of thatch and had pointed tops. The huts were scattered throughout the village without fences to separate them, nor did the doors have locks. The huts were, however, grouped together by lineage, and it was clear where each extended family lived. Each quarter had a "quarter chief", who was the oldest male of the family or the one with the strongest, most aggressive, or most warrior-like traits. My grandfather was the chief of the Wongan quarter.

Villagers moved easily from one hut to the other, and everyone knew everyone's names and business. Those who had had the good fortune to have traveled outside of the village to the city dreamed of one day having a "city" house, built of cement cinder blocks with a shiny zinc roof.

My sister, Tolema, was four years old when I was born. She was the most beautiful girl I knew and she was fun to be with. Liberia is predominantly a patriarchal society, so when I was born, my parents celebrated because I was the first boy and would carry on the Wongan name and the lineage of my father. Notwithstanding, Tolema was still valuable to our family and the village. Not only would she eventually play the roles of mother and homemaker, but she would also become a productive member of the village workforce, farming; carrying water, wood, and food from the farms.

Tolema and I loved to play with each other as well as with the other children in the village. Rainy days were our favorite play time. Liberia is a rain-forest country with distinct dry and rainy seasons. When it rained in the village, it really rained; the rain drops were big and it was as though someone was pouring very large containers of water on our heads. We would run around, dance, jump, scream, and laugh in the rain. Sometimes, the girls would take off their *lappas,* or body wraps, and the boys would shed their bombor or loincloth. The female breasts were never covered, the lappas were wrapped below them, and the girls and women would often take off their *lappas*, leaving on only their under cloth, which covered their genitals. The bombor or loincloth was a long length of cloth which passed between our thighs to cover our buttocks and genitals; it was wrapped around the waist and tied in the back to create a pouch. We enjoyed playing football, or soccer as it is called in the USA. Unlike the sturdy round balls that I see nowadays in New York City, our balls were oranges or limes.

In the village, we had a wide range of delightful foods to choose from, whenever they were available. Life was hard during the rainy season, when my parents and the other villagers were unable to walk through the jungle mud to get to the farms. Otherwise we had rice, cassava, corn, papayas, bananas, mangoes, and oranges, as well as meats such as chicken, goat, pork, snails, groundhog, and large field rats. Every day we ate generous portions of rice with classic West African *Palava;* savory sauces made with fish, chicken or some other kind of meat, hot chili pepper, and ginger. Rice with *Palava* sauce and *baa*, soft dough made from cassava and dipped in soup were my favorite foods. Meals were cooked in a large iron pot. Dinner was a family affair, and when dinner was ready, Mama would call us. All our family members gathered around and ate with their hands from the same pot or the same large bowl. Mama always asked me if I had eaten enough, and usually encouraged me to eat more.

There were no schools in the village. Instead, parents would take their young children to the farms to observe or participate in the family business. Each morning before leaving our hut for the farm, Mama would give Tolema and me plantains, leftover rice, or cassava for breakfast. We had to walk about a quarter of a mile through the jungle. During the day, while our parents worked, we watched them or helped with the chores they gave us. The machetes that my parents carried were extremely sharp, and they used them skillfully. Finally, it would be time for lunch, which often consisted of roasted corn, cassava, and mangoes.

As a child, I had no fear, but my parents, who knew about danger, often warned us to stay close to their sides because they feared we would be bitten by a poisonous snake. We didn't have tigers, lions, or any of those other big predators, but we had snakes, snakes that could kill. One evening when we were returning home, my father grabbed my hand. "Don't move," he whispered. A few inches from me, a large snake lay in the narrow trail ahead of us. I am not sure how he did it, but with what seemed to be one swift move, my father swung his machete and cut the snake in two. Tolema screamed, but Mama held her safely.

A few days before Tolema's ninth birthday, while we were all on the farm, she started crying nonstop. Mama and Papa decided to leave the farm early to take her home. I had never seen my sister cry so much or so long.

"Tolema, what's wrong? Tell me," I pleaded with her repeatedly, but she never answered. That night, Mama told me Tolema had a high fever. As was the custom, Mama consulted with the village "doctors" for help. These village doctors weren't trained in the medical field but they were skilled in bush medicine and knew the right plant for the right illness. Then there were also those who worked witchcraft and believed that witchcraft was a potent remedy for certain situations.

The Gio tribe believes that a Supreme God created the world including human beings but they also believe that this Supreme God is unreachable and so they do not worship that god directly. Because the Supreme God is too holy and unreachable, communication with him has to be mediated. Thus the villagers believed that a lesser spirit called *Du* works as a mediator between the Supreme God and themselves. *Du* lives in each person and is the spirit of the person. My parents held this belief also, and so they practiced ancestral worship in which the spirits of our dead family members are honored and consulted for help and guidance. Along with giving Tolema the bush medicine, Mama pleaded with our ancestors' spirits to help her daughter, my beloved sister. But early the next day the unthinkable happened. Tolema died.

Tolema was dead!

My little five-year-old mind tried to understand what that meant. Mama told me that Tolema was gone to be with our ancestors, so Tolema's body would be buried in the ground later that day.

"Why did she leave us to go with the ancestors? Didn't she like to be with us? Tell her to come back," I begged Mama.

"She can't come back, Gontor," Mama said.

I always believed Mama. She would not lie to me, and now she was telling me that Tolema wouldn't come back. What did she know that she wasn't telling me? Why couldn't Tolema come back? No one had answers for my childhood questions. I just knew that Tolema left behind a big taste of sorrow. Every time I remembered her, which was often, I cried. I was now my parents' only child. Although there were many children in the village with whom I could play, playtime was not the same without Tolema.

Mama got pregnant in 1963, the same year that Tolema died. She had a baby boy in August of the following year. Papa named him George Wongan. George was not given a Gio first name because Papa had decided to follow the new trend of giving Gio babies English names as a sign of prestige.

My parents were not afraid to work hard but depending solely on the small crops they planted had locked us into a life of abject poverty, with no hope for a better life. In 1964, the year George was born, the dry season lasted longer than usual, resulting in a severe shortage of food in Teahplay and other nearby villages. Borrowing from other villagers to tide us over through this difficult time was not an option because they, too, were in desperate need of food. As peasant farmers, we didn't have enough crops to sell for money, and even if we had, there were no trade routes or markets available to us.

"Naar, I have to go to the Ivory Coast to look for food," Papa said to Mama. "I can't stand by and watch my family die from hunger."

"Zlahn, do what you have to do. Are you going to take us with you?" she asked.

"No, Naar, I'm going alone. Stay with the boys. I won't be long."

The *Nuon River* separates Liberia from the Ivory Coast. Anyone leaving Liberia for the Ivory Coast just had to take a short swim, or a ten-minute ride on a raft or canoe to cross over into the Ivory Coast. The Ivory Coast is a bigger country than Liberia and has trade routes for merchandise that were not present in Liberia at that time. While Papa was gone, Mama breast-fed George and she and I ate cassava and chicken soup. Cassava was the crop that best withstood the dry season but we only had enough to last for two more days. Fortunately, Papa returned later that day with rice, cassava, plantains, and other goodies. I don't know where he got them, because Mama said he had no money. The following day, Papa and I fished in the *Nuon River*. Papa was an expert fisherman and would always come back home with a big catch of various kinds of seafood. That day, we caught about seven fish and some crabs.

Papa's method of teaching me about endurance and survival

remains in my memory. When I was about six years old, on our way back from the farm, he took me to the Nuon River. It was very hot and so Papa dived from the river bank into the river. He loved to swim and would always invite me to join him in the water but I was afraid of the water and always ran away. This time, however, I didn't run because Mama was with us and, although I felt safe with my father, I knew Mama would not take the kinds of risks Papa took.

"Come in, boy!" Papa shouted.

I was scared to go into the water so I pretended that I didn't hear even though he shouted the command repeatedly.

"Come in boy!" he yelled more loudly, still smiling.

He was smiling, but my little mind didn't trust his smile. It was only after Mama encouraged me that I moved closer to the water.

"Gontor, go ahead. It will be ok," she urged.

With Mama's assurance, I jumped into the water. In retrospect, I don't know what I was thinking because I couldn't swim, I just trusted Mama when she said everything would be ok. When I jumped in, I immediately started swallowing water. I tried desperately to stand but had nothing to stand on so I went under; father grabbed me then held me under my belly.

"You're going to learn to swim today," he said.

My fear of water returned, and I started protesting, but Papa ignored my pleas.

"You can make it, and you will make it today," he insisted.

He made me stretch my legs out and told me to move my arms. I did as he instructed and felt a little relief from my fear knowing that he was holding me. That day, because Papa would not let me quit, I learned to float and swim. Not quitting was also his lesson, when he taught me how to hunt animals and birds.

The Firestone Tire Company ran plantations in a more developed village many miles away from Teahplay and needed men to harvest its rubber. Men came from all over to seek the seasonal jobs available. Papa's work on our farm was not sufficient to feed our family, but he had committed to raising a family and he would not renege on his commitment. He used to say: *"A man is a man that can withstand the storm, whatever the storm may be."* These words never left me; I can even hear him say them now. About two months after George's birth, Papa left the village to search for work on one of the Firestone plantations. Mama explained that he was trying to make life better for our family. Two of his younger brothers, Mangon and Kayee, had already left the village in search of a better life. They had been recruited by the government, which had sent out messages to the Zone Chiefs of the various villages in the Counties, asking for young men who were willing to join the military or the police force. The government promised them a city job with training and, when they retired, a pension.

Uncle Mangon who had changed his Gio name to Samuel, was now working as a soldier in the Liberian Army, and Uncle Kayee, who had become Henry, was an officer in the Liberian Police Band. Because they had accepted the government's job offer, they were able to enjoy a better life than we did. Papa hadn't gone because he was much older than his brothers and, unlike them, he had a family in the village. He continued to farm and, now that things had gotten worse, he left in October 1964 to find work. The LAMCO Iron Ore Mining Company was also looking for men, and Papa felt that he would find employment in one or the other company.

Working on the rubber plantation and in the mine was backbreaking, slave work. Papa lived on the plantation and was away from us for such a long time that I began to think that I would never see him again, but Mother kept reminding me that he would soon return, and that our lives would be better. The plantation owners didn't give time off, there was no sick leave, and definitely no vacation time so, if Papa came to visit, it would mean time away from work and time away from keeping his word to feed his family. I missed my father so much, but mother did her best to care for us. I slept with her arm under me each night, went wherever she went, and helped to care for my baby brother. I had made new friends since Tolema's death, and started playing in the village again.

When Papa returned to the village in April 1965, a few months before my 7th birthday, I was very glad to see him, but Papa's meagre wage was unable to change our lives. The only thing that changed was that Mama now had some help with the work on the farm. He went back to working on the farm and took a very special interest in teaching me the skills that he said I would need. Before he left for the plantation again, he had taught me how to use a sling shot and how to set traps for animals. Papa insisted that I had to learn these things because one day I would be a man. Furthermore, he repeatedly advised me that *"A man is a man that can withstand the storm, whatever the storm may be."* Mama's efforts to teach me household chores also took on a sense of urgency. While teaching me she would say *"You have to learn to take care of yourself, because we won't always be with you."* In addition to working on the farm, Mama would cook, wash, and clean—skills that she passed on to me. I would beat the clothes on the rocks or washboard to make them clean and help her as she deemed fit. I loved being with Mama, as she showed such great care and patience when she was teaching me. By the time I was seven years old I was more skilled in domestic chores than most children twice my age.

Without my knowing it, my parents were preparing me for something that would change my life forever.

Brothers - George and Mark, and Mama- Guataye Wongan

Zlahn R. Wongan - Papa

Village Life in the 1960s

Chapter 2

Misery in Monrovia

"The Promised Land always lies on the other side of a Wilderness"
—Havelock Ellis

"Gontor, you are going to school," Papa said, one day, while we were taking a break on the farm to roast corn and cassava.

"School? What is school? Where is school?" I asked. My entire world was the village. As a seven year old, I couldn't imagine that there was a bigger game than Teahplay, but Papa was speaking excitedly about possibilities that would create a better life for our family.

"Well, when I went away to work on the plantations, I also went into Monrovia and stayed with your Uncle Henry for a week," he said. "Uncle Henry said that you could live with him and go to school. The city is beautiful. You will love it. You can learn English and be like one of the important people."

Mama must have seen the frightened look on my face. I had never been away from her or the village and I couldn't see myself being anywhere without her.

"Gontor, you don't have to be afraid," she said quickly. "You won't be with strangers. You will be with your family. Do you remember we told you about your Uncle Henry who is in the Police Band in the city?"

Papa had taught me to believe that I was a warrior and so I always tried to look fierce and unafraid whenever he was around me. He was staring at me now, and I felt as if I had to be tough and had to agree with him that I would be, as I can see now, the anointed and appointed savior of our family. But I couldn't do it alone.

"Ok," I said. "But Mama, I want you and George to come live with me."

"No, Gontor," she said. "I can't leave the village now, but I will come to look for you. And don't worry your little head; your Uncle Henry will take good care of you. He's family, and family takes care of family."

For some reason, I did not leave right away for Monrovia and life with Uncle Henry. In fact, that did not happen for a while, and I often forgot about what my parents had told me. Then, in November 1965, Mama packed a bag with my belongings. It wasn't much, but she told me that Uncle Henry would take care of the rest. Papa would stay with George and work the farm and other members of the family would assist while she brought me to Monrovia.

Just as the day was dawning, Mama and I left the village. She said we would go to the village of Garnta, the closest point from which to get transportation into Monrovia. The only path leading out of Teahplay was a muddy, unpaved 4-foot-wide trail with thick jungle on either side. The first day we only walked for about seven hours, but it seemed like days before we reached Garnta. And what a welcome relief when we did!

In town, we found a lineup of four "taxis" operated by individuals who made a living transporting people in their private vehicles.

"Monrovia! This car going to Monrovia!" one man was shouting. Besides him, there were three other drivers looking for passengers—one with a car and two with minivans. The driver who called out to us first already had two persons sitting in the front of the vehicle and three persons in the back.

"Come in, mother!" he beckoned to Mama.

"No, lady, come, we have more space!" another driver shouted. I don't know what factored into Mama's decision, but she chose the first car. There we were all eight of us in the packed car on our day-long journey to face whatever the City of Monrovia promised us.

When we got out of the car and stepped onto the crowded streets of Monrovia, I was not at all excited. Instead, I was afraid. "Mama, I want to go back with you," I whispered in her ear.

"Gontor, you know you can't. Remember we talked about it?" She looked directly into my eyes as she spoke. I could feel the tears beginning to form. A profound sadness suddenly engulfed me, and I knew I couldn't do what my parents asked me to do. I couldn't stay in a strange place with strange people for an unknown period of time.

"Mama, don't leave me. Please," I pleaded with her, the tears streaming down my face now. Mama didn't look at me. Instead she stared straight ahead of her with a blank expression.

"Mama, please take me back with you."

Mama didn't answer me, but she knelt on the rough cement sidewalk and hugged me tightly. She was crying, too.

"Gontor, I love you," she said. "You know I love you. Tell me you know I love you."

"Mama, I love you, too," I sobbed.

"No, Gontor! Tell me you know I love you! Tell me!" Her voice got louder as if she was angry with me.

"I know you love me," I answered between sobs. What was happening to Mama? Almost as soon as her apparent anger at me appeared, it disappeared. She hugged me very tightly, making it difficult for me to breathe.

"Gontor, I will be thinking about you every minute of every day." She was looking directly in my eyes again. "I will mention your name to our ancestors and I will come to look for you."

"Mama, I don't..." She didn't let me finish.

"Sssh, Gontor! It's going to work out. Things will be better for all of us," she tried to assure me. "You are going to play a big part. You are

going to help make life better."
Mama seemed so sure. She must be right. I believed her.
"I love you, Mama," I said, still crying.
"I won't be leaving right away, Gontor," Mama said. "I will stay with you a few days to help you adjust to living here. Come; let's go in to see your uncle."

Mama seemed to know the way to Uncle Henry's house. We walked through Monrovia until we reached a little cement house, and Mama went up to it. As soon as she knocked on the door, it opened, and a man stood looking at us.

"Hey, Naar, you made it!" He seemed excited.

"Hi, Henry," mother greeted him.

"And this is little Gontor? Your papa told me all about you. Come on in. Welcome to my home."

Mama and I followed him, with the small bag that she carried. When we entered the house, Uncle Henry introduced us to his family. We met his wife, Martha, and then his son, Patrick, who was about two years old. Patrick was never given a Gio name.Mama stayed at Uncle Henry's house for four days. During the day, Martha and Patrick were at the house; however, they spent the nights at Martha's family's house because uncle only had one bedroom in his house. Both Uncle Henry and Aunt Martha were very kind to us. They made sure that we had food to eat and asked us frequently if we were ok. In the mornings, Uncle Henry left early to go to his work as a policeman whereas we stayed in the yard all day.

"Mama, I miss my friends," I complained.

"I know, but you will meet new friends," she replied. "I will tell your friends in Teahplay that you are ok." Having her with me made me feel safe. I made myself believe that she would stay in the city but my delusion was short-lived. Early one morning, Mama called me to a corner of the yard.

"Gontor, I'm leaving today," she said. I simply looked at her, not knowing what to say. I didn't know how to make her change her mind about me staying in the city. Pretending that I was very sick came to mind, but I quickly dismissed it because I hated lying to Mama.

"Did you hear me?" She was looking directly into my eyes. I nodded. Mama was my security blanket now it was being taken away from me for an undetermined time. Uncle Henry and his wife had been kind to me, but I felt I belonged in Teahplay with Papa, Mama, George, and my friends.

"Mama, when will you come back to look for me?" that wasn't what I wanted to ask her, but those were the words that escaped my lips. It seemed as if Mama really wanted me to stay, and I didn't want to disappoint her. She seemed so sad already, I didn't want her to cry again. If I stayed I would stay because my staying would make her happy. It would make her dream come true.

She smiled. I smiled with her and she hugged me again, as though she didn't want to let me go. I promised myself that I would be strong for Mama but the tears started forming in my eyes again. Mama wiped away her tears and tried to speak but no words came. We kept hugging each other while our tears flowed.

"Soon, Gontor. I'll come back very soon," she said with a smile.

For weeks after Mama's departure, a profound and abiding loneliness and sadness rested on me. I didn't feel like eating and I cried myself to sleep every night. During the day, I would sit by myself outside in the yard of the little cement house and as soon as it was dark again, I would find my corner on the floor inside Uncle's one bedroom house. Uncle Henry would check on me when he came home from work, and when he noticed my sadness, he would encourage me to "be a man".

But, I didn't seem to be able to stop crying. One night he heard me.

"Sammy, what's wrong with you now?" he asked. "Why you crying?"

"I miss Mama and Papa and George," I replied.

"Stop the crying and go to your bed," he ordered me. "I don't want no crying in here. I need to sleep." That night, I tried very hard not to cry but I couldn't stop the tears and I couldn't stop sobbing.

"You hear me! Stop crying like you're a girl!" he yelled at me. "Be a man!" It appeared that, to my uncle, being a man meant not showing any emotions.

"Don't let me have to make you stop the noise in here," he warned. "Go to sleep." I don't know when I fell asleep, but when I awoke, it was daylight and Uncle had left for work. Aunt Martha frowned at me. "Sammy, you can't keep us awake at nights. Your uncle is not going to put up with it."

"I want my mother," I said to her. "I want my mother."

"Forget about your mother. Wasn't she the one that brought you here? Well, she brought you here for a reason. Remember, you're going to school!"

"I don't want to go to school. I want to go home." My tears started to flow again.

"Sammy, you'd better stop that crying," she warned. "Your uncle can't stand crying. Furthermore, you are a boy. Don't be a sissy with all this crying." I heard her, but not even the memory of Papa's word's, *"A man is a man that can withstand the storm, whatever the storm may be,"* could soothe me. I remember crying most of that day and that night with nothing to comfort me.

My unabated sadness irritated Uncle Henry and Aunt Martha. Instead of consoling me and seeing me for the child I was, instead of responding to me as parents would, they turned on me and shouted, "You are an ungrateful boy!"

Hadn't Papa asked his youngest brother to "take care of my boy as if it were I taking care of him"? Now, Uncle did not treat me at all as if he were my father, but started a reign of terror over me. Within a short time after my arrival at Uncle's house, he was beating me viciously almost daily for no reason that I could think of, except that he must have hated my father and also me. As far as my uncle was concerned, Papa was just a poor illiterate farmer from a remote and backward village, and worst of all, Papa was dark skinned. These were terrible deficits in my uncle's eyes. Since I, too, was black and needy, I reminded him of what he despised. His contempt for me was demonstrated in the ways he isolated and beat me. He would beat me with his belt or with his heavy hand. He couldn't have beaten the son of his enemy any more than he beat me. I learned quickly to always be careful around him, careful not to look at him when he spoke to me, careful not to ask questions, careful not to speak, careful not to move, careful not to breathe, lest it might upset him.

Since I couldn't speak English and English was necessary if I was to attend school, Uncle Henry created an accelerated learning track for me and became my teacher. Since he had no training and little intuition for teaching, his methodology was rigid and crude. Thinking of it now, I can understand his motive for wanting me to learn English quickly. After all, English is the official language in Liberia and the language used in the schools; it was logical that I should learn the language. But my uncle spoke to me in a mixture of Gio, our tribal dialect, and what I assumed at the time was the language he was trying to get me to learn. He spoke something to me in Gio then told me to say it in English. I didn't have a clue how to do so.

"Say it!" He shouted at me in the new language. I must have taken too long to open my mouth; before a sound could come out, he'd slapped me.

"Say it!" He screamed the unfamiliar words at me again then spoke in both Gio and the new language. He kept saying A-B-C, I'm not sure how I caught on to those letters or how many times he repeated it, but I am sure of my dread of another blow. This cruel ritual went on daily. He would call me, and when I answered in our dialect, he would shout "Say *yes!*" When I tried, he would say, "Don't talk." When the beatings during these teaching sessions became too much, I would run away from him, thus inviting more beatings.

One day, he added another teaching strategy to his arsenal, *repetition while squatting*. Whenever I got a word wrong or took too long to speak, he would have me repeat the word while squatting and standing. "Five squats!" or "Ten squats, faster!" he would bellow. Squatting tired my legs so that I couldn't run.

I was only seven years old, a child who wanted to play and have fun, but when Uncle Henry had a birthday party for his son, Patrick, I was excluded. My place at Patrick's "grand" birthday party was in the corner of the room or someplace outside. This was not only true for that first year but for all the other years I was there as well. I would hide in the corner of the big room as Patrick, his parents, and their friends celebrated. They could see me cowering in the corner, but no one acknowledged my presence. I felt like a castaway, like I didn't belong. I began to think that something was wrong with me. I watched with envy and anger as my light-skinned cousin beamed with happiness when he got his birthday cake and presents, and as his light-skinned mother and father told him how special he was.

Meanwhile, from November 1965 to September 1966, I endured my uncle's crude method of teaching me English. About a week before the school year started, Uncle Henry told me that he was done teaching me and that he had registered me at the Seventh Day Adventist School on Broad Street. So, at the age of eight, after a year away from home, I was about to enter the first grade—which is why I had come to Monrovia, after all.

The school was about four blocks away from our house. When the first day of school arrived, Uncle dropped me off at the door and told me that he would come to pick me up when the school day was over. He didn't bother to make sure that I was settled in the classroom. I didn't know anyone in the building and no one knew me. I was nervous, confused, and afraid. Furthermore, I was trembling because I thought the teachers might beat me to make me learn, as Uncle had. Other children and the adults were talking in English, but in spite of a year of beatings, I didn't understand most of what they said although I acted like I understood by nodding when anyone spoke to me.

A bell rang and all the children started walking—or running—into a large room. I followed them. A lady stood in front of us and started speaking. Near her was a man.

"Good morning, boys and girls," she said. "Welcome to your school."

"Good morning," I responded with the other children. That much I could do.

"We are now going to have our devotion before we begin," she continued.

Devotion? What was a devotion? I had never heard that word before. My eyes quickly scanned the room to see what the other children were getting. I thought the teacher was going to give us something.

"Bow your head and Mr. Brown will pray for you," she said.

"Lord, bless these children," Mr. Brown began to pray. He prayed a long prayer, and I didn't understand most of what he said so I returned to my worries about what my time in this new school would be like. What could I do to avoid getting another beating? I didn't want to get beaten in front of all these children. What would I say to them? How would I remember the English words? Most of the children spoke English fluently. How could I escape?

"I don't want to be here," I said to myself.

"Ok, children," the teacher's voice woke me from my reverie. "Time to go to your classrooms. There are three classrooms so listen for your names. Go to the teacher standing beside the door with the number I say when I call your names."

She talked so fast. What did she say? I was too afraid to ask so I decided to just watch what the other children did.

"Moses Adams, number one," she shouted. Moses started walking toward the first classroom with the teacher standing by the door. I was just about to follow him when the teacher called another child's name along with a number. That child walked to the second classroom. I noticed that the other children didn't move so I stayed put. The teacher called many additional names then I heard my name.

"Sammy Wongan, number three," she said. By the time she called my name, I understood the routine so I went to the teacher standing at classroom three. There, we sat on small chairs with no desks. My teacher, whose name I can't recall, seemed like a kind person. Notwithstanding, I still couldn't shake my fear that she was going to beat me a lot. She welcomed us and told us that she would be our teacher for the year. That morning, she said we would be reading and learning to add. My poor heart started beating rapidly, and I felt like I was about to choke.

She wrote math problems on the board such as $1 + 0 = ?$ and $1 + 1 = ?$ She then asked the class, "One plus zero equals what?"

What does she mean by "plus", "zero" and "equal"? I had never heard those words before. I hoped she didn't ask me. I stared at the floor, hoping that she wouldn't call me to answer the question. Yet, I felt like she was staring at me. It was a sensation of someone about to grab my neck from behind.

"Sammy, do you know the answer?" she asked. I stopped breathing. I was dead now. At any minute I expected to feel the sting of her belt or a whip.

"Sammy, did you hear me?" she asked again. "What is one plus zero?"

For some reason, I couldn't speak and kept staring at the ground.

"Sammy, no need to be shy. Look at the blackboard," she urged me. "Hold up your head. Look at me."

My head felt heavy. I managed to move my eyes upward instead of my head.

"Do you know the answer to what is one plus zero?" she asked again. This time, I shook my head.

"It's ok Sammy, you'll get it next time," she tried to comfort me.

That day, I was too tense and distracted by my fear of the unknown and by my fear of being beaten if I got the answer wrong to concentrate on what she was saying. Luckily, the teacher didn't call my name for the rest of the day. As the day passed without my receiving a beating from the teacher, I began to think that I might like school. It was a welcome break from having Uncle as my teacher.

Uncle came to pick me up as promised.

"Sammy, how was school?" he asked.

"School was good," I answered without looking at him. Immediately, I started fretting that he would ask me what I had learned. I was relieved when he didn't.

"Sammy, I'm going to take you to school and pick you up for the rest of this week. That way you will learn how to travel by yourself." True to his word, after the first week, I was on my own. He was diligent in making sure that I left the house for school.

For breakfast, which was not always served, because Uncle could not afford it, we had rice with water, fried or boiled plantains, or cornmeal porridge. There were days when I had nothing for breakfast and, since I never brought a lunch to school, by the end of the day I would be very hungry. Only a few children could afford to bring lunch. The school didn't have a lunch program so I often ate only one evening meal for the day.

It was my time in school with other children who spoke English that finally allowed me to become fluent in it. As I learned English, it became clear to me then that speaking it was a matter of survival for me in this hostile city.

Perhaps speaking English would help me to avoid more of the misery I had already known in Monrovia.

Fortunately, I did not know what was to come.

Henry K. Wongan - Uncle

Trail roads in the village (1960s)

Chapter 3

The Unexpected is Always Happening

*"First your parents, they give you your life,
but then they try to give you their life."*
— Chuck Palahniuk

Mama was standing in the yard! I couldn't believe my eyes. I screamed and ran to her and held onto her legs. She couldn't lift me up because she was pregnant and her belly was too big.

"Mama! Mama!" I kept screaming and dancing and giggling.

"Gontor, my son!" Mama said laughing. "I told you I would come back to look for you." She could hardly bend but she kissed me on my forehead and rubbed my head. It really felt good to feel Mama's touch again. When Uncle Henry heard my screams, he ran to where Mama and I were standing. He was shocked to see my mother; obviously he had no idea she was about to visit.

"Naar! What are you doing here?" he asked. I watched carefully to see if he was going to act nice to her. "Come in. You're pregnant! How did you make it into the city?" His voice was surprisingly friendly toward her.

Who was this man? He could just turn on his charm on and off like a faucet. Now he was treating Mama kindly, as if he cared for her.

"I had to come to look for Gontor. We miss him, and since your brother couldn't make it, because he went back to work on the Plantation, I decided to come," she answered.

During this time news had reached Mama, I don't know how, that Uncle Henry was brutalizing me. She had found a way to make it to the city to talk with my uncle about what she had heard. Uncle didn't even bother to ask about the well-being of anyone in the village. He was more eager to find out why Mama had come to the city. He invited her into the house where his wife and son were. That night uncle's wife and their son slept in her family's house. As usual, I slept on the floor and Mama slept in the bed with uncle.

In the morning, Uncle's wife and their son returned to the house, after which Uncle left and went to work. In the evening after dinner, Mama told him she wanted to discuss something with him. We didn't have much yard space so we all gathered in front of the small house.

"Henry, I heard that you have been mistreating Gontor," she said. "When I heard, I didn't believe it so I wanted to come see for myself and talk with you about this matter."

I looked at my uncle and saw the familiar mean look return to his face. I knew too well that he was just about to turn his wrath on Mama.

"Who the hell told you that?" he said in an intimidating voice. "Tell me who! I want to know who!" He stepped closer to my mother as if he was about to strike her. I wouldn't let him hurt her. I told myself I would kill him if he touched her.

"Is it true Henry?" My mother was not afraid of him. "I can't believe it. Would you beat your own flesh and blood, your older brother's son, and treat him like a slave? He's a Wongan and family takes care of family!"

Oh, no, I thought. Mama was going to get it. Uncle leaned straight in to her face. His wife, son, and I just stood staring at them, afraid of what would happen next.

"How dare you come to my house and ask me those questions? Woman, do you think you have a right to come here to address such an issue with me? Zlahn couldn't come to deal with me as a man so you decided to be the man?" He smirked and a wicked smile crossed his face.

"Your brother couldn't come, but I am here and Gontor is our son, your brother's child..." he didn't let her finish her sentence.

"Shut up!" He yelled and pushed her. Miraculously Mama didn't fall to the ground. "I don't want to talk about this anymore. That's it!"

I felt my fist closing and anger starting to boil inside of me. How dare he treat Mama like that? In my mind, I could see myself beating him up, but I knew he would just throw me across the yard like a piece of trash. Mother didn't say anything else. She was crying and hugged me tightly. Uncle and his family left the yard.

"Mama, let's escape early in the morning," I whispered in her ear.

"No, Gontor, we can't do that," she said. "I can't make the decision to take you back by myself, and I don't know how soon I'll see your father again. You have to stay." The tears were flowing fast and her *lappa* was wet. She loved me and I knew she wanted a different outcome for me, but I was their only hope for a better life.

"Mama, you think I should stay?" I wanted so to please her.

"Yes, Gontor, you have to stay. You can make it. Remember what I told you and what your father told you about being tough, like a man, whatever the storm may be?"

When uncle came back, it was dark. Mama and I were already inside. I was lying on the ground and she was in the bed. When he entered the room, I pretended that I was asleep. It sounded like he was changing his clothes, then he got on the bed. Shortly after I heard Mama whispered, "No, Henry, don't."

"What do you think, you can just come to my house for nothing?" he replied.

"No, don't. Please don't." She was pleading. "Stop!"

I raised my head slightly, careful not to be discovered, and saw something that I will never forget. There was my uncle forcefully holding my mother down on the bed. Mother was resisting but she was no match for him. I heard mother groan and cry softly. Whatever Uncle Henry was doing to her was definitely against her will. I had to do something; I had to do something, anything. Again my fists were clenched and thoughts about beating my uncle badly raced through my mind but I knew he would just beat me viciously. All I could do was to be quiet and helplessly cry silent tears as I listened to the sounds of Mama's soft crying. I dared not let my uncle know that I was awake and I didn't want to embarrass my mother. I believed she hoped that I was asleep. Like me she was helpless. We lacked the courage to openly rebel against this culture which says that if a brother's wife comes to visit, the man has sexual access to the wife even when the wife says no, as my mother said no to this merciless, selfish brute.

In the morning when I saw Mama, she didn't look me in the eye but tears were streaming down her face. I could tell she was trying to hold back the tears so she could be strong in front of me, but she was too sad. I didn't ask her any questions. I glanced at her face and then I hugged her legs, and that was all I allowed myself to do. She hugged me tightly and kissed me, her tears still flowing.

"Gontor, I will be returning to the village today," she said, still not looking me in the eye. "I want you to take care of yourself and remember that your father and I love you. George is ok. We will be ok. You can make it."

I didn't know what to say. Tears were streaming down my face, as well. I wanted to carry the hope of my parents but also wanted to be a child, happy in my native village. I wanted to be Gontor again. Mama and I hugged for a long time. She didn't want to leave me; I believe leaving me behind was the hardest thing she had had to do in her life. Uncle went to work, but Aunt Martha and Patrick stayed home. Aunt Martha didn't offer Mama anything to eat. In fact, she looked at Mama with disgust and kept asking her when she was leaving. I walked with Mama to the side of the road and watched her get into a pickup truck that was taking other people out of the city. The pain I felt as I watched her leave me behind was indescribable. It was a pain that I was to feel so many other times in my life. It was the pain of something breaking within me.

Looking back, I often wonder why Mama didn't take me back with her that day. She saw for herself how two-faced and mean Uncle Henry was. Were my parents so desperate for a better life that they chose me to be the sacrificial lamb for the salvation of the family? Did they quiet their ambivalence and worry for me by rationalizing that the payoff would one day be worth the hardship that I had to endure in the city? What consequences would Mama have had to face if she had abandoned Papa's plan for the family without his knowledge or consent?

It was our tradition for the man to be the head of the household. Women might have a say but the man made the final decision. Mama was trapped between her love and worry for me and Papa's grand but risky plan. After this visit, she tried to make it to the city again to visit me but she was unable to. She gave birth to a boy. She also had a stroke that twisted her mouth, slurred her speech and limited her movements. She had no access to medical care so she was forced to rely only on bush medicine. Life became more difficult and she had no money to make the journey.

* * *

For the next two and a half years, my life continued to be difficult. I lived in heightened fear of my uncle. It seemed there was nothing to stop his cruelty, now that he had dominated my mother. It seemed to me that my time with Uncle would never end. As a child, I couldn't understand why my parents didn't take me back to the village when they heard of how Uncle Henry was mistreating me. Although their actions might seem to lack compassion, I believe that their desire to protect me was hampered by their limited financial resources, the poor condition of the roads for travel, Papa's strong desire to distance me from farm work and his strong belief that my education was the

Breaking Point: A Journey to Self-Awareness and Finding Purpose in Pain

family's only path out of a difficult life of abject poverty.

But, in January 1968, after the December holidays, Uncle Henry suddenly shipped me off to live with a friend. He told me he didn't have space to keep me because we were all living in a one bedroom zinc-roofed house—and both Patrick and I, as growing boys, were occupying more space. Simply put, I was a burden and Uncle didn't want to keep me. At his friend's house, I was to earn my keep.

Over time, I was to stay with three of his friends. When one was finished using me and grew tired of me, I was shipped off without warning to another. For the first six months away from Uncle, I stayed with John, one of his coworkers in the National Police Band of Liberia. All John required me to do was to clean his fifteen-by-ten foot, one-bedroom home. He didn't care much about me, but he never beat me. He was a sick drunkard and, whenever he was sober enough to cook, he usually remembered to make a plate of food for me. At the end of the school year, in July 1968, John told Uncle that he could no longer keep me.

A month before I started the third grade that September, Uncle took me to live with a woman who was one of the privileged and uppity blacks whose ancestors had repatriated from the United States of America. During the almost two years I lived with Esther, she sometimes treated me kindly, but mostly she threatened to beat me, although she never did. While she allowed me to go to school, she did not allow me to do homework or read while she was awake. Instead, as soon as I arrived home from school, she started giving me work to do—sweep the yard, wash the plates, and other chores to keep me always moving. While she—and Uncle—called me a houseboy, I was really a house slave: scrubbing, cleaning, cooking, and jumping to respond to the orders she barked at me. I was the perfect child laborer. I was not paid a penny and I was given only the minimum of food, clothing, and attention.

As it was with my uncle, my head was always to be held down in her presence as Esther ordered me not to look at her. During the time that I lived with her, she often went out to bars and brought home light-complexioned American men.

Esther gave me three notebooks to last for the entire year, and so I had to write sparingly in them so that they would last as long as possible. This meant that, in order to pass my tests, I had to memorize everything I learned at school. The unintended consequence of this rationing led to the sharpening of my ability to memorize and apply information. This led to my becoming an "A" student in the third and fourth grades.

School became even more of a refuge for me. I had a white American Peace Corp teacher, Robert Schwartz, who took an interest in me. I had freedom to ask questions in his classes as he always encouraged the class to participate and always praised us when we did. Mr. Schwartz awakened my interest in mathematics, science, English, geography, and history. In his class, I learned to appreciate my abilities and for the first time, I felt capable and proud of myself. He made me realize the unthinkable about myself: house slave that I was, I was also smart and I could succeed just like other smart students. I felt proud of my abilities and achievements, but I had to keep my successes to myself because, apart from Mr. Schwartz, no one else around was interested in me and my parents, who would have been, were miles away in the village.

One summer during the two years I was living at Esther's; Papa paid a surprise visit to Monrovia.

"Papa! Papa!" I couldn't believe my eyes. "Oh, my God, Papa, is that you?"

"Hey, Sammy. Come here, boy," Papa said. "How are you, my son?"

I was almost eleven years old and in the fourth grade, but Papa lifted me up. It felt so good to feel his touch again. It was almost five years since I had last seen him. He looked different -- slimmer and much darker.

"Sammy, you look different," Papa said looking at me from head to toe. "You are going to be a fine young man, taller and bigger than me.

Breaking Point: A Journey to Self-Awareness and Finding Purpose in Pain

Sammy, you look good."

"Papa, I'm so glad to see you." I said, so excited. "I'm so glad to see you. How is Mama? How is George? How is everybody?

"They are okay, also your baby brother, whose name is Mark," he told me. "Now, you tell me. How are you? Your uncle told me that you have been doing well in school. He told me that his friend is taking good care of you. Tell me, Sammy, how are things going?"

I had learned in the time I was being brutalized by Uncle Henry and his friends to overlook my own needs. My intent was always to survive. When Papa asked me how I was doing, I was unable to get out of this mode. I was afraid he would get angry with me, too, and so I told him what I thought he wanted to hear. Uncle Henry had told Papa that I was doing well in school only because he knew that is what Papa wanted to hear. The truth is that, after Uncle Henry shipped me off to his friends, he never checked to see how I was doing.

"Papa, I'm okay," I said, in a guarded tone. "I'm just so glad to see you. I longed to see you. Did Mama tell you anything?"

"I longed to see you, too, Son," he said. "Sorry I couldn't come to see you earlier. I thought about you day and night but it just wasn't possible for me to come. I have been working at the diamond mine and the plantation. Son, life is very difficult there, it's slavery work."

"But, did Mama tell you?" I asked.

"Did Mama tell me what?" Papa asked.

"Did she tell you about Uncle?" I asked.

"What about your uncle?" Papa had a puzzled look on his face.

"I don't know. I just thought she might have said something about Uncle." I was filled with disappointment. If Mama had told Papa about Uncle Henry brutalizing me and raping her, Papa wouldn't talk to me about that. In our culture, children didn't have any part in adult business. We were taught that *'children must be seen and not heard'*. We children knew that when adults were talking, we had to walk away. And maybe, my father was blinded by desperation. Maybe he thought I was tough enough to endure anything in order to get an education and a chance at a better life. Maybe he reasoned that the means justified the end result they sought.

"Your mother did tell me that you had a little difficulty when you were with your uncle," he said. "Your uncle can be rough sometimes, but he means well. He promised me that he would take care of you."

Papa obviously didn't want to endanger the "grand plan".

"That's what he told you?" I asked. "Did Uncle tell you he would take care of me?"

"Sammy, things won't always go the way we want, but that's life," father admonished me. "You have come through the worst. Things are going to be okay. See, you look good, and you're getting your education. That's the important thing—your education."

"Papa, I'm doing well at school." I was excited to say this, because Papa was pleased. "My teacher said that I am smart and I get good grades. I love school."

"See, Sammy, I told you things would work out." He smiled at me. "Your mother and I are praying for you. You are going to make it, Son. Be strong."

"Papa, did you bring anything for me?" I wanted to know what he had in his bag.

"No, Son. I didn't have anything to bring," he said. "I haven't been to Teahplay yet. Work at the Plantation just finished. The job there was just for a time. I came from the Plantation straight to Monrovia. I went to see your Uncle Henry and he told me that you were staying with one of his friends, who is helping him to send you to school. Henry has been very helpful to us. The plan is working."

"Yes, Papa," I agreed. I could not tell him that I was wretchedly unhappy, because every time I had spoken up in the last years, I had been beaten. Papa would not have beaten me, but I had learned not to trust my own feelings and speaking up went against the training of the last four years. By eleven, I had learned to hide my true feelings so well that this trait would affect relationships throughout my life. I would even forget for long periods of time that I was hiding my feelings. It seemed like the natural way of things.

My parents, Zlahn and Guataye Wongan were my inspiration. To me, they were the epitome of love and care. Growing in the village, I admired the way they loved and cared for each other but more so, how they cared for my sister, baby brother, and me. Furthermore, they were survivors and they taught me how to survive. In their world it was all about daily survival, thriving was merely a dream. Seeing Papa again brought back a flood of memories. About four years had passed since I had last seen or heard from my parents. I was growing up without the care and protection of the two people who should have been the rock of my existence.

Looking back, I now realize how important early relationships with one's parents can be. That early relationship can either make or break a person because it influences self-esteem and behavior patterns in later life. My poor, uneducated parents had given me something priceless that has stayed with me throughout my life. That something was my lifeline in my early days in the wilderness of my life. It inspired hope in me so that, although they were not physically with me, they were with me in spirit every day that I was away from them.

During those years of brutalization and desperate loneliness, I often wondered where my father was and what he was doing. My memories of him were mostly of him in the fields on the farm where he would work tirelessly in the broiling sun or the pouring rain during the day or times when he would take me to hunt for animals, or evenings when he would sit briefly outside our mud house to socialize with others. Snuffing tobacco helped to relax him, so he would grind tobacco leaves, put it on his tongue then let it melt gradually. I was fascinated by this and would ask Papa to let me try it. I later found out that this was really a stimulant and must have provided a high for him.

Looking back, I can imagine how difficult life must have been for my parents then. Exposure to and acculturation into the American lifestyle has influenced my perception of what my life was like. Before I left the village, I thought we were living the good life. I had nothing to compare my life to at that time. Moving to Monrovia was my first eye-opening experience, my first barometer with which to measure my life in the village. I concluded that in spite of the abject poverty that existed in the village, we had something that money couldn't buy. We had community, people who cared for each other more than they cared for things or status. They appreciated what they had, but life was tough. Some of the villagers, like Papa, had been exposed to the concept of the "better life" that education could bring. So, they wanted more.

When I was left in Monrovia, I was exposed to the Liberian version of city life, with its conveniences. There were outdoor toilets whereas, in the village, the bushes had served as our toilets and leaves as our toilet paper. In the city, there were street lights, and buildings made from cement. I saw white-skinned people for the very first time as well as a mixture of cultures and peoples such as Syrians, Lebanese, and Americans. I saw electric lights and motorcycles, ships on the seacoast, and TV. In the village, light was provided by the moon, kerosene lanterns, or wood fires at nights.

By 1970, I was twelve and in the fifth grade. I had been living with Esther for almost two years. Unexpectedly, I was shunted off to a third friend of my uncle's, a Mr. Kamara, a banker from Sierra Leone now living in Liberia. Mr. Kamara was married to the daughter of the Liberian Ambassador to the United Nations, Mrs. Kamara, who had studied nursing in America and England. Although they had a woman called Annie to care for their children, they found many other chores for me and continued the practice of treating me like a slave. Little did I know that living with the Kamaras would change the entire course of my life.

I had to help clean their big house, wash clothes, cook, iron, and do whatever else pleased them in order to earn my chance to go to school. Not once did they praise me or even say thank you. My resting place at nights was in a five-by-six-foot storage room on a thin mat on the cement floor, without pillow or sheet. They got to use the toilet first, regardless of any urgent need on my part. Furthermore, I couldn't use the toilet when they were nearby and they forbade me to take a shower in the bathtub at any time. I had to bathe with a bucket of water in the back yard.

Dinnertime was another dehumanizing experience. The Kamaras ate first, as I stood on alert in the kitchen waiting to fulfill any request they made. When they were through, I could eat. (I was never invited to sit with them at the dinner table.) My dinner was the burnt crust at the bottom of the rice pot or leftovers from their plates. Many times all they left were dry bones or nothing at all. Those evenings were the worst because my stomach growled with hunger, and I cried myself to sleep.

One evening, the Kamaras planned a very special dinner party for which they bought a lot of food. Annie, the nurse, who was also a native Liberian, and I worked slavishly to ensure that the food was cooked and everything met the meticulous requirements of the Kamaras. I was very excited and hopeful that there would be sufficient leftovers to fill my belly because I had not eaten much all week. I took up my position behind the door and peeked as they and their guests ate.

"This food tastes really good," Mr. Kamara commented with his mouth full. "Give me more of that chicken."

As his wife passed the chicken to him, I felt saliva springing from the sides of my mouth and made a silent plea to my ancestors to let them leave something substantial on their plates. Their children were also laughing and eating happily.

"Eat up the food." Mrs. Kamara urged her children. "Don't leave any food on the plate. We can't waste food." I wondered if she remembered that I counted on them to leave some food in their plates so that I could eat. That night I was sorely disappointed. The Kamaras and their guests cleared their plates, leaving only bones. I cried silent tears as I cleared the table, but no one noticed. If they noticed the tears, no one asked me what made me cry. I thought about telling my uncle about how badly they were treating me but quickly realized that this would be a big mistake. Telling him would be an invitation for him to beat me severely, probably to death this time. I said nothing.

I decided to hold onto Mama's affection and Papa's word *"A man is a man that can withstand the storm, whatever the storm may be."* I had promised Papa and Mama that I would get an education as they had planned, to help the family. The memories and words of my parents inspired hope; they were my lifeline in the wilderness of my young life as I struggled to resist breaking under the stress.

Chapter 4

Crossing the Atlantic Ocean

"In spite of unseasonable wind, snow and unexpected weather of all sorts - a gardener still plants. And tends what they have planted ...believing that spring will come."
— Mary Anne Radmacher

The unexpected was always happening. One evening, after I had been with the Kamaras about a year, I heard Mr. Kamara shout, "Are you out of your mind! We can't bring him with us; we're leaving in two weeks. It's Annie who has to come with us."

"At least, listen to me," Mrs. Kamara pleaded.

It was after dinner. Annie and I had already cleaned up, and I was just about to leave the kitchen to go to my bed in the storage room when I overheard Mr. and Mrs. Kamara talking.

"No, you listen to me! What you're saying makes no sense. Sammy doesn't have a passport. He doesn't have a visa. Now you tell me, how can he come with us?"

"My father will help. Just listen to me and you will understand why we have to take him with us." Mrs. Kamara continued to plead with her husband. I didn't have to strain to hear them. Mr. Kamara was talking loudly and his wife was trying to get him to listen to her. I didn't know that they were talking about me until I heard Mr. Kamara call me by name. They never called my name unless they were commanding me to do something. I realized then that I was the subject of their conversation and I was totally confused as to why. They stopped talking, and I realized that Mr. Kamara might be coming to find me. Before I could run out of the kitchen which adjoined the living room, Mr. Kamara opened the door.

"What are you doing there?" He seemed angry at me. I didn't know what to say so I just stared at him. "Move out of my way and go find something to do," he ordered me. I didn't know why he had called my name and why he had entered the kitchen, because he just turned around and went back into the living room and resumed talking loudly. As soon as he left the kitchen, I resumed eavesdropping near the door. My name was called several times. There would be consequences if they caught me listening but I was eager to know why my name had been called.

"After we made all the plans, now you want to change them." Mr. Kamara was still complaining. "Why do we have to take Sammy with us? Now you tell me why this makes sense."

"I called Father today to give him the date of our arrival in America, and he told me that he didn't think we should take Annie with us because, the last time he visited us, she stole $300 US from his pocket," she explained.

"Ah! Ah!" Mr. Kamara burst out laughing. "Annie stole $300 from him, and your father didn't say anything? Why not?"

"I don't know," Mrs. Kamara replied. "Actually, Father said that he was planning to just forgive her and forget about it."

"So now he wants to bring it up. How does he know it wasn't Sammy? I bet Sammy was the one who took the money."

"No. Father said that when he went to take a shower and left his pants in the room Sammy was at school. It couldn't have been Sammy. It was Annie who took the money. We can't take her because she's a thief. Furthermore, as Father pointed out, if we take Sammy with us we can save money. We don't have to pay him. He is a hard worker and he can take care of the children and, when they are in school, he can go to school." Letting me go to school was the agreement they had made with my uncle. I was a houseboy for them in exchange for them allowing me to get an education. Strangely, even when they could have reneged on their promise, they kept me in school.

The idea of saving money grabbed Mr. Kamara's interest; almost immediately his concern about the feasibility of the new plan flew out the window.

"If your father can help us get Sammy's papers quickly, then tell him to start working on it immediately. We don't have time to waste; it's two weeks until our flight leaves."

Mrs. Kamara was delighted.

"Sammy!" Mr. Kamara shouted my name. Not wanting him to realize that I hadn't left the kitchen, I took a little time to answer. "Sammy! Where the hell is that boy!" he bellowed. I ran into the room without answering.

"What happened, boy? You didn't hear me calling you?" He yelled at me as soon as I entered the room. "Tell your uncle tomorrow that we're taking you to America."

"To America. . ." Frightened by this abrupt and shocking news, I tried to ask him a question but, before I could finish, he cut me off.

"Go! Just tell him what I said."

I couldn't sleep that night. All I could think of was that I didn't want to go anywhere with them. I'd heard others talk excitedly about America but, I had a sick feeling at the idea of my going there. I just couldn't shake the thought that the Kamaras would take me to America and dump me. Furthermore, my parents had no knowledge of this plan. They had sent me to live with my uncle to get an education, not to leave the country.

As I tossed and turned that night, I believed my uncle would understand that I didn't want to go and would tell the Kamaras that they were out of their minds for wanting to take me out of the country, especially at such short notice.

Yes, I would stand up for myself, I told myself. I would not go with them. I was thirteen years old now and this time I would not let myself be pushed around.

That next morning, I ran to the police headquarters where my uncle worked. He saw me before I saw him.

"What you doing here? What you doing here?" he asked in a stern voice. Somehow this time, I didn't feel afraid of him. He was the only one who could save me from the plans the Kamaras had hatched to take me away from Liberia.

"I don't want to go. I don't want to go with them," I gasped, out of breath.

"What the hell you talking about?" he yelled.

"The Kamaras want to take me to America! I don't want. . ." Before I could say another word my uncle slapped me across my face.

"You're going. Get moving!"

That was it. My resolve to stand up for myself collapsed. The last seven years of being brutalized kicked in, and I submitted. It was the only thing I knew to do. I don't know what strings Mrs. Kamara's father pulled but, within two weeks, I was "adopted" by the Kamaras and my name was changed from Sammy Gontor Wongan to Sammy Wongan Kamara. I'm sure my parents didn't give permission for this adoption. I had a passport and a visa and, within the two weeks, I was on a plane to America. I was 13 years old and had never gone anywhere near a plane. I was terrified about traveling on the plane and didn't know what to expect. Now, flying across the Atlantic, I was frightened, anxious, numb, and fearful of what the Kamaras would do to me when they no longer needed me.

I didn't trust them one bit, but couldn't do anything to save myself. The idea of running away had not seemed viable. Because I felt that way, I was, in fact, a captive of everyone's desires and decisions. Thoughts of my parents, from whom I so desperately wanted love and acceptance, also raced through my mind. I didn't get to see them to say goodbye. My uncle didn't ask their permission to send me. In fact, they didn't even know I was leaving the country. My uncle just gave me away without, as far as I knew, even getting the address of where I would be living in America.

I cried silent tears on the plane, careful not to let the Kamaras see me cry. The food they served had no taste, and it seemed as if we were in the plane for days. I missed my parents so much. I wanted to believe that, had they known, they would have protected me and taken me away to live with them. The Kamara's four children, nine, eight, seven, and five years old, were cuddled up with their parents in the middle row of seats. I sat in the seat across from them with no one to hug me, no one to quell my fears and wipe my tears. No one to explain where I was going and what would happen when I got there.

Fear was my companion and my friend. That sick feeling that I had had when I had first learned that the Kamaras wanted to take me with them, haunted me and would not leave. It kept me company each time I awoke after nodding off. The only thing that brought some relief was thinking of my parents and especially, of the admonitions they had given me during my formative years in the village. It was as though they had boarded the plane with me and I could hear them trying to encourage me to be strong: *"A man is a man that can withstand the storm, whatever the storm may be."* I also heard Mama's voice saying: *"Remember, I won't always be with you so you have to learn to take care of yourself."* I held on to those words for dear life.

When we finally landed at the John F. Kennedy Airport, the first thing that struck me was its size. It was huge in comparison to the lowly Roberts International Airport in Liberia that I had departed from. We took a car over a big bridge to where the Kamaras had an apartment. As we drove through New York, I was stunned by the tall buildings, the wide roads, and the number of vehicles on the streets. Their friends in America who knew that the Kamaras were relocating had helped them secure this apartment. It was in one of the tallest buildings I had ever seen, built of red brick, and, when we entered, we went into something that looked like a closet. It took us from the bottom of the building to the 4th floor.

That summer of 1972, when we arrived in America, the Kamaras reiterated what my role in their family would be. I was responsible for supervising their children in their absence—a role that had been Annie's—and accompanying them to and from school. After taking the children to school, I would then be able to go to school myself but I had to make sure that I was available on time to pick them up afterward. My responsibilities also included helping to cook, clean the apartment, iron, and do the laundry. I was to do all of this for free.

"I will show you where the laundry room is," Mrs. Kamara said.

"What is a laundry room?" I asked.

"What do you think?" She shook her head in exasperation. "A laundry room is where people wash clothes. I will show you."

I was eager to see this laundry room. As far as I knew, clothes were either washed on washboard, by beating them on a rock or washed by hand in a basin, and then they were laid flat or hung on a line to dry. Later that day, Mrs. Kamara, the children, and I went into the elevator. This time, it went down to the basement. In a big room, white machines were humming. I was amazed by what I saw.

"Mrs. Kamara, how can the machine wash clothes?" I asked. "Will they be clean like when you wash them by hand?"

"Of course," she replied. "You will see. Before you put the shirts in the washing machines, pour a little soap on the collar and the cuffs then rub them hard. When the machine stops, that means the clothes are washed. Just put them in the dryer. Then fold them when they are dried." This was very fascinating. I enjoyed doing laundry, as it was the easiest chore I had. In Liberia, laundry had been much harder.

Mr. Kamara gave me two pairs of pants, some shirts, and a pair of sneakers for school and told me that he would get me a coat and warm shoes because, in a few months, it would start getting cold. In Liberia, we sometimes have what we called cold weather. In our Gio dialect, we call cold weather *Bounene;* cold as we knew it in Liberia was the only cold weather that I could imagine.

My supervisory responsibilities included watching the children play downstairs in the courtyard of the apartment. I sometimes played ball with them but, mostly, I just watched them play. In New York, my life with the Kamaras improved somewhat. I still couldn't sit at the dining table with them, but while I stayed alert to help them when they called me, they allowed me to use their plates and eat in a corner of the kitchen at the same time that they were eating. Where would I bathe, I asked myself, tormented by the thought. They wouldn't let me use their bathtub, in Liberia. Would I have to go down into the courtyard? I didn't want to exposure my genitals to anyone, which I would have had to do if I washed in the courtyard. I couldn't go without bathing. The Kamaras had a balcony outside the living room. Seeing it, I told myself that I would rather bathe on the balcony than downstairs in the courtyard.

The day after we arrived, Mr. Kamara released me from my tormenting thoughts. "Sammy, you have to bathe in the bathroom," he told me.

I couldn't believe the words coming from his mouth. I could use the same bathroom as the Kamaras! I said nothing when he spoke, because I didn't want Mr. Kamara to change his mind.

"It's different in America," he continued. "So bathe inside. But you have to wait until after we take our showers and, when you are finished, don't forget to clean the bathtub."

"Ok, Mr. Kamara," I said. "Thank you very much."

In retrospect, I wonder why I bothered to thank him. Now I know, of course, that if he had insisted that I bathe outside it would have brought problems to his doorsteps. He would have been in trouble with the law. But I did not know that then.

Mrs. Kamara hated the idea of me bathing in the same bath tub as she and her precious family. Her veiled contempt for me first became apparent when she started making sarcastic comments each time I used the bathroom. She often warned me about scrubbing the tub thoroughly with disinfectant. Although I diligently cleaned the tub, she was never satisfied and often insisted that I clean it again. Her contempt for me seemed to grow daily. She told me that I was too ambitious and I needed to stay in in my "place". They sent me to school but showed no interest in my progress.

* * *

A few months later, in September 1972, I started attending John Philip Sousa Middle School on Baychester Avenue in the Bronx. I was placed in the 7th Grade. This was another culture shock. The school was big, and the classrooms were larger than any I'd ever seen. I felt out of place. I'd never seen so many children all together. The students were mainly African-American and Puerto Rican. A few were of Italian descent. I didn't know anyone at the school. My fear of speaking was not as intense as it was when I started attending school for the very first time at the Adventist School in Liberia. Nevertheless, I didn't know what to expect. Many of the children were talking and laughing together. It seemed as if they knew each other. Others, who were probably new like me, didn't seem as uncomfortable as I. We were directed to go into a very large room that could accommodate the entire student body. The seats were situated in a very peculiar manner and in front of the seats was an elevated stage.

A man dressed in a suit and tie addressed us. He turned out to be the principal of the school.

"Good morning, everyone! Welcome to a new school year at John Philip Sousa Middle School," he said. "This is a fun school. Your teachers and I are committed to helping you get a good education."

He proceeded to give information and instructions about the school and the expectations. He also emphasized the importance of appropriate behavior, obeying school rules, and asking for help from the school staff when we needed it. He repeatedly stated, *"We are here for you"*. That statement was very reassuring. Knowing that there were people who were willing to 'be there for me' caused some of my pent up fears to dissipate.

Settling into the routine of school at John Philip Sousa Middle School was, to my surprise, much smoother than I had imagined it would be. I looked forward to lunch at school, which was served in a large room that was referred to as the "cafeteria". Students had choices. Lunch was free and could be macaroni and cheese, cole slaw, potato salad, chicken, vegetables, fruits, bread, or other goodies. Milk was served daily.

My history teacher took an interest in me and started taking me to the other 7th Grade history classes so that I could share information about Liberia. Liberia's history has some connection with American history in that, in the early 1800s, this country had repatriated former slaves to Liberia. America was instrumental in the formation of the Republic of Liberia in 1847. The constitution of Liberia was patterned after American's constitution and the main city of Liberia, Monrovia, was named after President James Monroe, the fifth President of The United States. At first I was very timid about speaking before the classes, but my teacher was very supportive and inspired confidence in me. He always said: "Sammy, you can do it, but you won't know that unless you try." I took his advice and realized that the more I talked about Liberia the more confident I felt. I was sharing information that most of the students were hearing for the first time.

My academic performance was outstanding, and more advanced than that of the other students in my class. This led my teacher to recommend that I be promoted to the 8th Grade after only about two months in his class. I shared the news of my promotion with the Kamaras' children but not with their parents. Whether the children told them or not, I don't know, but they never asked me about it. In fact, Mrs. Kamara had begun to discourage me. She would make comments about how education was wasted on some people, and some people thought that having lofty dreams could change their lives. Memories of my time at this school are mostly pleasant. The only upsetting experience was being teased because of my accent. I did notice the difference between the way most of the students and staff spoke and the way I spoke. Like me, they spoke English but the sounds and inflections when they talked were much different than mine. My accent became fodder for a group of boys in my class.

"Here comes Tarzan!" they would yell when they saw me. One day, one of them came up to me in the hallway while the others watched and giggled.

"Hey, Tarzan," he called out to me. "How is it in the jungle?" The others burst out laughing. Their laughter bothered me a little. I guess I should have been more offended by their insensitivity but I was more curious and wanted to find out about this Tarzan. I had never met or heard of him and so I wasn't sure what my reaction should be.

"Who is Tarzan?" I asked one of the boys. My question made them laugh even harder.

"You're Tarzan!" the boys yelled. "Idiot! You're Tarzan!"

"Tarzan, go back to the jungle," another boy in the group jeered.

They never told me who Tarzan was, but I started to guess that they were trying to belittle me. Looking back, I'm amazed at their ignorance. It was they who were remiss, and not I. These were Black boys who looked like me—and yet they felt superior. The only difference between us was that we had different accents. I asked my teacher if he knew who Tarzan was. He told me that Tarzan was a fictional movie character who was supposedly raised in an African jungle by apes, after his parents died. I didn't know anything about this fictional figure. Had I, I might have taken those boys on as they jeered me. But then, maybe I wouldn't have, because I was not trained to be an aggressor; I was taught only to defend myself from physical attacks.

One day in the lunch room, two Italian boys tried to recruit me to become a "weed salesman."

"You can make a lot of money," one boy urged me. "Join our team."

"Yea," the other boy piped in. "It's $5 a pack. You would get $2 for each pack that you sell."

"You can do this, man," the first one continued. "When you go around talking about your Liberia stuff you can get customers."

"I am not interested," I finally answered. "No, thanks. Go try someone else."

"Who do you think you are, nigger?" the first boy shouted at me. I thought they were calling me *Niger* like the Niger River in West Africa. They both cursed me and asked me if I thought I was better than they were.

I only spent one year at John Philip Sousa Middle School and graduated in June of 1973. After that, I went to Harry S.Truman High School, which was even bigger than John Philip Sousa Middle School. It was newly built; the floors were shiny and the walls were clean. In middle school, I had started learning how to imitate the accent of the American students. At home and on my way to and from school, I even started practicing the curse words I heard every day, in order to try to fit in, but I felt too uncomfortable to use them in public. An inner voice insisted: "*this is not you*". The inner conflict was too much, so I dropped those words from my vocabulary.

High School work was much more difficult, but I had developed enough discipline to stick with it. My favorite subjects were math, English, science, and history—especially history. I didn't need help to do my school work, but I was very happy when the Kamaras' oldest son started taking his siblings home after school. This freed up some time, even though I was still responsible for the care of the children, as well as for helping them with their homework. I was also still responsible for the domestic chores. Nevertheless, although Mr. and Mrs. Kamara forbade me to study or read while in their presence, life with the Kamaras now afforded me more freedom to read than it had in Liberia. I was beginning to feel more at ease, living with them.

This was, however, the calm before the storm.

PART TWO:
THE LAND OF OPPORTUNITIES AND STRUGGLES

Chapter 5

Nightmare

"Sometimes it's easy to walk by because we know we can't change someone's whole life in a single afternoon. But what we fail to realize is that simple kindness can go a long way toward encouraging someone who is stuck in a desolate place."
— Mike Yankoski

When I was about 15, I could feel change coming again. The sick feeling in my stomach that I had first felt when I was in Liberia returned and, with it, a premonition that something bad was about to happen.

That something perhaps had its origins in the house parties the Kamaras threw. Their relatives and friends would fill the large living room and kitchen and sometimes the crowd would spill over into the two bedrooms in the apartment. In Liberia, Mr. Kamara worked as a banker and he had known many important people. Here in America, he continued to work as a banker, in downtown Manhattan. Mrs. Kamara worked as a registered nurse. I didn't recognize the relatives and friends who came to their parties, but they appeared to be very important people, too.

They would smoke and drink a lot while playing music loudly. The air in the apartment reeked of cigarette and marijuana smoke. I hated being there. Occasionally, perhaps unknown to the Kamaras, relatives and friends invited me to smoke, but I always refused it. I had heard about people being addicted to drugs and I didn't want to be one of those people. It was perhaps my refusal to accept the marijuana that eventually led to my being seen as a threat to the relatives and friends. They must have been afraid that I might get them into trouble.

A few weeks after my 16th birthday, what I had dreaded occurred. I came home from school one evening and, when I tried to enter the apartment, the children said from the other side of the closed door, "You can't come in. You don't live here."

"What do you mean I don't live here? I live here. Open the door."

"No!" The children shouted in a chorus. "Mommy said you don't live here. You can't come in." They refused to open the door. I was shocked at being locked out, fearful, and desperate. I went to a telephone call box and called the police. The police came to the apartment door and ordered the children to open the door. When the children opened the door, I repeated my story to the police and ran to the closet near the front door to show them my clothes and other items that belonged to me. The children tried to persuade the police that they didn't know me.

"Let him in," one of the policemen said in a commanding voice. "Don't make us have to come back."

That was it. The police didn't say another word. They just closed the apartment door and left me there. What had just happened? Had something really happened in my favor? I was in utter shock but very relieved to still be in the apartment. My relief was short-lived. A few minutes after the police left, I heard the familiar turning of the key in the door. When it opened, in stepped the woman whose disdain for me had become almost tangible. Among other things, she couldn't stand the fact that, being from the lower class, I was excelling academically and got better grades than her own children. Her eyes met mine, and I could feel the searing heat of her evil look. As an Americo-Liberian, she hated natives like me; she hated that I was doing well at school.

"What are you doing here? Leave now!" Her words pierced me.

Breaking Point: A Journey to Self-Awareness and Finding Purpose in Pain

"Mrs. Kamara, I have nowhere to go. I live here," I muttered.

"You what? You don't belong here. I want you gone as soon as my husband comes in here tonight. You're not welcome here." She continued to slash me with her words and she couldn't see how terrified I was, even though I repeatedly asked what I had done wrong. I was like a piece of toilet paper that, having been used, was being flushed.

That day marked the beginning of the end of my life with the Kamaras. When Mr. Kamara came home from work; he told me that I couldn't live with them anymore. His wife didn't want me there.

"Because I am a good Muslim, I will let you stay until December, but after that you have to leave," he said to me. I looked at him, stunned. Where did this man expect me to go? He and his wife had stolen me away from my family and my country. "Where am I going to go?" I was bold enough to ask him.

"I don't know and I don't care." He shrugged coldly. "I just know you can't live here anymore."

It was October; the winter was fast approaching. The increasing cold frightened me; I could hardly guess at what a winter in New York without a home would be like, but I knew it would be worse than anything I had ever known. Mr. Kamara had already told me that I would not be allowed to take anything from the house. Two families, whom the Kamaras knew from Liberia, lived on the upper floors above Mr. Kamara's apartment so, one day after school, I gathered my courage and went to their doors to beg them to take me in. The first family consisted of a man, his wife, and his mother. When I told them my story, the man said, "We can't help you."

"Sometimes people with stories like these end up becoming big," his mother said to him. However, she didn't suggest or insist that her son help me, even though I could tell that she wanted him to.

The next family was just a man who lived by himself, so I believed. I knocked, thinking that he was my last hope. He opened the door and invited me in. I immediately seized the opportunity to make my plea.

"Please help me. I need somewhere to live. . ." I said hurriedly.

Before I could say another word, he cut me off.

"You have to leave. I'm going to take my shower." He abruptly shut the door in my face, as though I didn't exist. I can't describe how I felt. It was a multitude of feelings mixed together. I was alone in the world—not good for anything and definitely unwanted. I went to the Kamaras' apartment, to the only bed they gave me, a spot on the floor, and cried silent tears. There was no one to help me, no one to care.

Late that October, I shared my situation with the soccer coach and the guidance counselor at Harry S. Truman High. They took pity on me and bought me a winter coat and a pair of winter boots. Another unexpected event occurred, and this time it was in my favor. While returning to the Kamaras' apartment one day after school, I met Leon, one of my old classmates from John Phillip Sousa Junior High School. We were very glad to see each other, and I immediately told him about how I was being thrown out. He couldn't believe what I told him and thought I must be joking but I wasn't smiling so he realized that it was a serious situation. He said he was sorry to hear my story. Then he invited me to his house to get advice from his mother.

Arriving at his house, he eagerly introduced me to his mother as his friend from Africa, who was in need of help.

His mother looked at me with questioning eyes but said nothing.

"Good evening, Mrs. Johnson," I said.

"Good evening, young man," she finally answered.

I held my breath hoping that she wouldn't send me away. She was my only hope at this point. She looked at me sternly but asked gently, "What is your problem?" I quickly shared my story with her, beginning with how I had been made to leave my homeland against my will to come to America. She gave me a very worried look and then asked me a strange question.

"Do you believe in God?"

"Yes, I do," I replied.

"Then pray to Him," she advised me. I didn't know what to do. I was so nervous. Should I kneel? Should I stand? I thought she would pray for me, but she was telling me to pray for myself.

"I don't know how to pray," I told her.

"Pray to Him like you're talking with me but you have to be serious if you want your prayer to be answered. Make a vow to the Lord and fulfill it," she advised. I hesitated. In the village, we didn't pray directly to the Supreme God. In Monrovia, I had heard about the Christian God but the closest I came to Him was a little New Testament Bible that I believe I got at school. I felt that I couldn't dare talk with God, as she was telling me to do.

"It would be better if you prayed for me." My palms were becoming sweaty.

"No," she said. "You pray to God just as you have been talking to me. Ask Him for what you need." I finally knelt down.

"Lord, I heard about your miraculous works," I muttered. "How you heal the sick and raise the dead and deliver people who are captive. I also heard that you provide for people. I need a family that will care for me the way my biological parents would, and help me finish my high school education. Lord, if you would bless me with a decent job and bless me with a family of my own, I will serve you all the days of my life."

When I was finished, she added, "Say 'in Jesus name'." I did, and then she said the words I was dying to hear.

"Well, as you can see." She still looked dubious. "I don't have much space but you can sleep on the sofa." She didn't know that sleeping on the sofa was a promotion for me after sleeping on the floor at the Kamara's apartment. I started grinning and wanted to hug her but I didn't, because I didn't really know her. I felt so relieved and repeatedly thanked her, but I couldn't help thinking, *Here I go again, moving into the home of another stranger.*

I didn't know that Leon had a sister until I went to his house. She greeted me but seemed to have no interest in speaking with me and walked away to her room. Leon chatted with me and kept asking me if I was ok. He told me that he and his sister had been born in Jamaica, but when they were young; Mr. and Mrs. Johnson had adopted them and had taken them to the USA.

When Mr. Johnson came home that evening, I was sitting in the living room on the sofa.

"Hi, Edris, how are things?" he asked as he entered the room.

"Hi, Ben," she replied. "Everything is ok, but I have a surprise for you."

"What?" he asked quickly.

"Sam, this is my husband," she said to me. "His name is Reuben"

Mr. Johnson stared at me without saying a word. I looked at him not sure what to say.

"Reuben, this is Sam," she continued. "He's one of Leon's friends."

Mr. Johnson stared at me again and said a quick "hello" in a soft voice, then left the living room. Didn't he want to know who I was? What did his silence mean? Was he going to tell his wife that I have to leave? My heart started pounding. Mr. Johnson reentered the living room; he had changed his clothes.

"Hi, Dad," I said timidly.

A faint smile passed quickly across his face and he nodded but said nothing.

That night, I slept in my new "bed" at the Johnsons' residence. Because I wasn't sure if the Johnsons would really let me live with them, I decided to return the next day to the Kamaras apartment to see if they had changed their minds about me leaving. When Mrs. Kamara opened the door and saw me she asked, "What are you doing here? You are not allowed to come into this place anymore. Get out! And don't you ever come into this building again!"

Dejectedly, I returned to the Johnsons' home.

The deadline given to me by Mr. Kamara was approaching. By then, I had started sleeping at the Johnsons every night. I asked Mom, as I had started calling Mrs. Johnson, if she thought I should get my belongings from the Kamaras. She agreed that I should get them. When I went to the Kamaras apartment, Mr. Kamara opened the door.

"Sammy, you know you are not supposed to come here anymore. What do you want?" he asked.

"Can I have my clothes, please?" I asked timidly. Some of these were clothes that the Kamaras had bought for me when I came to America. There were also the sneakers and winter coat that the counselor and one of my teachers had bought me.

"No!" He raised his voice as he spoke. "Look, you don't belong here. Don't come back!"

"What about my immigration papers? My passport? Can I have my papers please?" I pleaded.

"Excuses! Don't you ever come back here again!" These were his final words to me before he shut the door in my face. I wanted to cry but no tears came. I had nothing but my high school identification to prove who I was. I ran back to the Johnsons house in a state of confusion. By then I was crying.

Chapter 6

Rescued at Sea

"Call it a clan, call it a network, call it a tribe, call it a family. Whatever you call it, whoever you are, you need one."
— Jane Howard

I didn't want anyone to see me cry so I wiped away my tears before I knocked on the door of the Johnsons' house. Mrs. Johnson opened the door and immediately noticed that I had been crying.

"How did it go?" she asked directly. "Are they taking you back?"

"No," I said, fighting the tears that were threatening to spill over.

"You can stay here," Mrs. Johnson said.

Her words brought immediate relief. I felt unburdened, as if someone had lifted two hundred-pound bags of rice from my shoulders. I heard myself say, "Thank you, Mom."

The Johnsons' home became my safe haven and Mr. and Mrs. Johnson became my rock, my new parents. They allowed me to call them "Dad" and "Mom" yet I still longed for my biological parents. I had no clue how to get in touch with them. I had started saving my tears for the day I saw my biological parents again. I told myself that I had to survive in this new country until I could find my way back to Liberia to look for my parents.

But that was for another time, the Johnsons were my family now,

I told myself. The shock of mistreatment by my uncle, my own flesh and blood, after having grown up in a loving family in a village where people looked out for the well-being of each other, had scarred me. I had mixed feelings about having a surrogate family. I concluded that family could either be a blessing or a curse, and I had certainly experienced both. This made me wonder about other people's experiences with their own families. At nights, while lying on my very comfortable sofa, I often wondered what family meant to other people. Do all families have both good and rotten eggs—good and bad people? Who really needs a family anyway? A loving family, the Johnsons, had come to my rescue and restored my faith in family. I knew that *I* needed one.

The Johnsons cared for me as if I were their own biological son. Mom fed me lots of various and delicious Jamaican foods: oxtails, rice and peas, curried chicken, curried goat, cow foot, ackee, salt fish, and other such excellent dishes. I will never forget my first Thanksgiving dinner with them in November 1975; right after the Kamaras finally threw me out. I was allowed to sit at the dining table, after Mom and Dad introduced me to the family and friends who had joined them for dinner. It was as if I was having an out-of-body experience. I just couldn't believe that she thought I was worthy enough to sit at the table with her guests. Furthermore, she and the young lady who assisted her— for once it was not me—were the ones who had prepared the meal.

During dinner, I was hesitant to touch the food. Others at the table were filling their plates with the good things on the table.

"Sam, take anything you want," Mom urged me. "Come, eat something."

I glanced quickly at the people at the table then timidly put a little rice and chicken on my plate. I felt out of place. This was the very first time I had sat at a dining table to eat. Was this really happening to me? I had more food in front of me than I had ever seen, and I was free to eat whatever I wanted. I thought about my parents in Liberia and wished I could share this joy with them.

"Sam, you're not eating," Mom said in a disapproving voice. "Eat up the food. Eat as much as you want. Take more than that."

I quickly ate the rice and chicken that was on my plate. Then hesitatingly, I filled my plate with other foods, meats of all kinds, vegetables, rice and peas, puddings, and cake. After eating that second plate, I went for a third serving.

"Sam, are you eating?" Mom asked as she passed by my chair.

"Yes, Mom, it tastes good," I said, grinning. By the time I was finished eating, I could hardly move. As everyone else had finished eating and left the dining room, Mom and the young woman who helped her along with another woman began clearing the table and washing the plates. I got up and started helping.

"Sam, leave the plates and go watch TV," Mom ordered me.

"I want to help you..." I said, but she interrupted me.

"We don't need your help," she said. "Go watch TV and relax."

This was too good to be true. I began to feel uncomfortable, not doing anything. Things had turned upside down. Mom and her guests should be relaxing and watching TV while *I* cleaned up. I began to worry that Mom and Dad were testing me to see if I was lazy. Was this actually a test? Fear filled me. They are all watching me, I thought. They were all talking about me. Dad was sitting in his favorite chair and intermittently added to the conversation in the room. I kept watching to see if he was watching me, disapproving of me watching TV while his wife worked. All kinds of negative thoughts crowded my mind.

Instead of enjoying the TV, which I was not used to watching, I just sat and stared around the room, not wanting anyone to think that I was having fun viewing TV when I should have been working. Before I knew it, I fell into a deep sleep. When I woke up, I was alone, and the room was dim. A light was coming in through the living room window. It was morning, and I realized that someone had covered me with a blanket while I slept.

Breaking Point: A Journey to Self-Awareness and Finding Purpose in Pain

Mom seemed to be going out of her way to keep me from working too much around the house. I usually got up first in the mornings, as I always did in Liberia and in New York with the Kamaras, and I always found work to do. Mom would often stop me, insisting that I go sit down. Her care for me was tangible. She was not the hugging type, but she made me a robe that I still have to this day. It kept both my body and soul warm. She gave me good advice and, when necessary, she scolded me sternly, but with love and compassion. Dad was a man of few words, yet to me he exuded strength. It was as if nothing could touch his spirit. With them, I felt loved for the first time since I had left my biological parents and my playful, loving, and connected childhood in the village behind.

Although the Johnsons were the kindest and most caring people I knew, they never displayed any overt signs of public affection, such as holding hands, hugging or kissing each other. They were from the old school. Nevertheless, they dealt with each other lovingly and respectfully.

Mr. Johnson was a chauffeur and drove a stretch limousine that carried around people of means from Manhattan to various places in the Tristate area of New York, New Jersey, and Connecticut. He was also the pastor of a Seventh-day Pentecostal church in the Bronx. He was a humble man of few words, but had a very robust laugh whenever he was amused. He displayed the same temperament at home as he did at church. When he spoke, he would often rub the top of his head. When you asked his opinion, it was as if he was weighing and counting his words, being careful not to use up his supply for the day. But when he was preaching and was filled with the Holy Spirit of God, his voice thundered through the microphone and he would jump so high that we thought he was trying to touch the ceiling. The Johnsons shared their limited resources with church members and others who were in need.

Dad had to work to make a living, because he did not get a salary from the church. At home, I often wondered what he was thinking when he sat in his chair. Did he hate me? Did he love me? Would he also eventually ask me to leave? As time passed, Dad seemed to become more comfortable with me, or perhaps simply more accustomed to my presence. Mom was also my spiritual mother, because she taught me biblical lessons and offered me spiritual guidance and insight. In her late forties, she was heavy-set, with a light chocolate brown complexion. Her personality was a complex mix of tenderness and strictness. She was a plain-looking woman who was stern and outspoken; everyone knew that she would speak her mind simply and in a straightforward manner. Yet, she was a very good listener and a wise counselor. Because she was a good communicator, she was one of the teachers in the church. When needed, she was not afraid to speak loudly or shout at someone, but she was by no means vulgar or rude.

After I went to live with them, I continued attending Harry S. Truman High School. Although I had lost contact with my biological family, I still held my father's dream for me close to my heart. I was now older and understood the importance of an education in bettering one's lot in life. Nothing would get into my way, now that I was in America, attending what I considered to be a topnotch high school in a big fancy building, with sophisticated desks and chairs. I would get my education and one day show Papa and Mama that their dream of me helping the family had come true; that I hadn't endured hardship in vain. I would see Papa and Mama again. I just knew I would, so I never missed a day of school and got "As" and "Bs" on my report cards.

During this time, I attended church with Mom and Dad and took a real interest in the fellowship. I participated in the worship and even started giving testimonies of thanksgiving in church. Mom taught me a lot about the Bible. Her teaching, coupled with my gratitude to God for providing me a surrogate family and a job, contributed greatly to my decision to become a Christian. The church brethren embraced me and received me enthusiastically. Every time I participated in a church activity, I felt the love of the brethren.

"Pastor Barnett, meet Pastor and Sister Johnson's African son," the church sister said as she introduced me to the pastor of a church that we were visiting.

"What's your name?" he asked me.

"Sammy," I replied. The sister held my hand and took me around the fellowship to introduce me to other church members. This experience was not only repeated at the church Dad pastored, but also at the sister churches we visited. I was even invited to greet the church and to share my testimony. I was often very nervous and hesitant to speak in front of the congregation.

One weekend, we were at a church convention in Washington, DC, where members from various churches gathered for fellowship.

"Brothers and sisters," one of the pastors addressed the church. "Today we are glad to have our beloved Pastor and Sister Johnson with us. Let's praise the Lord!"

"Praise the Lord!" the church replied in a chorus.

"Before the preacher comes forward, Brother Sam is going to share his testimony," the pastor continued. "He is the son of Pastor and Sister Johnson, and is all the way from Africa. Did you hear me? I said 'He's all the way from Africa!' "

"Praise the Lord!" the church members shouted energetically. "Praise the Lord!"

"Before he comes, Church, stand up and give God the highest praise," the pastor urged. "Let's shout hallelujah seven times for this young man. God has been so good to him." The members shouted hallelujah seven times and some of them started jumping and rejoicing in the Holy Spirit.

I was overcome by the excitement in the church. My heart started racing, and my hands were trembling. I looked to Mom for reassurance. I had never spoken before so many people in all my life. The atmosphere was charged, and the exuberance of the church members heightened the feelings of expectancy. My mind went blank, and suddenly I didn't know what to say. Everyone started clapping, and I could feel that all eyes were on me. I didn't move. Instead, I stared at Mon as though I were in a trance.

"Sam, go. The pastor called you to testify," she urged me. I still didn't move. "You can do it. Just tell people what the Lord has done for you. You know your testimony, now go."

"Come on, Brother Sam," the pastor called again. "Come share your testimony."

I finally got up and walked slowly to the front of the church, trying to collect my thoughts. They were jumbled. What should I say first? What if I made a mistake? Why would these people want to hear about me anyway? Who was I? I was not important.

"As you all know," I mumbled. "I'm from Africa. I was brought to New York City by a family who threw me out into the streets after three years here." The room became suddenly quiet, and all eyes were focused on me. I stared straight ahead and continued.

"I had no family to take me in. One day, I met Leon, the son of Pastor and Sister Johnson. I told him my story, and he took me to his house so I could share my story with his mother."

The people looked amazed as I shared about my life. Some were even crying whereas others started rejoicing in the Holy Spirit. Something magical happened that evening. I felt the sweet feeling of belonging to a group of people who had opened their hearts to receive me. They didn't judge or scorn me; they embraced me just like the church members at Dad's church had done. I felt good. I decided at that moment to give my life to the Lord and be baptized, so that I could truly enjoy the loving acceptance that the church offered, so that I could feel that I belonged. In the fall of 1976, I made the decision to be baptized. Dad told me, however, that I had to be sure that I knew what I wanted to do.

"Baptism is a serious thing, Sammy," he admonished me. "I need to see fruits of repentance: fruits such as consistent prayer, compliance with the church rules and regulations, as well as active participation in the church."

Breaking Point: A Journey to Self-Awareness and Finding Purpose in Pain

I must have borne enough fruits to satisfy Dad because he finally decided to baptize me a year later. One day in December of 1976, I was one of four youths who stood ready for baptism next to the church's pool, located in the basement. Most of the church members were gathered before the pool, singing hymns and choruses, as we each professed our faith in God and our determination to be true followers of Christ. When signaled, I stepped into the pool with Dad and the deacon.

"Today, you will turn your back on the world," Dad proclaimed as he held my hands. "You're about to enter a new life. Are you fully persuaded to walk with the Lord?"

"Yes, Dad," I replied. "I'm ready."

"Brother Sammy Kamara," Dad said. "According to the profession of your faith and your testimony, I now baptize you in the name of the Lord Jesus Christ for the remission of all your sins." As he said the words, he held both my hands together and covered my nose. Assisted by the deacon, Dad placed his left hand at the back of my neck and pushed my upper body backward into the water. As he did so, I held my breath. I was a baptized member of the church. It felt good to belong.

After my baptism, I joined the youth choir and continued to participate in the youth department. I was also a member of *The King's Children Youth Choir* and traveled with the choir to minister at various churches throughout the northeastern USA.

I had found a family and a church.

It seemed that my life would ease up!

Rebuen N. Johnson - "Dad"
Foster Father

Edris M. Johnson – "Mom"
Foster Mother

Chapter 7

Beginning to Work

*"Opportunities are usually disguised as hard work,
so most people don't recognize them"*
— Ann Landers

Things did look up for me in the next years. The summer before I graduated from Harry S. Truman High School, I got a summer internship at the New York Botanical Garden in the Bronx, through the HUB Summer Internship Youth Program. It would be years before I understood what a gift this was.

The training that my biological father had given me on our farm served me well during this internship.

About fifteen young males from various high schools had been selected to participate in the program. We were all gathered at the entrance of the operations building when a White man came out and greeted us.

"Good morning, young men," he said in a commanding voice that was thick with a German accent. (I was later to learn this man, like me, had migrated to the US, he was also a retired US Army lieutenant.) "I am Mr. John Lavin, the head supervisor of operations. Are you here to work today? Are you ready?"

"Yes, we are," we answered, most of us timidly.

"Alright," he said. "Begin by picking up all the papers around this building." We all immediately started picking up the debris, but as soon as Mr. Lavin went back inside the operations building, all the other interns stopped working. Some talked with each other and others just stood around. I kept working and eventually had picked up most of the litter. While I was still working, I heard Mr. Lavin's voice at the door. Hearing him, too, the rest of the interns made a mad dash to join me in picking up papers.

Mr. Lavin stepped out of the building and watched us for a moment or two. "You," he commanded, pointing at me. "Come with me."

I was still busy picking up papers and didn't realize that he was speaking to me.

"You," he commanded again, just as I looked up and saw his finger pointing at me. "Yes, you. Come with me."

What had I done wrong? I followed him timidly into the building. Why had he called me—and not the others—into his office? I was so scared. I felt as if Esther or Uncle Henry was reprimanding me and I immediately began to fear that bad luck had followed me, even to this internship opportunity. Mr. Lavin was going to send me home, I just knew it. I would have to tell Mom and Dad that I had been sacked.

"Have a seat," he ordered as he himself went over to sit behind his large desk. "What is your name?"

"My name is Sammy Kamara," I mumbled, looking down at the floor.

"Where are you from?" He noticed that I was staring at the floor and frowned. "Hold up your head."

"I'm from Liberia." My voice was barely audible, and I was barely able to look this White man in the face. When I said "Liberia," a broad smile crossed his face.

"Oh, I see," he said in a softer voice. "Who is the president in Liberia now?"

"William R. Tolbert, Junior," I replied in a slightly stronger voice.

"As a matter of fact, I was a consultant to the US military when they helped the Liberian Government to amend the Constitution of Liberia," he informed me. "So I worked in Liberia for a while. I remember various streets, Broad Street, Water Street, the Ducor International Hotel, the Mansion, and many other places in Monrovia."

I was excited to learn that he knew about my homeland. I allowed myself to smile, but I contained my excitement. What was happening here? I asked myself with my usual wariness. Could this be some unexpected good fortune coming my way?

"Mr. Lavin, I really want to work," I said with more confidence.

"I can see that," he said in this new, mild tone. "Ok, I'm going to take you to the custodial department to work today." When we went back outside to join the other guys, Mr. Lavin instructed them to continue picking up trash. Then he took me to the custodial department.

I was excited that evening to be able to tell Mom and Dad that I definitely was in the internship program and that I would be working in the custodial department. With a job, I would be able to pay my expenses and no longer be a financial drain on Mom and Dad. They had been so kind to me and now I could not only pay my own way, but perhaps possibly help them out.

The next day, I reported to the operations building with the other interns. After greeting us and giving the others their tasks, Mr. Lavin escorted me to the custodial department. This became my daily routine for the rest of that summer. I would gather with the other guys and then Mr. Lavin would escort me to my work site.

After all the years that I had worked for nothing, after I had been exploited and given hardly enough food to survive on, or any clothes to wear, it was a deep satisfaction for me to be paid for my work. Each paycheck seemed like a miracle. In all, this was a good summer, and, at the end of the internship program, I went to Mr. Lavin's office. "Mr. Lavin," I told him, "I really enjoyed working at The Garden."

I said this with more confidence than I knew I had. Something had begun to happen to me. "Please consider me for next summer."

"No problem, Sammy," he said in a friendly tone. "Come and check with me next summer. I wish you all the best."

In June 1977, three months before my nineteenth birthday, I graduated from Harry S. Truman High School. I went to the graduation ceremony alone. No one was there to witness my achievement and to congratulate me. Mom was away on one of her frequent evangelistic trips to another state, and Dad was working to earn the income to keep the family afloat. Leon and his sister had no interest in attending. As much as I wished Mom and Dad had been with me, I yearned even more to have Papa and Mama witness me graduate—especially Papa. I wanted to see the pride and joy on their faces. I wanted us to all hug and cry and scream at my progress toward the realization of our family dream. I could now begin to work toward getting them out of poverty. But alas! They were many miles—and many years—away. Nevertheless, I did my own little celebration by leaping for joy and pumping my right fist, thumb up, in the air. "Yes, I did it!" I shouted.

The weekend after graduation, I talked with Mom about my future. Now that high school was over what would be next? Mom was in some ways like Mama. She was honest, caring, and full of good advice.

"Mom, I want to go to college," I told her. "The guidance counselor at school has talked with us about attending college after graduation."

"Sam, it would be wonderful if you could go to college," she said. "But how is that going to happen? We have no money to send you to college."

"I want to study engineering," I said ignoring her realism about money. "I want to work on helicopters or airplane engines, or I want to be a helicopter pilot."

"Sam, that sounds very good." She sighed. "But as I just said, we cannot afford it. Where is the money going to come from to send you to college? We are not people with money."

"So what am I going to do now?" I asked, a bit sadly. While at Harry S. Truman High School, I had learned about mechanics and really wanted to build a career as an engineer. Did my dream have to be sacrificed again? There must be another way for me to study further.

"Well, the only logical thing is to get a job," she advised me. "What about going back to The Garden? Didn't you say that they said you could come back for summer work?"

"Yes, Mr. Lavin said I could go back."

"Well, that's the opportunity that God has provided," she pointed out. "Pray, and then go check with the man."

"I will, but that is a summer job," I explained. "That won't help me to go to college."

"Sam, start with a summer job. It's better than nothing," she said. "You never know what God will do. When the summer is finished, you can look for another job. You may not get a job with big money, but you should look for a job with benefits."

"What benefits?" I was puzzled by that term.

"I'm talking about health insurance, a pension when you retire, and any other help that the company might give to their employees. First, seek out summer work. Go see if the Garden will take you back. Then you can plan for long term work."

Some of my peers who had graduated with me were going on to college and I had hoped to be with them. I was very disappointed that I wouldn't be, but I didn't allow myself to be angry at Mom and Dad. They had done their best for me—they had already done so much. I wasn't their biological son, yet they had taken me into their home and heart. They had provided for me without asking for any compensation. If they had been able to send me to college, I'm sure they would have invested in me. But they did not have any extra funds.

So in the summer of 1977, I went back to The New York Botanical Garden.

"Good morning, Mr. Lavin," I said.

"Good morning, Sammy!" he answered in his cheerful voice, which was as Germanic as ever. "Glad to see you. How have things been?"

"I graduated from high school," I said, feeling pleased with myself.

He rose from his desk and headed out the door. "Come with me," he said, and led me out to one of the golf carts. "Jump in, Sammy. Why are you standing there?"

When we arrived at the custodial department in the Watson Building, Mr. Lavin took me to Mr. Vinny Pitaro, who was the head supervisor for the custodial department. I hadn't told Mr. Lavin that I had come to seek a job because I had graduated. He seemed to remember that he had promised me a job when I graduated.

"Pitaro, here is Sammy. He is going to be working with you from here on," he said. "He worked here last summer, if you remember."

"I do." Mr. Pitaro turned to me: "Sammy, welcome back," he greeted me, and shook my hand.

Mr. Lavin offered me a temporary position as a Junior Building Custodian. It was not the usual summer job that the Garden offered interns—there would be another batch this summer. The position was available for six months. This was the opportunity I needed. I had my foot in the door and I planned to work diligently to keep that job. That day, I stayed and worked all day, not even thinking that Mom might be worried about where I was. I ran home that evening to share the good news.

"Mom! Mom! Guess what!" I yelled with excitement as I entered the house. "I got the job!" I wanted her to be the first to know, because she was the one who had suggested that I ask Mr. Lavin for a job, in the first place.

"Praise the Lord!" she said. She was excited for me. "You have something to thank God for."

During those six months, I did my best to deliver good service to The Garden. In December 1977, a permanent career-track position for a Junior Building Custodian opened up. Full-time employees of The Garden are also employees of the New York City Government. This opening was therefore a union job with benefits such as health insurance, a pension, a uniform allowance, and so on. In spite of the plan for me to obtain a full time job and my clear need for such a job, I didn't plan to apply. In my usual way, learned over years of being put down in Liberia, I thought that I was not qualified.

But, there was more. When the Kamaras kept my documents, Mom had advised me to apply for a replacement social security card, so I had one. Notwithstanding, because I did not have my immigration documents in hand to prove that I had entered the USA legally, I thought I was in the country illegally. This was my belief, even though I could recall Mr. Kamara telling me that I had entered the country with a permanent resident card. All fall, while Mr. Pitaro encouraged me repeatedly to apply for the position, I still didn't apply.

"Sammy, why haven't you applied for the position?" Mr. Pitaro asked me one day, perhaps a bit frustrated with me.

"I don't think I am qualified," I said to him.

"What do you mean you aren't qualified?" He looked incredulous. "You're one of the hardest workers around here. You definitely qualify. Fill out the form, and I will approve it. The job is yours."

It hadn't occurred to me that the job was not in open competition, that it was mine for the asking. Only Mom and Dad and Mr. Lavin had ever had such belief in me. I couldn't believe that Mr. Pitaro did, too. I was reluctant and nervous as I completed the form. I now felt I had to submit it, because of Mr. Pitaro's commitment to me. As promised, I was offered the position and, so in December 1977, I became a permanent employee with the City of New York at the New York Botanical Garden.

Receiving a paycheck every other week for a permanent position provided me peace of mind—not to mention a degree of financial stability. I was being paid about $2.65 per hour, which wasn't much, but it was certainly better than not having an income. Thoughts of Mama and Papa frequently invaded my mind. If only I could share my new found "wealth" with them! I agonized over not being able to send them money to help ease the hardships they must have been facing at home. I turned to the Lord again in prayer, earnestly asking God for some way to reconnect with my family. Thoughts of my family in Liberia always made me feel hopeless. This heaviness sometimes lasted for weeks.

How could I reach them? I didn't want to ask Uncle Henry to help.

In fact, I admitted to myself that I hated him. When I remembered the way he had mistreated and neglected me, I often felt intense pain and anger. I was now a Christian and the anger did not seem to be a Christian response. Nevertheless, now that I was a grown man, I wanted to meet him face to face, man to man, to make him pay for the wrong he had done to me. I wasn't sure how this pay back would work, but nonetheless it occupied my imagination daily. I had frequent flashbacks of his wrongdoings and in these flashbacks I fought back.

Years had passed since I had come to America, yet the pain of being away from my family and not knowing what was happening to them surfaced again and again. In my late teens, my need to connect with them was becoming excruciating. Thoughts of my family in Liberia began to invade my mind when I least expected them and caused me to lose focus on my tasks. To bring myself some relief, although I hated Uncle Henry, I accepted the fact that he was my only hope to make contact with my family again. In the spring of 1979, I decided to write a letter to him. I addressed the letter to the Liberian Police Band where he last worked when I was there:

> Dear Uncle Henry,
>
> I hope this letter finds you in good health. Actually, I hope you get this letter. I don't have your address so I finally decided to write to you at the police band.
>
> How are my mother and father doing? I miss them and long to hear from them.
>
> Please write back soon. Please tell them that I am ok. I would really appreciate it.
>
> Thank you very much, Uncle.
>
> Yours truly, Sammy

I didn't tell Uncle that the Kamaras had thrown me out, just as I had suspected that they would. What had he been thinking of when he abandoned me to them? Did he really think they would raise me as their son? I also didn't inform him that I had graduated from high school and that I was working. I didn't tell him that I had found good surrogate parents in Mom and Dad. I didn't tell him any of these things because he hadn't cared what happened to me when he might have helped me. Why would he care now?

That year, I sent two other letters to the police band. Each had a return address, but I never heard back from Uncle Henry, nor were the letters returned to me.

Chapter 8

Small Successes

"When heavens smile on a man, the earth has no other choice than to respond to his needs"
— Ikechukwu Izuakor

Working at The Garden had provided me with an opportunity to meet people in the larger world – the White world. Employees included Europeans, South Americans, people from Asia, and the Caribbean. I was the only African working there at the time. The Garden was a fascinating world where I learned bits and pieces of each employee's culture. One experience stands out in my mind to this day.

Mr. Pitaro had assigned me to work on the second floor of the Watson Building where the Office of Dr. William C. Steere, the President of The Garden at the time, was located. Each morning, I would clean Dr. Steere's office and hurry to leave before he arrived. On a few occasions, he would arrive just as I was almost finished. He would say good morning and then proceed to make himself tea or coffee. One morning, Dr. Steere did something that I never dreamed could happen.

"Sam, have a cup of tea with me." He smiled and pointed to the cups and hot-water kettle. I could not believe what I heard! The President of the Garden was inviting me to have tea with him.

"Thank you, Dr. Steere," I muttered. I was bound to make a mistake if I stayed to drink tea with him. "But I have to put away the cleaning supplies."

"Sam, just take a minute and have a cup of tea," he invited again.

"Thank you, Dr. Steere," I replied. As he had asked, I poured myself a cup of tea. My hand was shaking and I kept warning myself not to spill the tea or drop the cup.

"Have a seat here." He pointed at the chair beside his desk.

"Thank you, Dr. Steere." I sat, mostly looking at the tea in my hand while glancing at him occasionally. Dr. Steere was drinking his tea. My heart was beating so hard I thought Dr. Steere could hear it.

"Drink your tea," Dr. Steere urged. I had thought to leave with the tea, because I didn't want him to think I was wasting time and not working. I was still very much a "slave houseboy" and had little confidence in myself. Was Dr. Steere just testing me to see if I was lazy? Had I done something wrong? Or was he subtly trying to get information about me? Why would the President of The Garden, of all persons, want to have tea with me?

"Sam, I'm writing a book," he said. He knew my name because he knew that I had been assigned to clean his office. "Many people think that writers just sit and write a book, just like that, but it is not easy. Sometimes I get stuck. It takes time."

I just kept nodding my head, too afraid to say anything. I hurriedly sipped my tea and said, "Thank you, Dr. Steere. I wish you well with your book. Thank you for the tea, Dr. Steere." I gathered my cleaning supplies and hurried out of his office.

Dr. Steere did not realize that his offer of kindness was intimidating and made me feel very uncomfortable. His kindness to me was most likely his way of showing appreciation for the meticulous manner in which I cleaned his office daily, but I knew we were from two "different worlds", and I felt myself unworthy of being invited by him. I was not yet able to accept kindness without suspecting that it masked something negative. That had been the norm for most of my life.

At The Garden, I met other important persons such as professors and researchers. Initially, I was intimidated by them and socially awkward in their presence, the way I had been with Dr. Steere. In time, however, I started to realize that they were human beings just like me. Furthermore, they regarded me with kindness. Their down-to-earth approach to me finally broke down my guard.

Wow! Was this really me talking to them? I often asked myself this as I met these people. At first, I was highly suspicious and often refused their offers of breakfast, coffee or some other kindness, because I wondered if they were trying to set me up to lose my job. It took me almost a year to accept their invitations without worrying that something negative would happen. I couldn't help remembering the "rich" people that I had encountered, both in Liberia and when I was with the Kamaras. Those people had scorned me. I couldn't use their cups and utensils. I couldn't eat with them because of the strict social taboos and the boundaries they had created and demanded that I observe. Surprisingly, these people of the American upper class treated me nicely. I appreciated it, but kept wondering when they would start treating me badly. Some part of me was more comfortable being mistreated. I knew where I stood, then.

* * *

As a child attending school in Liberia, I was aware that William V. S. Tubman was the president of Liberia. Following a succession of other Liberian presidents of Americo-Liberian heritage, Tubman led Liberia for about 27 years, from 1943 to July 1971, when he died while still in office. Tubman helped to modernize Liberia's infrastructure in Monrovia with his economic "Open Door" policy to bring in foreign investors. These investors were lured to Liberia by lucrative tax breaks and other privileges. By the 1950s, the city of Monrovia had paved streets, a sanitation system, hospitals, and literacy programs. Tubman greatly influenced Liberia's political and economic growth

Breaking Point: A Journey to Self-Awareness and Finding Purpose in Pain

and development during the 20th century. During the 1950s, Liberia reportedly had the fastest growing economy in the world, after Japan's. By the time Tubman died in 1971, Liberia had the largest mercantile fleet in the world, although it was alleged that some of these ships were merely flying the Liberian flag for tax benefits. It had the world's largest rubber industry, was the third largest exporter of iron ore in the world, and Liberia was benefiting from over $1 billion US dollars in foreign investment.[1]

Tubman was both loved and hated. According to one writer, Fred van der Kraaj, Tubman was "sincere and oppressive, lauded as a patriot and accused of selling the country to foreigners, chauvinistic defender of Americo-Liberian interests, and an ardent supporter of the noble cause of national unification between the Americo-Liberian colonists and the tribal (native) population of Liberia."[2] Paradoxically, Tubman helped to initiate various social and political changes, such as unification efforts to bridge the gap between the Americo-Liberian elites and native tribal Liberians. Yet, after an assassination attempt in 1955, Tubman's autocratic tendencies became apparent as he brutally cracked down on political opposition.

When Tubman died in 1971, he was succeeded by his vice president; William Tolbert, Jr. Tolbert was also of Americo-Liberian heritage. (His grandfather was born in Charleston, South Carolina) At the time Tolbert became president, politics and government were concentrated in the hands of less than three per cent of the population—the Americo-Liberians -- and the "modern" economy was controlled by foreign investors from countries such the USA and Lebanon. The indigenous tribal majority was excluded from both political life and the developing modern economy of the country. While this does not excuse the ruthlessness of indigenous people like Uncle Henry, it does explain their insecurity.

---

1 http://www.ourcampaigns.com/CandidateDetail.html?CandidateID=212966
2 *The Open Door Policy of Liberia – An Economic History of Modern Liberia* (Bremen, 1983) – Fred van deer Kraaj

Tolbert tried to make his own mark on the development of Liberia by reversing some of Tubman's policies and instituting various polices of his own. For example, he tried to promote polices to improve the standard of living of the masses—policies such as "Total Involvement for Higher Heights" and "From Mat to Mattresses". The progressive reforms to help the masses, however, encountered strong opposition within his own political party, the True Whig Party, which had ruled Liberia since 1870. Tolbert faced other challenges. He had employed many of his own relatives in his government. One brother was the Minister of Finance, and another was President Pro-Tempore of the Senate. Furthermore, the Mayor of Monrovia was his cousin.[ii] His critics accused him of "...nepotism, corruption and the continuation of privileges for a few and poverty for the masses."[iii] Tolbert began to secure more power for himself. In October 1975, he was elected President in elections where he was the only candidate. He extended his term of office from four to eight years.

Tolbert's presidency came to an abrupt end on April 12, 1980 when he was assassinated in a vicious and bloody coup at the Liberian Presidential Mansion. This was during my third year at The Garden. I still had not heard back from Uncle Henry and was worried by the news that was coming out of Liberia. How was this impacting my family? I had no way of knowing. The assassination coup was led by the native Samuel K. Doe, a Master Sargent in the Liberian military. Doe and his men also executed members of Tolbert's government; who were mostly, if not exclusively, Americo-Liberians. With this blood bath, Doe ended more than one hundred years of minority rule over the masses, and for the first time in its history, Liberia was under military rule. Doe suspended the existing constitution and banned all political parties. He allegedly planned to return the country to civilian rule in 1985 after a new constitution was drafted. However, Doe fell in love with power and decided that he wanted to remain as the head of state.

Chapter 9

Lost Family

*"He who finds a wife finds what is good and
receives favor from the LORD"*
— Proverbs 18:22

I was interested in finding a woman to be my wife, but none of the sisters in the church caught my eye. The list of qualities that I sought in my future wife was reasonable, I felt. I desired a young lady with whom I would feel comfortable worshipping God together, someone who loved the Lord dearly. She should have love and respect for me, should be faithful and trustworthy and should contribute to the well-being of our family. I didn't know the sisters in the other churches and the church leaders were very strict; they didn't believe in what they called *boyfriend-girlfriend relationships*. They also didn't believe in dating or courtship because these could stimulate lustful drives. To avoid this, we were admonished to keep our eyes on the Lord and, if we found ourselves emotionally interested in someone, we were to seek the Lord's approval and, if we got it, we had to get married within six months or as quickly as possible. Our church discouraged long-term engagements. The prevailing belief was that, to avoid sexual sin, it was best not to delay marriage.

Shortly after I started seeking the Lord, I noticed a church sister named Laura, who was being tutored by Mom. She was about 5 feet

4 inches tall with a caramel complexion. I learned later that she has a combination of Indian and Black blood. Her biological mother was of Indian descent, and her father was from Jamaica. Because of her Indian heritage, her shoulder length hair was coal black and soft. She was small-boned, with small hands and feet. Her voice was soothing. Although she didn't have a curvaceous body, she had kissable lips and small, dark brown eyes. She was pretty and her smile was quick.

Laura had been in the church much longer than I, and, like me, she was being tutored by Mom about the Bible and life. Mom spoke well of Laura and told me that she had never heard a bad report about her. She was an avid student of the Bible; she abided by the church rules; she was reliable and an active participant in church services and other activities; and she was very helpful, domestically.

While I respected her highly developed knowledge of the Bible, I was also drawn to her silky hair. I often imagined running my fingers through it. I could definitely see her as my wife and the mother of my children. I convinced myself that sharing my life in marriage with her would add to my joy and happiness. After all, we shared religious beliefs, and we had known each other since I was seventeen years old and she sixteen. I was actually only five months older than she and I felt comfortable and safe with these facts. I kept getting more excited about being with her, and held very high expectations for our future together.

Since the church leaders frowned on the idea of dating and courting, I sought advice from Mom about how to develop these romantic feelings into something tangible. I felt that I could talk with her about anything. In fact, I had grown to love her and Dad very much and she was the first person I ran to when I had any questions about the Bible and life.

"I can't tell you whom to marry," she said in a firm tone, when I shared my thoughts. "All I can say is that all that glitters is not gold. I don't know if this girl is the right or wrong person for you, because living with a person is way different than seeing the person a few times a week."

"So what should I do?" I asked. I wanted her to tell me what to do, because I didn't want to make a mistake, but she refused to budge from her statement that she couldn't do so.

"Well, all I can say is, make sure she loves you. She has to love you, also, and both of you should seek the Lord before making any decision." She stared at me and gave me a mysterious little smile. "I will pray for both of you, that's all I can do."

After speaking with Mom, I decided to do the manly thing and approach Laura. She lived with her stepmother who usually come to the house to help Mom with dish washing, cooking, and other chores. Her stepmother had raised Laura from a young child, and was Mom's very close friend. I timed my approach carefully. Mom had gone outside, and no one else was in the house. Laura was in the kitchen washing the dishes, and I stood the doorway.

"Hello," I said softly

She turned to face me. Fearing rejection, I was a little nervous. Notwithstanding, I approached her with caution, careful not to spoil the moment and my chances with her.

"I want you to know that I like you," I said confidently. She looked at me and smiled, then turned around and resumed washing the plates. That was a smile of acceptance -- at least I interpreted it as such, so I pressed on. Moving closer to her I asked, "Did you hear what I said? I mean that I love you." She looked at me again and smiled but said nothing.

"What do you have to say?" I asked.

"Mmm," she responded and continued washing the plates.

That was it; there was no significant display of emotions, no bells and whistles, no hooey-gooey feelings—just her bland acknowledgement of my expressed feelings. I took her smile and soft response to be an expression of her feelings, that she understood that I loved her. And I understood that she didn't reject me.

That moment marked the genesis of my relationship with Laura. Since the church and her parents didn't allow dating, we never dated or cozied up with each other. A few months after, I proposed to her at her mother's house.

"Laura, I would like you to be my lovely wife"
"Ok," she responded.

Although she never once said that she loved me, I told myself that she must love me, or she wouldn't have agreed to marry me. So, I suggested that we inform our parents of our intention to marry, thus beginning our walk along the tightrope that led to our wedding day. I call it a tightrope because I had to learn the art of maintaining balance while walking along the tensioned wire stretched between church and parental restrictions, and my desire to develop a more intimate relationship with her before we married. There were no movies, no trips to the park, or to other places of leisure, where we could relax and learn about each other. Apart from seeing her at church, or during her visits to the pastor's home, where I still lived, I was only allowed to make short visits to her house every now and then, and only when her stepmother was present. Her stepmother's strict rule was that we had to talk in the living room, while her stepmother moved around the house. Our parents were afraid that *something* could happen. We barely spoke when we were together. These were dry and non-stimulating encounters and our conversations were very formal and holy. We had to tread carefully because we were on "holy ground". Furthermore, her stepmother set a curfew, at which time I had to leave the house. I always left just before her stepmother's bedtime, which was usually about 9 p.m.

Adhering to our commitment to toe the line meant we had never even kissed before marriage and only engaged in occasional holy hugs. We were both virgins and had to wait until our wedding day to become sexually involved. All I knew about her was what I saw at church, on church trips, or during my short, monitored visits to her house. We didn't talk about what we wanted in our life together, our likes, our dislikes, or our dreams. The closest we went to talking about our future was when I told her that I didn't have a career job as yet, but would be getting something better, and that I would take good care of her. I considered my job at The Garden to be temporary, because my career plan was still to become an engineer. She informed me that she was working at an insurance company, so that if we lived within our means we should be ok. We didn't talk about having children. Only after marriage did we talk about having a boy and a girl.

I loved her. She was graceful and very committed to the Lord and that made me love her even more. I imagined her as a caring, soft spoken, young woman. This must be God's answer to my third prayer. My first prayer was for God to provide me with parents that would care for me and treat me with love just like my biological parents did; my second prayer was for God to help me finish school and get a decent job; my third prayer was for God to give me a wife that would fear Him. This Christian God was much more responsive than the spirits of my ancestors.

Prior to our marriage, I made a vow to God that I would be a fully committed and loving husband and care for her as my treasure. I would love her with all my heart in the sight of God, whether she loved me or not, because I was accountable to God, who had responded to my prayers. This wasn't just idle mental chatter. I made a vow to the God of heaven, not to her only. To me, it was an even more solemn vow. If I could, I would have written these vows with my own blood to prove my dedication to her. Regardless of any ups and downs, I vowed to do whatever I could do to repair any damage and resolve any problems that we might face. My heart was totally turned over to God and now it would also be totally turned over to her. I made my life commitment to Laura and erased thoughts of every other woman, long before I said my vows in the church. Reflecting the vows we would eventually repeat in the church, my feelings were "until death do us part."

* * *

Being with the Johnsons and being integrated into the life of the church made me feel that I belonged. Now I was getting ready to make a major change in my life. Not knowing what was happening to my birth family was a heavy burden to bear. As the time approached, I thought daily about Mama, Papa, and my brothers but I had no way of reaching them to share my new found joy. I struggled daily with that lack of knowledge. I wanted my biological parents to witness the wedding ceremony and celebrate my coming of age. When I thought of my family, it wasn't a case of out of sight out of mind: it was a case of absence making the heart grow fonder. I was making a new life for myself here in America, but I was still searching for ways to reconnect with my parents. One night, in the fall of 1980, as I lay awake, staring at the ceiling I decided to write Uncle Henry again. This time I decided to send it to the Liberian Police Headquarters in Monrovia.

I wrote the letter and prayed over it for days before I put it in the mail. I asked God to help me find favor by allowing Uncle Henry to receive this letter so that I could reconnect with my parents.

Two months later, in December 1980, a miracle happened! I received a letter from Uncle Henry! When Mom handed me the letter, I fell to my knees in disbelief. Although I had prayed to God many times about hearing from Uncle Henry, now that my prayers had been answered, I was in total shock. I can't recall telling Mom thanks, I felt too numb to speak. Not wanting to break down in tears before Mom, I went to the bathroom to read it.

> Hi Sammy
>
> This is your Uncle Henry. I got your letter. Your family is ok. You took a long time to write but it is still good to hear from you. Your parents are ok. Your father came to visit me the other day. Don't forget to write soon and send a picture so I can see how big you are."
>
> From your Uncle Henry

Reading the letter eclipsed the joy I had felt as I opened it. Uncle

Henry did not even bother to ask about my well-being. I became angry at myself for expecting, or needing, him to ask. Had he tried to find me at all, over these years? Or was it a case of out of sight out of mind? I allowed myself to seethe before replying to him. Don't be ungrateful, I told myself, at least you now have contact with him and he is the road to reconnection with your family. That night, I replied to Uncle's letter and a few days later I dressed in a suit and tie and had a photograph taken to send to him.

Uncle Henry wrote two other letters to me in 1981. He did not once ask me how I was doing—if I was still with the Kamaras or if I had graduated from school. In each of those two letters, he asked for money because life was hard in Liberia. And he kept telling me that my parents were fine. I know my parents couldn't read, and even if they could, I had no other way to communicate with them. Uncle Henry was my lifeline to them. So I started sending money home to my parents, through Uncle Henry.

Shortly after sending my photograph to Uncle Henry, I started having very severe headaches. At various times during the day, my head felt as if it was boiling. Sometimes it felt as if it was about to explode or as if something was trying to rip my brains out. To ease my torment, I would drink Guinness Stout. Little did I know that the beer was only adding to my troubles. The headaches would ease up, but return the next day with a vengeance. Yet, I didn't seek medical help. I told myself that I had to grin and bear it. I just had to press on through the pain because I had to go to work.

While at a prayer service at church, two of the church sisters started speaking in unknown tongues. One of the sisters began to speak in English and stated that my mental torment was related to my sending a photograph to Africa. She further stated that they were jealous of me. The plan was to destroy my brains and, if possible, kill me. That night many prayers were offered on my behalf. Subsequently, although I still had bad headaches, I no longer felt as if my brains were being ripped out, and my headaches were less frequent and less intense.

Chapter 10

Oh Happy Day!

*"Nothing can bring a real sense of security
into the home except true love."*
— Billy Graham

In deciding to marry, I was like a wave rushing to the shore. It had not occurred to me that once I reached the shore, like a wave, I would lose my energy and be subsumed by an undertow.

We decided on a date for our wedding ceremony and reception about seven months after I had revealed my feelings to Laura and we had informed our parents. Because of our church beliefs, it seemed natural to us that, strangers as we were, we would commit to a life together. Despite the church's emphasis on marriage, we didn't receive any formal or structured premarital counseling on what might make a good marriage—for instance, the importance of compromise, accountability, and maintenance in marriage. Dad, who delivered the counseling, was not a trained minister or marriage counselor so he prayed with us and encouraged us in the Lord. Mom also gave us some godly advice and prayed with us. Premarital counseling was not seen as a necessity because we were two Christian believers of the same faith and denomination. This was supposed to mean that we were only required to seek the Lord before we proceeded with marriage and all would be well.

As I recall, ministerial education was not emphasized in our church at the time. In fact, the official position was that there was no need for ministers and teachers of the church to go to seminary. They only needed to fully trust and rely on the Holy Spirit to teach and guide them.

Furthermore, discussion of sexual matters was forbidden in public. It was an unspoken taboo; not once did we have any discussion of the subject. If someone were to ask a sexually-related question, the speaker was immediately dismissed with the terse comment that church was not the place for subjects like this. I cooperated with the rules, teachings, and expectations of the church. In fact, I often defended them, but somewhere in the recesses of my mind, I knew there had to be a better, more progressive and helpful way. After all, it was as if we were denying or denouncing important parts of ourselves in deference to the emphases on "spiritual" things.

Today, I know that the church I so dearly loved needed to begin to embrace and practice holistic ministry to its people. Our church needed to make necessary changes, such as training and developing its ministers, reexamining doctrines and theological certainties, and making competent counseling services available to members. Church officials needed to provide marriage enrichment opportunities within the church, instead of merely condemning divorce, and insisting that married couples stay "bound for life" without offering the help required to make their marriages work as God intended. There needed to be more openness, including teaching about maintenance and accountability in marriage. We ought to create a supportive environment of Grace, not legalism, in which people could feel free to be open, honest, and vulnerable with each other.

Could my beloved church make these changes? Only time would tell.

* * *

"I now pronounce you husband and wife," Dad announced on June 28, 1981. It was such an honor to have him serve as the minister, performing the marriage ceremony that united my bride and me. That day, I was 22 years and ten months old, and she was 22 years and 4 months old.

Laura looked radiant in a long white bridal gown, trimmed with decorative lace. Her head was adorned with a matching small white tiara and she carried a beautiful bouquet of assorted flowers. My eyes were fixed on her. My heart was racing with excitement that today; our world would know that we were husband and wife. Very intimate thoughts of being together crossed my mind, but I immediately dismissed them because we were standing in the holy church before a man of God.

Her father had died during our teen years. Her stepmother, along with members of her side of the family, friends, and members of our church, were gathered to witness this milestone event in our lives, but her biological mother was absent. My darling wife had been born in Jamaica, in the Caribbean. Before she turned five, her father married her stepmother, and the two of them raised her. I met Laura's father a couple of times before I became interested in her. He was a quiet and unassuming man of few words. He'd look at you and not initiate a greeting, but would respond if you greeted him first. At the time, Laura did not have a relationship with her biological mother, who had left Jamaica to live in England.

Her stepmother, Estella, was a very kindhearted, devoted Christian woman. She was soft spoken and easy to get along with. She had raised the girls, her own biological daughter and Laura, with much care. We attended the same church, so I had the opportunity to observe how considerate and caring she was. She seemed to love Laura as her own daughter, and appeared to defer to her often. I never observed Estella scold or disagree with Laura. In fact, she seemed to have a high regard for her. I never observed Laura disrespect her stepmother. If Laura harbored resentment of her stepmother or father, it never showed.

Leon and his sister were not at our wedding. Mom was very disappointed about that. Mom had spent a lot of time training them and explaining life to them, but Leon and his sister felt that the Christian life and the church were boring. They thought that Mom and Dad were too strict. In their late teen years, the two of them decided to leave the home that Mom and Dad had provided for them. As I saw them leave to begin a life of revelry outside the church, I felt sad that they had forgotten the values they had learned. I heard that Leon became a Rastafarian, started using drugs, had children out of wedlock, and was a charlatan preacher. His sister had a child out of wedlock. Neither of them kept in touch with Mom and Dad.

Laura smiled a lot during the ceremony. I wondered what she was thinking. When we held hands, her touch sent shivers all over my body. When Dad said, "You may kiss your bride," I gave her a quick kiss on her cheek. Deep kisses on the lips in public were considered to be lustful, carnal, fleshly, and were therefore disapproved of by God. This was the belief that was implied by the church, and we accepted it. Nowadays when I attend weddings, I am amazed at how liberated the couples are when they kiss each other at the altar. The kisses I see are often deep and juicy. If we had kissed like that, we undoubtedly would have offended most of individuals from our church community at the time.

After the ceremony, we left the church and were driven in Dad's limousine to the New York Botanical Garden to take photographs. Even though we were now legally and publicly married, there was not much intimacy or touching between us. I believe she felt as happy as I did but I can't remember asking her if she was happy. That evening, after celebrating at our reception, we went home. We were now two grown adults, legally married, and could be as intimate as we wanted to be. Notwithstanding, we faced a big challenge: how do we become intimate with each other when we have spent so much time trying not to be intimate, not to touch each other, not to kiss each other? Initially, being alone with her felt strange and awkward. This feeling of awkwardness would later become a constant presence in our marriage and hindered intimacy between us.

Our upbringing and our religious convictions called for little or no public displays of affection at home or at church. We were careful not to be too fleshly- or carnally-minded. This meant that we had to be very conservative, even when we should have been open and vulnerable to each other. I believe we were afraid that the Holy Spirit would reveal our carnality and fleshly desires. So we mostly lived our lives as students from the "old school of prudence".

Our first home was on Fish Avenue, in the Bronx. We had a one-bedroom apartment in a private house. Laura was particularly close to her best friend from church who also worked with her at the same company. They talked a lot at church and on the phone. They appeared to be inseparable. Laura seemed very comfortable sharing thoughts and feelings with her best friend. She had other friends at church, one of whom was affectionately called BB. BB often visited us and assisted whenever she was able to.

Laura and I did our best to break down the emotional walls that existed between us. Sometimes she would allow me to hold her hand when we walked on the street. This was big! We went for walks, visited the Bronx Zoo, The Garden, and other sites in Manhattan. As we walked, we admired the various species of flowers and we delighted in the beauty of the different sceneries. These outings began to bear fruit in our marriage. We began to feel more relaxed with each other and this began to stoke the fire of our love life. My belief was that our enjoyment of sexual intercourse was shared. But we never ever talked about it. We were prudish. Furthermore, in the "old school of prudence," one never talks about sex.

Also, we rarely told each other "I love you," except on special occasions, like birthdays. Again, the old school had conveyed the message that love should be shown, not expressed in words. Laura's acts of kindness demonstrated her love to me. She faithfully washed my clothes, cleaned the house, prepared our meals, and shared intimacy with me. Also, she would call me at work, just to check up on me. She mostly called me Sam and so I felt a special delight when she called me "Darling." I reciprocated by bringing her flowers, working hard at my job, and helping with the domestic chores.

At the end of each work day, I would rush to get home before Laura came in. In those early times, the mutual love and respect that I dreamed of and longed for was present. The time we spent exploring and experimenting with our sexual desires was delightful and bonded us. I felt close to her and secure in our relationship. While my relationship with my second parents provided safety and a strong sense of emotional well-being, my relationship with Laura was providing the kind of emotional comfort and safety that I'd always longed for—ever since my parents left me with my uncle.

As our love continued to grow, one evening after dinner, while still sitting at the dining table, I brought up the subject of having a baby.

"Babe," I said. "I think it would be nice for us to start thinking about a child. What do you think?"

"Ok," she answered softly. "My only concern is our finances. Can we afford it?"

"Well, what we can do is start checking on the cost," I told her. "How much would it cost for baby food, clothing and shoes, a suitable and trustworthy babysitter, private school? How much would lost time from work cost?"

"Yes, we would have to check it out," she said and shook her head. "I don't think we can afford it. We don't make enough money."

"Well, we can pray about it," I advised. "See what God will do." She didn't respond but looked as if she was in deep thoughts.

"By the way," I continued. "What would you want? A boy or a girl?"

"It doesn't matter to me if it's a boy or a girl," she said.

"I would want us to have a boy," I said.

"Why?" she asked.

"Because having a boy would provide protection for the family if I were not around," I answered. "A boy could be in charge and take care of you."

"Yes, that makes sense," she agreed. "I wouldn't mind having a boy."

"Well, let's pray about it," I concluded "And let's begin putting our plans in place to prepare for our child." With that agreement, we started saving, by putting away a small portion of our salaries, not taking vacations, and curtailing our spending.

* * *

One day while I was working, an entourage of New York City press was on a tour of the Garden with New York City Mayor Ed Koch and Professor Sir Ghillean Prance. Professor Prance is a renowned British botanist and ecologist who worked at The Garden from 1963 to 1988 as Director of the Institute of Economic Botany and Senior Vice-President for Science. While at the Garden, he researched the Amazon region of Brazil extensively.

The meeting with Mayor Koch was to celebrate an award that had been presented to Professor Prance. Professor Prance wanted to show off The Garden he loved so dearly. As the group of dignitaries and press passed by me, Dr. Prance stopped and greeted me cheerfully then asked the photographer to take a picture of him and myself later than evening. Dr. Prance often stated that he admired me for my Christian conduct. He was a Christian himself, so he often invited me to have lunch with him and his friends. We would share thoughts about the Bible and pray during this time. He never passed me in The Garden without greeting me.

Professor Prance and I shared a friendship that was rooted in our shared Christian beliefs – we were brothers in Christ. This reality allowed me to feel at ease with him. Although Professor Prance was a man of high social standing and academic distinction, I didn't feel intimated or uncomfortable with him as I had when Dr. Steere invited me to have tea with him. Professor Prance and I always welcomed the opportunity to greet and chat with each other.

* * *

Church played a dominant and defining role in our lives. When not working, Laura and I mostly spent our time going to church together and participating in the many church activities and events. We even went to church conventions in different parts of America. We shared a mutual delight in being part of the church and in striving to please God in our lives. As faithful members of our congregation, we attended church all day on Saturday, 9:30 a.m. to 7 p.m. or later, depending on when the sun set. Then we attended Sunday evening evangelistic services, followed by weekday prayer service or Bible studies.

During this time, we took one vacation to Florida together. I don't remember the details of the vacation, but I still remember the special feelings I had as we prepared for the trip. Being with her made more of an impression on me than our destination, or the places and people we visited. We started talking again about our desire to have children. During that time, I suggested that we both should try to reconnect with our biological families so that our children could meet them and we could develop stronger family bonds. Laura was hesitant to embrace my suggestion at first, because her relationship with her biological mother was strained. I urged her to forgive her mother and see whether reunification between them was possible. After I made several efforts to get her to reach out to her mother, who lived in England, she finally agreed to contact her.

Sam with Edris & Reuben Johnson
June 1981 – Sammy's wedding. Picture taken at NY Botanical Garden

Sammy and Professor Ghillian T. Prance at the New York Botanical Garden

PART THREE:
BITTER-SWEET WATERS

Chapter 11

Holy Matrimony Without Sweet Communion

"Nothing else wounds so deeply and irreparably. Nothing else robs us of hope so much as being unloved by one we love"
— Clive Barker

I don't know if Uncle Henry thought I was dead but, after sending him my photograph and money for my parents, I did not hear back from him. In September 1982, however, I received a letter from William Diah. He said he was my mother's younger brother. I know my mother's father's name was Diah but I didn't remember who William was. At first I was suspicious, and wondered how he had gotten my address, but my suspicion was quickly replaced by excitement. First of all, I was hearing from home again, but more importantly, it was not Uncle Henry writing to me, but my mother's brother. The contents of the letter however, made me very sad.

    September 14, 1982

    Hi Sammy,

    I am William Diah, your mother's brother. I don't know if you remember me but I got your address from my brother

Phillip, your uncle. He is now living in the city. I hope you are ok. Your family misses you, especially your mother. She cries for you every day. But we keep telling her to trust God and see what he will do. Sammy, I have to tell you some bad news. Your father, Robert Zlahn Wongan stopped taking care of your mother and he is treating her unlawfully. She has to do everything for herself including farming and building a house. Your brothers George and Mark are in Teahplay. George and Mark are helping your mother along with me and her brothers. Here is a message from your mother *"Gontor, I am not well in my body, you should find way by any means to come let me see you before I die. I am old now, your mother."* It is very true that she is suffering from her head, if no way of coming now please send some money so she can take some treatment. If there is money I will be able to send for her to come to me in the city to take the treatment. Write soon.

Your Uncle William

This was the worst news I could have received. When did Mama become sick? Uncle Henry kept telling me that she was ok. I suspected that he hadn't given her the money I had sent for her on more than one occasion. I felt like beating myself up for trusting that lying bastard. Was Uncle William even telling the truth? If not, why would he tell such a cruel lie about Papa and Mama? I wanted to believe that Papa loved Mama –that if Mama was sick he would be the first one to rush to help her. My emotions were in knots. Who was Uncle William? Sure he *said* he was my mother's brother, but was he? I decided to trust him. I couldn't live with myself if he was telling the truth and I didn't try to help my mother. So I sent money to Uncle William for my mother. Did she get it? To this day, I don't know.

Two months later, in November 1982, I received another letter from Liberia. This time it was from Uncle Philip—whom Uncle William had mentioned in his letter. Uncle Philip reminded me that he was my mother's younger brother and William was her youngest brother. I remembered that when I was leaving the village, Uncle Philip told me goodbye. However, when I lived in Monrovia, he never visited the City. Why not? Did he not know how Uncle Henry was treating me? I guess he also didn't have the means to travel to the City, because he had to take care of his own family.

> October 27, 1982
>
> Dear Sammy,
>
> May this letter find you in good health and the Lord watching over you. Sammy you cannot imagine how happy we are that you are still alive. My sister, your mother is heartbroken because she has not laid her eyes on you for all these years. Your grandparents are dead. Your mother is very old now and doesn't have anything, because your father put her outside. I am the one taking care of her and I don't have money. Send money to help her. Your mother would like to see you in person if there is possibility. Send money. Your mother is suffering horribly. Since PRC[iv] took over our Liberia it's very hard especially for us doing yard or groundwork. We desperately need your help. May God watch over you my son.
>
> Your Uncle Philip

A sense of urgency besieged me. I had to go to see my mother. My mind was completely made up but, as soon as I thought of it, I remembered that I didn't have my travel documents. The Kamaras had everything. Furthermore, Laura and I had just gotten the delightful news that she was pregnant. It was as though I was trapped in a colony of fire ants. That same week, I received another letter informing me that Mama had gotten worse. Uncle Philip was asking for money to take her to a private hospital in Monrovia for treatment. He was also asking for money to send George and Mark to school.

My agony dragged on for days, but I did not share it with Laura until yet another letter arrived from Uncle Philip telling me Mama was getting worse. I knew I had to travel to Liberia soon, to see her. I also suspected that Laura would not want me to go. Whenever I shared news about my family, she acted as if she was not interested. She seemed more interested in how my decision would impact her and our child; than how it would benefit us as a family. I suspected that her lack of interest was related to misinformation she had heard about Africa being full of witchcraft and that African men had multiple wives. Her fear may have been that I would start another family, based on this African tradition.

"Babe, I need to talk with you about something," I said with heaviness. "It's about my family in Liberia."

"What about your family?" she asked.

"My mother is very sick. I need to see her," I told her.

There was complete silence. You could hear a pin drop.

"I am pregnant," she replied slowly. "Are you planning to leave me like this?"

"Of course, that's not what I want to do," I said, a little annoyed. "I just can't stand the fact that I'm not there with my mother. She needs me."

"She needs you?" Laura retorted. "*She* needs you? I guess she is the only one that needs you."

"You're not making this easy for me," I said, not wanting to upset her.

"Sam, do what you want to do." She turned away.

"Babe, I don't want to leave you and our child alone," I said.

"Anyway, I don't even have my papers to travel."

That night, I chose not to argue with her. She was pregnant and she was right. I couldn't leave her alone. This would be our first child; I had to be there with her. I decided to send money to take care of Mama, instead. Another letter arrived from Uncle Philip in early December 1982. He stated that he did not receive the $200 I sent to him because the postal system in Liberia is unreliable. He also mentioned that he read my letter to my mother and that she was overjoyed to hear from me. Mama cried and wanted to know what I was doing, whether I was working, and if I had a family.

I received good news from Uncle Philip in March 1983. He said Mama was feeling better and that my brothers were also well. But the $100 I had sent him was stolen. Uncle Henry wrote me once during this time to beg for money for himself and for my parents. I wondered what other value I had to Uncle Henry besides providing him with money. I am not a psychologist and I don't understand personality disorders, but I concluded that there was a serious defect in Uncle's personality. Couldn't he realize that I was a human being with feelings? Couldn't he imagine that I had longed for affirmation and even one word of comfort or care from him? Didn't he think that I remembered the brutish treatment he dished out to me when I was under his roof? Even if he chose not to hug me, couldn't he have listened to me, so that I felt heard and understood? Couldn't he have supported me when I felt hurt and vulnerable? Whenever I remembered his callousness and inconsiderate nature, anger and resentment often started percolating in me to the point where I wanted desperately to confront him. I resented his requests for money.

Uncle Philip and Uncle William also wrote. I had begun to trust Uncle Philip.

* * *

On June 15, 1983, two years after our marriage, Laura gave birth to our first child. I was in the delivery room, dressed in the surgical scrubs that the nurses had given me. I held her hands and soothed her until she was ready to give birth. The joy I felt when our daughter entered this world was indescribable. I felt light, and grinned like a silly little boy. I named her *Leah*. When she was born, I felt like I was on top of the world. It was a renewal of so many things, including my outlook on life. Her birth brought so much hope. Leah was playful and fun to be with. She loved to laugh and read. She was the only child in the house and so she got our full attention and care. I took her almost everywhere with me: to church, to The Garden, The Bronx Zoo, horseback riding, to theatrical plays, and to various parks in the Bronx. She loved every bit of it. Her laughter and wide-eyed excitement thrilled me. This was exactly what I wanted for her. I wanted her to have the carefree, healthy and happy childhood that I had lost when I left the village.

* * *

At the same time, the pain of not being able to be with my parents, especially my mother, persisted. Uncle Philip's updates about her, however, brought much needed relief. I could enjoy my wife and child and find some comfort in knowing that Mama was in Uncle Philip's care. Not much was said about Papa, but I was determined to also find out about his well-being. I loved him and cared about him, too. Furthermore, I wanted to know what had really happened between him and Mama. The letter I received from Uncle Philip in August 1983 contained a message from Mama.

August 1, 1983

Dear Sammy,

I pray that you are in health and that the Lord is still watching over you. Your mother is staying with me in

Monrovia for the time being. I took her to the doctor but I need US$400 for hospital expenses.

Here is a message from your mother. "Gontor, anytime you wish to send money to me, please send it in care of Philip Diah, because the money you sent last year to Henry Wongan I did not receive anything from him. I also advise that you send enough money to at least buy me a bed. What are you doing in the states? Are you working or going to school?" Sammy your mother is longing to see you and hear your voice. Send me your telephone number so I can try to get a call through to you so that she can speak to you. I don't have a phone but I will try to use my friend's phone.

From your Uncle Philip

Uncle William wrote requesting shirts and trousers for himself. George sent a letter through Uncle William, asking for financial help and also pleading to see me again, "I want my brother," he stated. In 1984, I received letters periodically from my family. Mostly, the letters asked for money to help with food, clothes, school, or healthcare.

Life for my relatives and other native Liberians of tribal descent has always been hard. There are three groups of people in Liberia, the rich, the poor, and the poorest. The average income at the time was between US$30 and US$40 per month. People had little or no access to healthcare. They mostly didn't have money to go to the doctor when they were sick or, by the time they sought help at a hospital, their illness was too advanced to be helped. Nutritious food was also in short supply. Those who lived in the villages often survived on produce from their farms; whereas those who lived in the city had to hustle for food, especially if they didn't have jobs. Illiteracy and unemployment rates among the masses were very high. Whether they lived in the city or the village, people pumped and carried water from wells. Many of them slept on mats because they couldn't afford mattresses, and those with beds sometimes had bedframes without mattresses.

In May 1984, Uncle William sent a picture of George. He also informed me that Mama was back in Teahplay and she was farming by herself. George was in the city staying with William, trying to go to school or get a job. Uncle William was asking for $200 to start a business to help George. The letter I received from Uncle Philip in August ignited hope in my soul. Uncle stated that Mama and the rest of the family were doing well. He said that Mama talked a lot about me to all the villagers and that they all knew me and longed to see me. Uncle also wanted to arrange for mother to come to the city to speak with me via telephone.

* * *

Prior to Leah's birth, communication between Laura and I had been respectful. Like every married couple, we had our disagreements but we were still working together to make our marriage what we believed God wanted it to be. When we had disagreements, we ironed them out quickly and forgave each other.

After our daughter's birth, our marriage started to chill and experienced a subsequent decline. I can't recall any particular event that led to this, but, if I were to try to pin down a possible explanation, I would have to say it might have begun when her biological mother visited us from England to see Leah.

Laura's biological mother had not seen her for many years and was now seeking to reconnect with her daughter. It turned out that she didn't like me. I think she believed that I was "too black" for her daughter and I didn't fit the pedigree she had hoped for in a son-in-law. She couldn't see how much I loved and cared for her daughter. She couldn't see my total commitment to our marriage; she could

Breaking Point: A Journey to Self-Awareness and Finding Purpose in Pain

only see a man whose complexion was too dark. One day during the visit, Laura and I had a disagreement. It was the kind of disagreement that we would normally have argued about then resolved between ourselves, but this time Laura shared the matter with her mother and her mother jumped in and sided with her against me.

"He is wrong for speaking to you that way," her mother said, loudly enough for me to hear. "He's not even fit to be talking with you. Never mind him."

I was angry. Who was she to be putting me down like that? She was overstepping her role, here. I didn't want to be disrespectful to her so I just walked out of the house and left them. It was a reaction I had learned during my brutalized childhood. To avoid further conflict, I didn't talk with my wife's mother for the rest of her stay with us. For the rest of her stay with us, she often stared at me with a disgusted look. It felt like Liberia all over again.

After her mother left, Laura and I started arguing over every little thing. When I asked her what was wrong, she wouldn't answer me. During this time, we had a very ugly and uncharacteristic encounter that had never occurred in our marriage and thankfully never occurred again. I can't even remember what we were arguing about but the way each of us reacted was regrettable.

"Shut up!" Laura yelled at me. "Shut up!"

"Don't talk to me like that!" I yelled back at her. "Don't you dare talk to me like that!"

It was a very heated argument. I was sitting on the bed in our bedroom as she stood in front of me. Before I knew it, she sprang at me and slapped me in my face. It wasn't the slap that dazed me. It was the realization that a woman had slapped me. In Liberia and I believe in all other African countries, a woman would never dare raise her hand to attempt to hit a man, much less to actually slap him in his face. To hit a man, especially in his face, was the very height of disrespect and dishonor. My response was reflexive.

"Do you know what you just did?" I grabbed both of her arms and stood up with her. I squeezed her arms and held her against the wall. "I could crush you if I wanted to. Don't you ever do that again! You hear me? Don't you *ever* do that again!"

The following day, I felt very remorseful about the incident and thought about it all day long. As soon as she came home from work, I approached her.

"Babe," I said. "Let me talk with you about what happened last night."

"Mmm." She stood by the doorway as I sat on the bed.

"It was not my intention to grab you and hold you against the wall," I said. "I don't believe in beating a woman, neither do I believe that a woman should beat me. Please don't do that again."

"You were wrong!" She raised her voice in defense of herself. "You shouldn't have been rough with me."

"You may say that I was wrong," I said. "But what was the cause of it? You shouldn't have slapped me. All this could have been avoided."

She continued to defend herself and to accuse me of being unilaterally rough with her. It was as if she had forgotten she had slapped me first.

"Well, don't you ever slap me again!" I said. "I don't slap you and I don't believe that a woman should beat me up. Do me a favor, in the future, don't let it happen again."

"Ok," she said.

She said okay but she would bring up the incident whenever we had an argument.

"Hit me!" she would challenge me. "If you think you are bad enough go ahead and hit me."

"Babe, I don't want to hit you," I would respond. "I'm not a woman beater. Don't provoke me."

I have come to believe this was one of the incidents that she held against me throughout the rest of our marriage. Receiving forgiveness from the one you love for something you did wrong is a basic emotional need, but she would not forgive me. I desired to be accepted for who

I was, with my warts and pimples, my faults and shortcomings; but for reasons she did not disclose at that time, she started withdrawing from me. In an effort to bridge the gap I sensed was beginning to form, I would invite her to go for walks or to jog with me. Or I would invite her to come to the park to watch me play basketball. But she declined each invitation. Each time she declined, I felt disappointed, but I didn't argue with her because I didn't want to cause problems between us. My desire was not to force her, so I decided to stop asking and left her alone for the sake of peace.

Chapter 12

Family in Liberia

*"In prosperity, our friends know us;
in adversity, we know our friends"*
— John Churton Collins

In 1985, Samuel Doe lifted the ban on political parties and formed his own party. The October elections were reportedly riddled with fraud and irregularities. Nevertheless, Doe was declared the winner by the election officials. About a month after his victory, on November 12, 1985, General Thomas G. Quiwonkpa, the former Commanding General of the Armed Forces of Liberia, attempted a coup to overthrow Doe. The coup failed, and the General and his accomplices fled. Doe was sworn into office on January 6, 1986. Instead of using his position to improve the lives of the Liberian masses as he said he would, Doe began to oppress the people. His oppressive policies isolated segments of the country. The military was increasingly comprised of men from his own Krahn tribe. The Krahn-led military began to retaliate against the Gio and Mano tribes in Nimba County, not because they had long standing tribal disputes, but reportedly because President Doe had given the Krahn-led military preferential treatment and authority over the other tribes.

During this time, although my family always asked for money

when they wrote, I looked forward to receiving letters from them, especially after hearing about the coup attempt in the news and the subsequent killing of many individuals from the Gio and Mano tribes.

I was glad to learn that my relatives were ok. It was Uncle Philip who wrote most frequently. I received another letter from him on April 14, 1986 informing me that our family survived the political upheaval of November 12, 1985 where many in the country lost their lives. My brothers were not able to attend school due to a lack of money and mother had begun to feel ill again. My mother was also requesting a photo from me to see how big her son was.

Mother was sick again. And here I was in United States, the so-called land of opportunity, while my dear mother was suffering back home. "I am going to go see her and nothing is going to stop me," I told myself. I went to see a lawyer, who asked me to get a copy of my birth certificate so that he could help get back my legal documents in the USA. I wrote to Uncle Philip in April 1986, sent him passport photos, and asked him to help me get my birth certificate from the Liberia Bureau of Records so that I could begin to replace the documents that the Kamaras had kept. I figured that if they had adopted me and given me their name, there must be some record of it. I just had to prove it.

Uncle Philip replied in May 1986 to inform me that the Social Welfare office in Monrovia would not accept my passport pictures. He said I had to pay more money. I had sent the required money for the processing of the birth certificate. How much more money did they want? Uncle didn't spell it out and I didn't think that he was trying to rob me. I suspected that the birth certificate office clerk needed a bribe in order to process my birth certificate, so I sent the extra money. I had sent my telephone number and money for Mama to travel to Monrovia. Now Uncle wanted to know who would pay for the telephone bill if he brought my mother to Monrovia to speak with me.

Money! Money! Everything came down to money. Laura and I weren't earning a lot of money. We had our bills and we had a young child to care for. But this was for my mother. Shame and guilt filled me. How could I be fretting about money when it came to Mama's care? She deserved every cent I had. Furthermore, I understood that my relatives were living desperate lives. They were barely surviving with what they had and often lacked adequate food, clothing, and shelter. I understood their plight, but I also desperately needed them to affirm me, to see my worth beyond the material things I could give to them. I felt that my only worth to them and others rested in what I could give or do for them. Nevertheless, I sent another $300 for Mama's care and to facilitate her coming to the city to speak with me.

Uncle Henry and his son Patrick had the nerve to write to me at this time. They told me that they were desperate and needed me to send them money. Uncle Henry claimed he hadn't gotten the money I had sent for my mother but I had my doubts about that claim. Again he didn't even ask how I was doing. Not once did he ask about the Kamaras. I wondered if he was aware that they had thrown me out. Did he not want to know what had happened to me? How I had survived? Didn't he have even one ounce of concern about me? Thinking about him only made me angrier. Yet, I sent him $100 of my hard-earned money. I decided to double my efforts to get my birth certificate so that I could get my passport to visit Liberia. Uncle Philip wrote me in November 1996 asking for more money, for $2000 to buy a house, so that I would have some place comfortable to stay when I visited Liberia.

I liked Uncle Philip's ambitious plan. Having a family home in the city would be a great blessing. For reasons which I did not allow myself to explore, I had not told my family in Liberia that I was married and had a child. In retrospect, I believe I was afraid to let them know of my success. I was also afraid that some of my relatives would become jealous of me and seek to do something bad to us, such as working witchcraft or voodoo against us. This belief in witchcraft or voodoo reflected the tension that existed between my Christian and cultural beliefs at that time. Yet, I imagined taking my wife and daughter to visit them someday. Having them meet my parents would be a dream come true. I decided to dream along with Uncle Philip, although I didn't have the $2000 he needed to realize his dream. I encouraged him to build unity in our family and asked for more details about his plans, but I didn't send him any money.

In January 1987, Uncle Philip sent two letters; one to inform me that he had received a letter from the Bureau of Vital Statistics regarding my birth certificate. They couldn't process my application because they needed my parents to sign documents and mother was not in the City. The other letter thanked me for expressing a desire for reunification and informed me that Papa had returned to the diamond mine far from the City and no one was able to find him. George and Mark were not attending school due to financial difficulties. Uncle wanted me to send a picture of myself, a tape recorder with my voice so that Mama could 'see' and hear me.

I no longer bothered to share my family's letters with Laura. She no longer made any pretense of caring about them.

* * *

I believe that during the early years of our marriage, we both recognized and focused on each other's positive qualities instead of the negatives. But as time passed, a lot of hurt diluted the love and care we had once had for each other.

Our uncoupling was less obvious to the public—and it wasn't obvious even to us. If I'm correct, it began with physical distancing then moved on to emotional distancing. Sexual intercourse became less and less frequent, along with touching each other. I longed to hug and cuddle her, but fear of her rejection handcuffed me. Kissing her on the lips was something she forbade. Our communication became weaker. She occasionally still called me "Darling" and I called her "Babe," but romantic talk between us eventually became meaningless. Our conversations were mainly dull and routine: "Good evening,"

"How was your day?" "What's for dinner?" "Do we have bread?" or "What are we doing for Thanksgiving?" We started focusing on negative traits, what we disliked about each other, instead of focusing on what we liked, and what originally drew us to each other.

It was almost a complete reversal of our initial coupling. Yet, most people didn't see the emotional carbon monoxide in our marriage that was killing us slowly but surely. We were very private and shielded our problems from public eyes—so many people mistakenly thought that we were the ideal family. Our relationship was like a tire losing air. Without repair, it was only a matter of time before the leaking air led to the tire going flat.

I guess I needed Laura's validation and affirmation in ways that neither she nor I were fully aware of. I was, after all, a person who had lived for years without being lovingly touched or validated. She was my wife, the person that I chose to be intimate with, and I longed to feel that she valued and needed me. I longed to have her hug me affectionately. Her emotional and physical withdrawal from me started eroding my already fragile ego and confidence. The more she pulled away, the more desperate I began to feel and the more I realized I had to do something to reverse our uncoupling, to win her again. But it was as if I was standing in quicksand. The more I panicked the faster I sank. Having my own wife and child meant the world to me. I vowed to do all I could to protect them. I started out by pleading with her to talk with me about her feelings.

"Babe," I'd say. "What's the matter? Did I do something wrong?"

"You should know," she replied.

"What is it that I should know?" I asked. "Please tell me."

"If you don't know, I have nothing to say," she would say dismissively and refuse to speak. This ended the conversation. I spent many years feeling inadequate and begging her to share her feelings and thoughts with me regarding the state of our marriage. I wanted her to tell me so that I could work on fixing it.

During this time, she got pregnant with our second child, who was born on May 23, 1987. We named her Joy. Unlike Leah, she was introverted, and although she would laugh at Leah's many jokes, she herself was not one to crack jokes. Joy loved to read and do the same things Leah did. Leah was her role model and Joy followed Leah wherever she went and did whatever Leah did. They were smart, and both girls did very well in school. In the early years of our marriage Laura and I had longed to have a son, however, as our marriage continued to deteriorate the desire to have another child after Joy started to dissipate. Neither of us wanted to bring another child into this unsettled environment.

* * *

Due to my continued diligence at work, in 1987, ten years after I had come on staff permanently, I was promoted to assistant maintainer in the Department of Operations. The Garden gave me opportunities to acquire the skills I needed for the job. Working in every shop in the Operations Department - electrical, painting, plumbing, masonry, carpentry, and auto mechanic - had helped to make me a well-rounded worker.

Since my life circumstances had denied me the opportunity to go to college, my ambition had focused on becoming a skilled maintainer at the garden. I always strove to do excellent work; however, I worked beyond what was expected of me, and knew I qualified for the position of maintainer when the position opened up. I had superior work evaluations and attendance. In fact, the promotion roster indicated that I was next in line for promotion to Maintainer. Yet, the then director of operation and his assistant did all they could to deny me the promotion to the position of maintainer.

* * *

Somehow, Uncle Henry heard about my efforts to get my birth

certificate and wrote on June 2, 1987 expressing his desire to help me. Of course, he was also asking me to send $200 to get this done as well as money for himself and Papa. He emphasized that I should send cash instead of a check.

Did Uncle Henry think I was a fool? I didn't trust him. Where was all the money I had sent him? When would Papa realize that Uncle couldn't be trusted? How could I get money to my father? According to Mama's brothers, there was now a rift between both sides of the family. None of them would tell me the reason, but my sending money for my parents seemed to have added to the conflict, since each side accused the other of stealing the money I sent. I decided to write a letter directly to Papa. I knew there would be no privacy because Papa couldn't read the letter himself but there was no other way and I wanted desperately to share my feelings with the man I loved and missed. I wrote two letters, one addressed to Uncle Philip and the other to Papa. I informed Uncle Philip of the urgency of getting my birth certificate from the Bureau of Records office in Liberia, sent money, and requested that he take my parents to the American Embassy to verify my identity.

I decided to write a letter to Papa imploring him to reunite with Mama. I knew Papa couldn't read so I asked the reader to take great care in conveying my thoughts to my beloved Papa. Regardless of what he did, he was my father and I wanted him to know how much I still loved him and wanted the best for him and the family. I wanted him to know that I did not forget his hard work and devotion to our family throughout the years. I also wanted him to know that I looked up to him and I was proud to have him as my father.

* * *

Helplessness is a terrible thing. As my parents' oldest living child, I should have been there to help them mend whatever was separating them. This feeling of helplessness was compounded by the gathering clouds that had begun to darken my relationship with Laura. We never had another physical altercation, but our words were fast becoming deadly missiles.

Chapter 13

Marriage Versus Family

"Man that is born of a woman is of few days and full of trouble"
— Job 14:1

Whoever uttered the words *"sticks and stones may break my bones but words will never hurt me"* either lied to all of us, or had a protective shield and unspeakable inner strength that allowed that person to withstand the damage of negative words. I know that words can kill. My self-esteem had already been punctured by the piercing negative words from my past. As a child, being called "stupid" and "a nobody" or being told that "you are good for nothing" or that "you will not come to anything in life" can really do severe and long term damage to a child's self-perception and self-esteem; especially when those words come from that child's trusted caregivers.

The words of affirmation and encouragement instilled in me by my biological parents sustained me through some deep waters and dark nights. Their positive words provided a shield from the attacking words of others that were meant to "kill" me, and my parents' admonitions prevented the total destruction of my self-esteem. The strangers I grew up with, after I left my parents, never praised or complimented me. Instead, their steady stream of abusive words was "killing" me slowly but surely. I internalized their negativity and learned to shut my mouth and not think anything of myself.

My relationship with Laura started to have the same effect on me as the words of the folks in Monrovia and the Kamaras had had, and this further eroded my dwindling self-esteem. I didn't have the inner fortitude to withstand the damaging effects of Laura's negative and debilitating words. Although I became a Christian in my late teens, my eyes were still clouded, and I could not see the good in myself. When I heard someone say that I was a handsome, kind, and thoughtful person, I would wonder who they were talking about. "Who, me?" I'd ask them. I simply could not see it.

I was not a saint, though. The negative words I lived with had seeped deep within me and shaped the negative words that I, in turn, would use on others. I learned how to cuss and how to use my words to wound in retaliation. I wanted others to hurt as I was hurting. I wanted to cut them down to size so that they would realize that they were no better than me that they, too, had flaws, and I deserved to be treated like a human being just as they deserved to be. This was my defense mechanism, although I also loved and cared for people. I loved and cared for Laura. *Zlahn* and *Guataye* and my Christian faith taught me how to care; they taught me how to love. The Village of Teahplay and my Christian faith taught me how to look out for the well-being of others. That's who I was, a caring person, but the environment I lived in did not allow me to act in a caring and loving manner.

* * *

The desire to get my birth certificate started driving me crazy. I had been praying about it for months and still nothing had materialized, although I had sent a lot of money to get it. Uncle Philip still had not arranged to have Mama speak to me. The angry feelings that were building in me mingled with shame. I shouldn't be feeling anger toward my family. But why was getting a simple birth certificate taking forever?

Uncle Philip wrote in October 1987 to thank me for the items I had sent. He said he didn't know who should get them. I couldn't remember who was to get them. I was more concerned about news regarding my birth certificate. All Uncle Philip could report was that they had sent the documents to the Bureau and had not yet heard from them.

When his next letter arrived I opened it hesitantly. I had had so many disappointments and lost so much money that I was beginning to lose hope that I would ever get the birth certificate I needed to replace my documents in America, and thus, travel to see my parents again. Uncle Philip had asked again for more money for hospital bills for my mother and clothes for my brothers.

Why the hell was Uncle asking me for more things? Where was my birth certificate? I immediately asked the Lord to forgive me. I didn't mean to curse but Uncle seemed to have priorities other than my birth certificate. Hearing that my mother was sick again was just too much. I wanted to go and see her.

"Babe, this thing is driving me out of my mind," I told Laura, trying to share my misery.

"What are you talking about?" she asked.

"I got another letter from my uncle and he's telling me that my mother is sick again," I replied. "I want to go and see her."

There was complete silence.

"Babe, did you hear me?" I asked her.

"Yes," she said.

"I haven't heard anything about my birth certificate yet," I continued. "How many years has it been since I started trying to get it from Liberia? I can't even remember," I answered my own question. "As soon as I get my papers I'm flying to Liberia to see my parents," I continued. She didn't even turn to look at me. "Babe, don't you have anything to say."

"No," she said curtly.

"Ok, forget it," I said, annoyed at her. "Forget that I even mentioned it. It's my problem."

Breaking Point: A Journey to Self-Awareness and Finding Purpose in Pain

* * *

Each letter I received from my uncle held hopes that I would soon get my birth certificate. As a Christian, I rarely curse, but when I received Uncle Philip's last two letters in December of 1987, I almost did. Instead, I prayed and cried. He was, yet again, begging for more money. He stated that Uncle Henry and Papa were accusing him of stealing the money I sent them.

I wondered which hole was swallowing the money I sent for my family. The strange thing is, if I sent $20 they would get it, but if I sent $50 or more they would claim they never got it. I decided that I wasn't sending any more money until I got my birth certificate.

In June 1988, I received a letter from a man named Doweah. I didn't know who he was. Was he one of Uncle Philip's scribes? I don't know if Uncle Philip was even literate. Someone different wrote his letters to me each time, with different return addresses. Each letter was in a different handwriting. He wrote quite frequently, how many people did he know? On June 9, 1988, I received a letter from an officer in the Bureau of Records stating that he needed more money to expedite the processing of my birth certificate.

Trying to get my birth certificate had begun to drain me emotionally. It was just one of the many other things that had begun to drain me.

I was about to enter deep into the wilderness, where I would again be brought to a breaking point.

Chapter 14

Reunion

"I Miss My Mother's Voice"
— Sammy Kamara

In the summer of 1988, while on our way back to the Bronx from a church trip to Washington, DC, I had a seizure on the church bus. That event marked the intensification of my pain and sorrow.

Growing up in Liberia and in the time prior to my marriage, I had never had a seizure and, as far as I knew, no one in my family had ever had one, either. To this day, I don't know what caused my first seizure. However, eight years earlier in 1980, while still single, I had had two terrifying nightmares. In the nightmares I was lying on a sofa, sleeping, when I felt like a force was trying to rip out my brains. The force looked like the impersonation of a white figure. It started fighting and I fought back vigorously for a while until I woke up from my sleep, still struggling. The second nightmare occurred about a month after the first. The same white figure was attacking me again. In my sleep I started shouting "Jesus! Jesus!" Then I awoke out of my sleep, shouting.

The nightmares preceded a series of severe migraine headaches that lasted for days. These headaches occurred periodically after my marriage and got worse whenever I was depressed, lacked sleep, overworked myself, or was stressed by events in my marriage. Sometimes, when I felt overwhelmed, I would drink a beer to ease my mind. I had no idea that these stressors and the beer were wreaking havoc on my health. The seizures, once I began having them, severely impacted the trajectory of my marriage and my life.

Believe it or not, after the first seizure, I did not go to my doctor. At first, after the Washington bus seizure, I would have a seizure once a month. Eventually, I started having seizures three or more times a week. During the seizure episodes, I would bite my tongue and my mouth would be sore for days. It was only then that Laura and I decided to go to the doctor. The doctor gave me a cocktail of medications but the frequency and intensity of my seizures did not abate. In fact, they continued to increase. After a few weeks, we had to rush back to the doctor. The doctor suggested that I might have to stop working for a while and go to a rehabilitation facility for treatment. After we left the doctor's office, we discussed our options, our bills, and the care of our children. We were still having serious difficulties in our marriage but, thank God, it was still intact, and Laura was able to be supportive of me at this time. I thought for a moment about the doctor's statement and the medical challenge I faced. I could not visualize myself being a burden to the government and not working to support my wife and my children. I took the bottles of pills and threw them away. If God couldn't help me, neither could these medications. I decided I would rather trust God than these pills.

* * *

I took great satisfaction in my church work and used the experience as a refuge from my unhappiness at home and the uncertainty surrounding my Liberian family. I had accepted positions as both a teacher of the adult Sabbath School class and as president of the young people's department.

The youngsters didn't have a Sabbath School teacher, so I had to choose between staying with the adults and working with the children. I decided to give up teaching the adult class so that I could teach the children instead. Teaching, advising them, and playing with them, delighted me greatly. Working with the children motivated me and stirred a strong desire to be in church every Sabbath. Sadly, in the midst of this pleasure of being with the young people, my seizures increasingly prevented me from meeting with them regularly.

* * *

The lawyer at the Liberian Consulate that was helping me kept asking me for my birth certificate. I intensified my efforts to get it by writing strong letters to Uncle Philip and Uncle Henry. I told them that if they cared about me and really wanted me to see them soon, then they should go out of their way to help me get my birth certificate

* * *

From 1988 onward, I became engaged in another desperate struggle: how to hold on to my job at The Garden. My seizures became a big secret that I felt I needed to hide from my supervisors. I dreaded the day when they found out that I suffered from seizures. I had convinced myself that, if they were to find out, I would immediately lose my job. Working at The Garden was a treasured opportunity. The Garden had provided me with my first income as well as opportunities to learn about mechanics and gain other skills in the operations department. Working in The Garden was how I was able to provide for my family. I was afraid that without this job I would be unemployable, and dreaded not being able to take care of my family.

Seizures usually occurred at nights or early in the mornings while I was asleep. After coming out of a seizure episode, I often felt empty and extremely alone. I yearned to be embraced and held. I needed to feel like I mattered to someone. By now I was becoming more skilled at numbing my feelings to protect myself from further hurt. In this way, I was able to keep soldiering on. Laura would support me by calling the ambulance and accompanying me to the hospital but she seemed to be afraid to be physically close to me after I had had a seizure. I wondered if she thought she would catch the seizure or become possessed by what she feared I had.

Many mornings, after a rough night of seizures, I could barely speak, because my tongue and mouth were so sore from the biting they received. When my supervisor gave me the job orders for the day, I barely spoke; I would just nod while praying feverishly that he would not ask me any questions. I didn't ask him any. I did my duties well and tried as much as was possible to keep to myself.

One morning still stands out very clearly in my mind. Very early that morning I had had a seizure. My mind was groggy but I was determined to go to work. I prayed and asked God to let it be a light day without too much challenging work. My prayer went unanswered because shortly after I arrived, the Vice President of Operations, Mr. Bob Heinisch, came into the operations shop where I was working.

"Hi Brother Sam," he greeted me. "I have a job for you."

My heart started racing when I heard his voice.

"I have broken metal that needs welding," he continued. "It needs to be done today for a security vehicle."

I nodded.

"So, can you do it?" he asked.

I nodded and said "Yep!" with a smile.

He left but I was terrified. I was sure that this was the day when my seizure condition would finally be discovered by The Garden. Welding was a part of my job that I had done effortlessly in the past. However, because of the seizure that day, my memory was cloudy and my hands were unsteady. Welding can be dangerous work. To do the job, I had to use arc welding equipment. When the welding rod touches the metal it creates a very hot fire which melts and seals the cracks in the broken metal. This work is intricate and requires even overlapping movements of the rod on the piece being repaired. My hands needed to be steady and my eyes focused to prevent me from injuring myself or setting the shop on fire. Just thinking about it was nerve-racking.

Nevertheless, I knew I had to try.

God was my only source of help in the mechanic shop that day. I prayed a silent prayer in tears: "Lord I can't think clearly. How am I going to do this? I desperately need your help."

This was my miracle. I felt the sensation of someone standing beside me telling me what to do: *Clean the surface of the metal, attach the rods to the welding machine, and move the rod slowly to the damaged area of the metal and in a steady, zig zag overlapping manner.*

Later that day when Bob returned for the piece, he was thrilled.

"Wow! Sam this looks good. Great work," he said cheerfully. "Thanks a lot, Bro Sam."

"You're welcome." I smiled as he left the shop, but I was rejoicing inside. God had come through for me that day.

* * *

Uncle Henry wrote again with his usual request for money. I had given up on him and really didn't want to hear anything he had to say. Yet, I still opened his letter with anticipation. I couldn't believe Uncle Henry. He was now asking me to send for him to come to America or send a $1000 to buy land. In addition to this, he needed more for his hospital bills and for his general care because the living conditions were critical. He cautioned me not to send money through Uncle Philip because Uncle Philip kept the money and that it was missing.

Why should I care about him when he hadn't cared about me? Did he think that I was a money tree that he could shake for fruit when he wanted to? And when did his son Patrick become my brother? I would be very drunk or completely insane to consider sending for Uncle Henry to come to America. Furthermore, how could I do that when I had not yet replaced my immigration papers? I wished he would stop writing to me. Uncle Philip had also begun to annoy me with his letters. Four of them arrived in quick succession. The one dated September 14, 1989, informed me that he still hadn't taken my parents to sign the documents at the American Embassy. He needed more money to do so. He told me to forget about my mother because she was seriously ill; if I wanted to see her again I should try to come by December 1989 or she might be dead.

* * *

In spite of the seizures, I still came to church and desired to work with the children; the exhausting effects of both the seizures, the medication I took to control them and my general unhappiness were taking an increasing toll on me. The toll began to exceed my ability to perform.

Many times, I put the best face on things while at church, but I just didn't have the degree of strength and motivation needed to work with the children by myself. That fall of 1989, I had to stop teaching them. Unfortunately, due to a lack of leadership, the Children's Workshop was forced into a temporary hiatus in 1990.

* * *

I received another letter from Uncle Philip. Uncle Philip told me that he was helping to take care of my mother in the absence of my father. I had given him my telephone number so he was eager to let me speak with Mama. One day in October 1989, my phone rang. I answered, thinking that it was just another call from one of our church brethren. I couldn't believe my ears. It was a call from Liberia.

"Sammy?" the voice asked. "Is this Sammy Kamara?"

"Yes, it's me Sammy" I replied. "Who is this?"

"It's me," the person replied. "It's me, your Uncle Philip."

"Uncle Philip!" I said excitedly. "You got my letter! It's good to hear you."

I don't know when or how Uncle Philip learned English, because when I was in Liberia he was still living in the Village of Teahplay.

"Sammy, I have a big surprise for you," he continued. "You won't believe who I have here with me."

"Who?" Could it be Mama or Papa? I was hesitant to ask.

"Your mother," he replied. He seemed to be excited for me. "Your mother is here with me."

My heart started racing, and I suddenly felt weak. I couldn't believe this was happening. It had been about twenty-one years since I had heard my dear mother's voice. I was so eager to hear her voice, but at the same time I didn't know what to say. So many thoughts were flooding my mind and so many different feelings were rushing through my body.

"Sammy?" Uncle asked. "Are you there? Sammy, are you there?"

"Yes, yes, Uncle," I replied. I felt very nervous. "I'm here. Where is Mama?"

"She's here," he said. "Hold on let me give her the phone."

"Mama," I said. I know I was happy that she was on the phone but for some strange reason I felt timid. "Hi Mama, How are you?" She didn't answer.

"Mother, this is your son, Sammy," I said in the little Gio that I remembered.

"Sammy?" she said, sounding confused.

"Yes, this is your son, Gontor. I am alive!"

"Gontor?" she said recognizing my name.

"Yes, this is Gontor."

"Gontor?" she asked again as if she couldn't believe it was me.

"Yes, Mama, it's me."

There was total silence. Then she said something in Gio which I could not understand.

"What did you say Mama?" I asked. "I didn't understand what you said. Say it again." It appeared that she didn't understand what I said, either. The language difference was like a thick wall between us.

I tried, but I just couldn't remember my Gio language. There were so many things I wanted to say to her. I wanted to tell her that I loved her I wanted to ask about Papa and my brothers. I wanted to know about the friends I left behind. I wanted to tell her that I would see her soon. I was now thirty-one years old so Mama must have been about fifty-six years old. Although her life was very hard and she was often sick, her voice sounded strong. My need to see her soon became even more intense.

"Mama, give the phone to Uncle," I told her. I don't know if she understood my instruction or if uncle realized that the conversation between Mama and I was stalled. Uncle came on the line.

"Sammy, your mother said she is overjoyed to hear you," he said. "She thought you were dead." Uncle was trying to translate to me as Mama spoke to him.

"Tell her I miss her," I said. "Tell her I long to see her. Tell her I'm going to see her soon."

"Ok, Sammy," Uncle said. "Sammy, we need..." He didn't get to finish. The call was cut off.

"Uncle? Uncle?" I called out in disbelief. I wasn't finished. I wanted to talk to Mama some more. This time it was anger and frustration that I felt. I didn't have a number to call my Uncle back.

It had been ten years since I had first penned a note to Uncle Henry to ask him to help me find my parents. Liberia had been a quiet country then. In 1989, it was slipping into deadly turmoil. I didn't know it then, but it was to be a long time before another contact became possible.

In December 1989, civil war broke out in Liberia.

Bob Heinisch and Sammy at the
New York Botanical Garden

Chapter 15

Mama

*"Nothing is perfect. Life is messy. Relationships are complex.
Outcomes are uncertain. People are irrational"*
— Hugh Mackay

Uncle never called me back or sent me a telephone number where I might reach him. With civil war now tearing the country apart, I had no way of getting information about my family. All I could do was watch the newscasts and read the newspaper reports helplessly. Headlines such as *"Civil War Rocks Liberia," "The Liberia Civil War is one of Liberia's Bloodiest," "Thousands of Liberians are being slaughtered"* only served to increase my fear. Where was my family? Were they still alive? All sorts of dreadful thoughts invaded my mind. I was terrified for my family.

The seeds of the civil war had been sown in the early years of Liberia's history. The Americo-Liberians in the minority ruled over the majority, who belonged to the various tribes. The 1980 coup led by Master Sergeant Samuel Doe was meant to reverse the years of oppression of native Liberians. Yet, what followed under Doe's leadership was further oppression of the very people he claimed to have fought for. Not only were the natives oppressed during President Doe's reign, but tension between the tribes themselves, due to Doe's policies of dividing the country, developed and intensified.

President Doe belonged to the Krahn tribe and granted favors to people of that group, while reportedly harassing and killing those from other tribes. He began to fill the army with soldiers from his own tribe, while marginalizing soldiers from the others. These tensions formed the groundwork for the invasion by Prince Johnson and Charles Taylor. Johnson is from the Gio tribe in Nimba County where I'm from. Johnson recruited his tribal comrades to rebel against and overthrow the Doe government.

Although Charles Taylor is a member of the Gola tribe, he is of Americo-Liberian ancestry. Taylor was educated in the USA, where he earned a degree in economics in 1977 from Bentley College in Waltham, Massachusetts. He returned to Liberia and was serving in the Doe government as director of the General Services Agency. While on a visit to the USA, Taylor was accused of embezzling thousands of dollars by President Doe, and he was arrested in Massachusetts. Taylor was held in prison from May 1984 to September 1985 while he awaited extradition to Liberia. The circumstances are unclear, but Taylor managed to escape from prison in the USA and was reportedly spotted in Ghana, then supposedly landed in Libya.[v] Taylor joined with Prince Johnson to lead the uprising against the Doe government in December 1989.

Because the revolt started in my home area, Nimba County, President Doe dispatched the Liberian army to counter the revolt by Taylor and his men. This was a very bloody operation, which resulted in many innocent civilians being randomly and wantonly killed. Reportedly, most of those killed were from the Gio and Mano tribes. The Gio and Mano tribes are the dominant tribes in Nimba County. As the war raged on, it was reported that both sides of the conflict recruited young children, some as young as 9 years old, to join the vicious civil war.

A letter from Uncle Philip in February brought welcome relief. I had not heard from my family since the telephone call with Mama and Uncle was suddenly cut off in October 1989. I also received a letter from him in April 1990. Uncle reported that all our people were displaced, and a large number of people had been killed by soldiers during the war between the government and the rebels. He desperately needed money to help my mother survive. In March 1990 he wrote:

> Dear Sam
>
> Sam, the illness of your mother was due to the shortage of blood and severe headaches and she was able to recover in a month. Sam, frankly speaking your father has not made any contribution toward your mother and your brothers and his whereabouts is unknown. Since my wife and your mother left for the interior before the incursion of December 24, 1989 I have not heard from them. The incursion has caused Nimba citizens to flee to Ivory Coast and Guinea for survival.
>
> Respectfully yours,
>
> Philip G. Diah

This situation with Mama and Papa really broke my heart. If only I were there, I know I could have helped them resolve their differences. What had happened to the love I remembered between them? What went wrong? Was it because Mama got sick often? I dismissed that thought because I felt that not even sickness could have changed Papa's caring and loving feelings toward Mama. I resolved to double my efforts to return home to Liberia to help to bring the family back together again. But in April 1990, I received a letter from Uncle Philip, warning me not to travel to Liberia until I heard from him. The political unrest there was intensifying and many people from Nimba were being killed. All of the villagers had taken refuge in neighboring countries and there was no way to enter Teahplay because the forces fighting the government were in full control of the area.

* * *

The stones of emotional and physical distancing continued to create walls between Laura and myself in our marriage; I began to think that our problems were becoming bigger than we could resolve by ourselves, so I suggested to her that we should seek help from Dad and Mom. Mom was our biblical and spiritual tutor, and Dad was the minister who had married us. Surely, they would give us sound advice while preserving confidentiality. Laura, however, didn't want anyone to know our business and declined to invite Dad and Mom to intervene. I also thought about asking her stepmother to intervene, but Laura also refused to let her help us. It was as if thick walls of stone were caving in on me, and I felt as if I was suffocating. I had to do something, so one day; I broke our code of silence and shared what was happening with Mom and Dad. Actually, I spoke with Mom and she told Dad.

"Mom things are not going well at home," I started. "Our marriage is going to hell in a basket."

"What are you talking about?" Mom looked alarmed.

"We are arguing all the time," I replied.

"What do you find to argue about?" she asked. "As children of God, you both should be able to work out your differences. You should at least be praying about whatever it is. Are you both praying?"

"We still have worship on Friday evenings," I answered.

"That's good," she said, looking pleased. "Keep putting the matter before the Lord. It's good that you are both praying together."

"That's the problem, Mom," I said. "We have devotion together on Friday evenings, but our marriage struggle is never mentioned."

"That doesn't make sense." Mom looked confused. "So what do you pray about?"

"Everything else, except the elephant in the room," I replied. "That's why I wanted us to talk with you, but Laura doesn't want to talk to anyone. She would be very upset if she knew I'm speaking with you."

"Sam, I don't know what to say!" Mom said. "All I can say is to keep hanging in there, and pray about it, try to see if you can talk things over with her. I will also pray for both of you. God is able."

I knew Laura would be upset with me but I was desperate for some help and I knew that Mom had wise, godly advice. Furthermore, she was very confidential. Talking with her could only make things better. But nothing changed. Laura and I tried to at least be civil with each other, but most of the time, it was as if we were roommates. She still cooked and washed my clothes, and we still greeted each other and went to church together. We sat beside each other at church and ate together. I still drove her to the train station each morning so she could catch the train for work. We still ate at the dining table as a family.

One evening, we sat at the dining table around a very appetizing meal. Our daughters looked happy, and Laura seemed relaxed, but I felt miserable. Here was I sitting at a table where we could eat whatever and however much we wanted. Before I had sat down at the table that day, I had been starving; now I couldn't stand looking at the food. My appetite had suddenly disappeared.

"What are your father and your sick mother eating?" an inner voice screamed at me. "And your brothers, have they eaten anything since morning? Look at you with all this food in front of you, while your family suffers with nothing to eat."

I burst into tears. Everyone looked at me, confused.

"Daddy, are you ok?" one of my daughters asked. At first, I nodded, and then I blurted out:

"I don't know if my family in Liberia has anything to eat," I said. "Sorry, I can't eat dinner with you, but you eat up your food."

* * *

We received bad news in the spring of 1990. Mother Johnson, as we sometimes called Mom, had a stroke while on one of her evangelistic missions in Ashokie, North Carolina. She was rushed back to New York, and, after leaving the hospital, was confined to a nursing home in the Bronx. The result of her sickness was a life sentence in the nursing home. Dad was devastated. He dutifully visited her, but it was evident that it was wearing on him. Seeing Mom in the nursing home was also very difficult for me. The stroke did major damage; one side of her body was totally paralyzed, and she could not speak.

Mom was my savior, my teacher, and my confidant. Who would listen to me now? Who would constructively criticize and correct me? Who would love me just for who I was? In spite of my family at home, most of the time, I felt alone. With Mom's stroke, a profound sense of loss and helplessness descended on me. This was to continue for years.

I was a member of the Board of Trustees at church, and in 1990, I was ordained a deacon, due to my faithful and consistent contribution. I was fully and completely committed to God and the church, and engaged in very little else, outside of church attendance and activities.

Chapter 16

What is a Christian Marriage?

"Sexual expression within a marriage is not an option or an extra. It is certainly not, as it has sometimes been considered, a necessary evil in which spiritual Christians engage only to procreate children. It is far more than a physical act. God created it to be the expression and experience of love on the deepest human level and to be a beautiful and powerful bond between husband and wife."
— John MacArthur

I didn't know this at first but time and circumstance have taught me that women and men are equally emotional beings. In other words, both women and men have strong emotional needs; needs for affection, care, concern, and respect. The problem or challenge is that each gender desires to have those needs satisfied in different ways. Women desire to be cuddled. They love to be listened to and spoken to. They want to hear "sweet" words, and to receive flowers, chocolate, help, and other acts of kindness. These demonstrations of affection are some of the ways that their emotional needs are met.

Women are complex beings. We men are less complicated. While sex is not the only means by which our emotional desires can be met, sex is the main or the most significant channel through which we find emotional fulfillment. Sex is not just a physical act for us; it is an emotional affair. Many women don't realize this; they just think that all men want is sex. I believe that most men want more than sex: we want women's respect, women's care, and women's love—and, yes, we want sex. This strong desire for sex makes us very vulnerable to women who realize that men desire sex more than they do. Denial of sex becomes a weapon in relationships. Some women may belittle the man, because he desires it so much. Even Christian women are not exempt from this type of behavior. If the woman only knew how damaging this weapon is to her man's ego, to his confidence, and to his sense of well-being, she would not use it. Then again, it may be that she uses it precisely *because* she realizes its effect upon the man.

As a Christian youth with a commitment to God, I had restrained from sexual intercourse before marriage, because I wanted to give the gift of my virginity to my wife. Initially, our sex life was robust and appealing. The first three years of our marriage was our happiest time. Like other couples, we weren't perfect, but we were on the same page.

From the end of our third year through the 26th year of our marriage, sex took a back seat. We made love once in a blue moon and, whenever that occurred, it was more because I kept begging and she finally agreed out of a sense of obligation or from pity, not because of passion or pleasure. I found myself in a very serious dilemma. Here I was, a young healthy man who loved sex, and who was hardly getting any. I was totally committed to God and while my commitment and love for my wife was somewhat diluted, it was still very strong. I was still committed to her and I honored my vow to God. Where would I go and what would I do? In spite of everything, I still loved and desired her. I had made a vow of commitment to her but more importantly I had made it to God. But I was burning. There were times when I hurt badly, because I was trying to contain myself.

I had started looking at pornographic magazines, not so much for self-gratification but to gain knowledge of what I might be overlooking in our sex life. I looked for tips about how to touch her, how to talk with her, and what areas of her body I needed to stimulate. Whenever

I tried to apply the tips, she would not tell me how this affected her. Sexual frustration was setting in and, as a result, I started developing a lustful drive for pornography, and thoughts of fooling around with other women started crossing my mind. I resisted them because I was not the kind of man that believed in using and discarding women. However, I must confess that I found myself taking longer looks at the sexy females I saw on the streets. I didn't believe in masturbation, so my sexual urges were intensifying. Crying out to God and fasting helped for a while but then I would go back to my bouts of intense sexual urges.

One night, I decided that I couldn't take it anymore. I wasn't getting any at home, but I told myself I wasn't going to solicit any of the church sisters for sex. There was an "Adult" store not far from my house. I knew that this store had pornographic movies and female escorts who would have sex with me for money. It was a fierce mental and physical battle; Sammy Kamara vs Sammy Kamara. Should I go or should I not go? Sexual desires had taken hold of my mind and eclipsed any thoughts of commitment to Laura or God. Praying did not even cross my mind. *I'm going to get some tonight*, I told myself and so I got dressed and left the house to go buy me some sex.

I parked across the street from the adult store and watched as both males and females entered and exited. Some seemed to be there only to pick up videos, whereas others left with escorts. Somehow, referring to the women as *escorts* made my intended action more palatable. I had told myself that I would never have sex with a prostitute. I wrestled with myself in the car, and worried about being seen by a member of the church or one of my friends. The decision was made in a flash: I would leave the car and move like a Ninja, very carefully but fast. I mustered enough courage to get out of the car, but as I moved toward the entrance of the store, a commanding but gentle voice said to me: "*Sammy! Sammy! Do you know who you are?*" Shockwaves of adrenaline rushed through my veins. I looked around to see who was speaking to me, but no one was near me. The voice continued speaking: *"What are you doing here? As a member of the heavenly royalty, is this the place for you?"*

I tried to move toward the door again but fear took hold of me. The voice I heard without seeing anyone brought me to my senses. I ran to my car as fast as I could to drive home but instead of going home, I drove to a lonely spot and bawled uncontrollably, while praying and asking God for forgiveness, and thanking Him for helping me in my moment of weakness.

That night, I didn't get any. I went to bed feeling lonely and unloved. The voice that had spoken to me must have been God's. No one else was there to see me, so I could have bought as much sex as I desired, but I couldn't do it. My consciousness of God and my commitment to Laura would not allow me to.

My emotional needs went unmet for most of my marriage but I was determined to hold on to my integrity and remain faithful in my marriage and my relationship with God. I tried numerous approaches to maintain my sanity: I frequently asked questions about sex in church, I prayed and fasted, I admired other women from afar, I bawled, and begged Laura for sex. Sometimes I had to run away from the presence of women as did the patriarch, Joseph, in the Bible.

There were two occasions when I felt a magnetic pull from church sisters who were apparently attracted to me. The pull was extremely strong, and I was very tempted but, like Joseph, I asked myself, *"How can I do this wicked thing and sin against my God?"* Admittedly this whole ordeal took a toll on my self-esteem and my confidence. Notwithstanding, God helped me in the midst of my storm so that the cables of my internal anchors did not fail. Holding on to integrity is often not easy; it takes much strength of will. I'm no better than other men who fall under the weight of sexual temptation; especially when that temptation is prolonged. But I can say that it is possible to hold on to your integrity under dire conditions. It is possible to be honest to oneself, to God, and to one's spouse.

* * *

The last time I heard from my family in Liberia had been in early 1990. This silence was like a heavy wet blanket on my spirit. Yet, I had to keep those feelings hidden at home. There was no use in bringing up my fears and yearnings with Laura. What could anyone do if I did tell them about the situation and my feelings? My life continued to trudge along and the world around me buzzed with activities, as if nothing was wrong in Liberia. There was little or no mention on the radio or TV of the wanton killings of innocent civilians in my country. To get some news, I would travel into Manhattan, to a vendor who sold magazines and newspapers from various countries.

The war escalated, and on September 10, 1990, the Los Angeles *Times* published the following report:

Liberian Rebels Shoot, Capture President Doe
September 10, 1990
RICHARD E. MEYER | TIMES STAFF WRITER

WASHINGTON — A rebel group Sunday captured President Samuel K. Doe of Liberia, a State Department official said, adding that U.S. observers believe Doe was wounded during a fierce gun battle in Monrovia.

"Our embassy has confirmed that he was captured," said the official, who asked not to be identified.

Reports reaching Washington said that Doe was taken into custody by rebel Prince Yormie Johnson, who declared himself in charge of Liberia. The reports said Doe was wounded in both legs. Asked whether Doe had been shot, the State Department official replied: "We assume it's true."

We later learned that, the day before the article was published, on September 9, 1990, President Doe had been tortured to death by Prince Johnson (and his comrades), leader of one of the warring factions in what would become known as Liberia's first civil war, which had begun nine months earlier in December 1989[vi]. I was tormented by this news, not knowing if any of my relatives had been caught up in the violence. Had anyone been killed? Uncle Philip had informed me that many of our tribal people had fled to the Ivory Coast or Guinea. I figured that Mama and my brothers were among them but where was Papa? Uncle said they didn't know where Papa was. Had Papa been killed?

During this time, my frequent seizures that often made me fall off the bed led to the dislocation of my right shoulder. I was scheduled to undergo major surgery on September 18, 1990, to repair the damaged ligaments that had resulted. The unknown can be a terror. All sorts of dreadful thoughts tormented me in the days before the surgery. What if I died? Who would take care of Laura and the children? Or what if the surgery went wrong and I became crippled? I'm right-handed, what would I do without the use of my right hand?

The day of the surgery, Laura was by my side. We didn't say much to each other but she stayed with me until they were ready to take me into the operating room. She looked worried, maybe a little sad.

"Everything will be ok," she said to me just as the nurses pushed my gurney into the operating room.

I couldn't tell how long the operation lasted, but as the anesthesia wore off, pain racked my entire body. The room seemed to be filled with smoke, but I could tell it was Laura standing by my bedside.

"Sam," she called gently. "How are you feeling?"

All I could do was groan and grind my teeth as hard as I could. Laura didn't touch me but knowing that she was there with me meant a great deal to me. I was discharged from the hospital the following day with painkillers and instructions about how to care for and protect my arm. She was my nurse at home. I was truly grateful for her attentiveness and care at this time.

My recuperation lasted for over five months. This meant that I was unable to work for that period of time. Not being able to work added to my misery. I was not one to sit around idly, not doing anything. So I found work to do around the house and even drove my standard shift car with one hand, my left hand, while my right arm was in a sling.

Chapter 17

Mixed Blessings

*"When we lose one blessing, another is often
most unexpectedly given in its place"*
— C.S. Lewis

The next year and a half, passed without much improvement in my general health and without any news about my family in Liberia. My quest to return to my homeland, which had begun in 1979 with a letter to Uncle Henry, was still on hold.

Early in 1992, not having heard from my family in a couple of years, I wrote a letter to Uncle Philip, hoping this communication would get through to him. I was overjoyed therefore when, in March 1992, I received a return letter from him. He was still displaced and living outside of the city. While he had been trying to find his way from the city to the village, government troops had taken away his documents, including the letters I had sent him. He no longer had my address, so he wanted my telephone number to try to reach me. When conditions in the country settled down he wanted me to come and see for myself the present deplorable conditions.

I was overjoyed to hear that Uncle Philip was alive, but what about Papa and the rest of the family? He didn't say a single word about them. Immediately, I replied to his letter, hoping that in spite of the chaos in

Breaking Point: A Journey to Self-Awareness and Finding Purpose in Pain

Liberia he would still get my letter. In May 1992, I received another letter from Uncle Philip, but it didn't mention my letter to him.

Uncle Philip wrote again in June 1992. In this letter he gave me the latest news of the family – some of my relatives were dead! Among the dead was Uncle Henry, who had been killed by government forces. His two wives and their children had survived but were scattered in various centers for displaced people. Papa and Mama were safe in the village but Uncle Philip's son, John, and my mother's father, Oldman Diah, had also been killed in the war. The living conditions were dire, and he wasn't working. In fact, he was writing from a refugee camp in Ivory Coast and badly needed financial help.

Uncle Henry was dead! I just couldn't absorb this news. No, Uncle Henry could not be dead; I wanted so much to confront him—make him apologize to me for his brutality. If he were dead, obviously, I would not be able to do that so I convinced myself that Uncle Henry was not dead. I would get my opportunity to confront him and make him pay for my mistreatment and for raping my mother. So many people had been killed; Uncle Philip must have received incorrect information. It must have been a case of mistaken identity. Uncle Henry could not dead.

I did know, though, that based on Uncle Philip's report, the situation in Liberia was terrible. My family members were refugees in another country, suffering. He wanted me to send money but I had no certainty that the money would get to him. After all, even when the country still had some degree of peace, most of the money I sent to my relatives never got to them. Should I send money and pray that my family gets it or would I just be sending money to thieves? I took a risk and sent money to the refugee camp in the Ivory Coast.

* * *

In 1992, on one of the rare occasions when we had sex, Laura got pregnant with our third child. This time, it was a boy! Both of us had mixed feelings about this pregnancy. On the one hand, we were ecstatic because, although we love our two daughters, we had initially wanted a son. On the other hand, due to the unwholesome state of our marriage, neither of us wanted to bring another child into this unsettled environment. He was born on July 12, 1993. We named him Junior. Four months after our son's birth, our third daughter and last child was conceived. We love all our children but were surprised by the arrival of both Junior and Loretta. During this time, our marriage was reeling like a drunkard. In addition to our marital troubles, we had to deal with financial challenges. We had spent a lot of money taking care of our children, including sending our older daughters to private schools. Eventually, we had to send them to public school.

It is amazing how much happiness and joy children can bring to a parent's life. God gave us these children as a gift, a gift that ironically made me feel whole in spite of the other areas of brokenness in my life. I loved to play with them. They made me laugh, and they made my life worthwhile. On many days their cute little faces, smiles, and playfulness dragged me back over the threshold of sanity. I felt a deep sense of responsibility and protectiveness for them. They were mine, and their mother's, too, and I was determined that no one would harm them. Not wanting them to be mistreated by any other man who might enter their mother's life if she and I separated helped me endure a marriage that was being drained of the love and care it once had. I didn't want another man to care for my flesh and blood, and I didn't want her to struggle to care for them without a man. I loved them too much to leave the responsibility of their nurturing and protection to someone else. I had to be there for them to give them the childhood I had dreamed of, but was never able to recover.

* * *

The attitude and action of the director of operations at The Garden and his assistant toward me was pure evil. As far as I was concerned their behavior was discriminatory as they denied me the promotion I was entitled to. I was hurt. The base part of me wanted to retaliate by tackling them physically, but I knew that thought was foolhardy. I decided, instead, to fast and pray for one week and then discuss the matter with my union representative.

In 1993, I brought the matter to the attention of my union shop representative at The Garden who then submitted a letter of grievance to the D.C 37 Union. A top representative from the Union headquarters came to The Garden and addressed the issue. My appeal was successful! Shortly afterward, the acting director was removed and I was promoted to the position of Maintainer. Oh, praise the Lord for victory in a hard fought battle.

* * *

Some of my co-workers at The Garden treated me with respect and others didn't. Nevertheless, these co-workers won't easily be erased from my memory. In the 1990s, Billy, a Portuguese man who is now retired and Tony, an Italian man who is now deceased, helped me to become a skilled maintainer like themselves. Billy helped to sharpen my auto mechanic skills and Tony taught me how to paint.

Then there are my current co-workers, Al and Mertz, who are rare, irritating, and humorous. The three of us work together as The Garden's unique painting team. Al is a tall African-American, about 275 pounds. He speaks very loudly, is rough, and jokes about almost everything – good or bad. Mertz is a short, slim, and neat Italian who interjects or interrupts with soft gestures and blames Al for almost everything that goes wrong.

At times these guys give each other a piece of their minds, but amazingly, in a split second, they reconcile with hugs and laughter, like loving blood relatives. At first, working with them was exceptionally difficult. But as time passed, we were able to make adjustments to achieve mutual understanding. Now we are a fun working team.

Sammy and his four children

Chapter 18

Solace

"We are driven by five genetic needs: survival, love and belonging, power, freedom, and fun."
— William Glasser

After the contacts with my family in 1992, there was silence. Again, I had no idea what might have happened to them. Not knowing was devastating to me, but I persevered in my hope of finding them. Sometimes I would testify at church about losing contact with my family. Occasionally, I would tell my children about my family but I mostly kept my feelings to myself.

Already a deacon of the church, I became a member of the Executive Board in 1992. By the fall of 1992, the Children's Workshop, which had been inactive since 1990, was ready to be infused with new energy. Two church sisters, Valrie Ricketts and Carol Mills, wanted to restart the Children's Workshop. Both had relocated from the Island of Jamaica to America during 1990 and 1991. Being in their twenties and full of energy, they wanted to contribute to the church via some meaningful ministry. The revival of the Children's Workshop was a clear need and so Carol Mills became the leader of the effort to recreate it. Pleased to know that the program would be available again, I decided to join their effort. The Workshop now had three teachers, and was not dependent on me for its guiding energy. In time, the name—Children's Workshop—was changed to *"Beulah Children and Teens Ministry."*

We worked well as a team. I was reenergized by the enthusiasm of these two young women and by their commitment to working with the children. Their energy and hard work in the ministry provided fuel for my soul and motivation that pulled me along on the days when I otherwise would not have been able to meet with the children. I was excited to see the children, once again, getting the attention they needed and deserved. We knew it was important to maintain good relations with the parents who trusted us with their children, and tried our best to do so.

As we all three worked together, the children's ministry started to grow—it even appeared to be growing faster than the membership in the general church.

I loved Valrie's sweet smile and infectious laughter. She was gentle, affectionate, and very friendly, and she made me feel alive when I was around her. Valrie was married and had a son so, although I was fond of her, and thought that I would love to have a wife with her temperament; I did not allow myself to entertain any other thoughts about her.

For her part, Carol was usually very serious and businesslike. Although we all worked collaboratively, she was the one in charge. I admired Carol's commitment, but had no further attraction toward her. She was mostly interested in academic and intellectual conversations, and she didn't seem to be affectionate or interested in domestic matters.

As the two women and I worked together, we joked with each other. They often laughed at me whenever I got upset and teased me about how my nostrils would open wider then. On my part, I would find something to tease them about. We planned trips for the children, their parents, and the additional ministry staff who later joined us. These trips were to The Garden and other sites of interest in the Bronx.

Through the nineties, thanks to Carol and the rest of the staff, the ministry grew both in numbers and in the quality of the program. I felt happy. Working in this ministry with its two bright and energetic leaders was a bright spot in my otherwise unhappy life.

* * *

I was elated one evening when I arrived home and found a letter from Liberia. The letter was from Uncle Sam, another of my father's brothers. He had been in the Liberian army when I was living with Uncle Henry in the City:

> December 3, 1995
>
> Dear Sam,
>
> I have the honour most respectfully to write you this esteem letter.
>
> My dear son, I am first of all very sorry to announce the death of your Uncle Mr. Henry K. Wongehn. Mr. Henry were killed June 3, 1990 by Krahn's soldiers while on his way struggling from Paynesville and at that time all of us were scattered and hiding ourselves from the said Krahn people. Even those of us like myself who are from Gio tribes in the Army A.F.L. were affected. I mean the Krahn were against the Gios by killing us too much and some of us escaped from their killing.
>
> But right now I have gone back to my usual work which is the National Army, the Armed Forces of Liberia (A.F.L.). From my escaping the bush since last year July the first, 1994 and since then, we have not yet getting salaries. So in this light I'm kindly asking you to possibly send me

Sammy Wongan Kamara

your present address and telephone numbers so as to call you at any time for communications.

And I am furthermore informing you that your mother is not well at all in her body. I myself been there to them at the interior which is Nimba County and I carried some drugs for her and she is still sick. Notwithstanding, there is no immediate family member to give us helping hand on the line of financial support. So I am kindly and seriously asking or begging your pardon to please send me at least $500.00, five hundred dollars to enable me to purchase some important drugs for her survival.

My son, right now it is not easy to live in our country which is Liberia. The money problem is very difficult and I want to please remember as I just mention that since July 1, 1994 I never receive my army salary. And secondly, I have a whole lot of children. Because of this hardship I am living in displaced center. The reason of which I'm in displaced center is because of the difficulties I am passing through. Therefore whenever somebody can't afford money that person can't go and rent somebody's house without paying rentage. This is the main reason I am just going from place to place suffering with my children in displaced center.

However, I thank the Almighty father that I have survived from the so-called and senseless war. So I am eagerly looking on the way for your favorable response and please send all my requirements.

Truly your uncle

Samuel M. Wongehn, (3rd) Third Infantry Battalion A.F.L.

Wow! Uncle Samuel had always been a man of many words. His letter wasn't yet finished as he added another page informing me that:

> I am again informing you that I have here a girl by the name of Juliana who is a 10 grader to be sent to you as your assistant. But before sending her to you, I want you to first of all send us your picture and your approval for the coming of the girl, and then we will also send you the picture of the said girl so as to see her for yourself. She is of course 26 years of age in which I trust her faithfully that she will better serve you deligently.
>
> My dear son, I am insisting that you must please send me that amount of 500.00 five hundred dollars or whatsoever amount that you can afford so as to buy drugs for your mother because your father and your mother are not together in our town and I'm the only person she is looking up to for assistance.
>
> May God bless you and give you prosperity.
>
> Your Uncle Sam.

Uncle Sam's letter at first left me without much of a response. Upon reading the passage in which he said he had a girl for me, I had to laugh, because I knew exactly what Uncle Sam meant. It was a part of our tribal custom for a father to seek out a girl for his son. When Uncle said that the girl would be my "assistant" and that she would "serve me diligently", he was referring to her becoming my woman or wife who would "take care of me" sexually and domestically. I didn't fully understand the custom when I was a child but I recall telling Papa that I didn't want him to select a woman for me. At the time, Papa had laughed at me and told me that I was too young to understand what a woman meant to a man.

When I had finished Uncle Sam's letter, however, angry thoughts of Uncle Henry filled me. As much as I tried to block these angry thoughts, I could not help noticing that Uncle Sam had also confirmed that Uncle Henry was dead. Uncle Sam had even given me the date and circumstances of his death. I tried to remember where I was and what I was doing on June 3, 1990. That was a significant day in the history of the world—at least of *my* world. My oppressor had finally been taken out by fate. Justice had ultimately been served, even though it was not at my hands.

As I thought about him, flashbacks of his raging face and how he had hit me flooded my memory. The hateful words he yelled at me began to replay in my mind. I hadn't realized how strong my need for revenge was. I wanted to beat him myself. The thought that death had cheated me made me punch the wall. Then I heard a voice whisper in my ears, "You have to forgive him."

"No! I don't and I won't!" I yelled back. I knew it was God telling me that I had to forgive my uncle, but I could not fathom why God would let Uncle Henry off the hook like that. It was like letting a murderer go free, without making retribution for his crimes. I wanted my revenge.

"You have to forgive him," the voice whispered again.

"Sorry, God," I replied. "I can't forgive him." My anger was at its boiling point. Why had he beaten me like that? If he had beaten me for doing wrong, I could have understood. But what did I do wrong? And if I did wrong, I was just a little boy; why not teach me the right behavior? Why did he mistreat me when I was not a difficult child? Why did he not give me even one word of encouragement? When people mistreated me and I told him about it, why did he side with them and beat me simply because I had complained to him? More importantly, why did he rape my mother? He had his wife, and Mama was pregnant."

I wanted to break his neck. I had learned martial arts so that, one day, when I returned to Liberia, I could confront Uncle Henry and defend my mother's honor. Now I was reading that he wouldn't be there when I returned. The tormentor of my childhood was dead!

I kept punching the wall until I was spent. Then the tears started falling, and I heard myself shout and wail. I don't know who heard me; I didn't care who heard me. After that day, I sometimes cried, and I sometimes bawled. It was as though something in me had also died. For several months afterwards, I had little or no interest in things that I used to enjoy: my children, basketball, and even God. I kept to myself although, when I went to church, I played my expected role. No one, not even Laura, knew how profoundly sad I was.

A few weeks after the December 3rd letter, fortunately before I had sent any money, Uncle Samuel wrote to ask me not to send anything to him in care of his friend because the post office was no longer doing things correctly, and his friend would take the money for himself.

I knew there were other Liberians in the USA and had I been in touch with them I might have had more reliable news, but I didn't know any of them. I tried to follow the news about Liberia wherever I could access it. There was very little about it on TV and in the US newspapers. Things were really deplorable in Liberia due to the instability in government. Since the aggressive attack by the insurgent Charles Taylor and his group, the National Patriotic Front of Liberia (NPFL), against the peacekeeping forces in Monrovia, warring factions in the country fought over who should make up a transitional government and prepare the country for national elections. According to TimeRime.com, a tentative peace agreement was reached and plans were made to hold national elections in 1997. After seven years of war, 80% of the people lived in extreme poverty.[vii]

In the general elections of 1997, Charles Taylor, a member of the Gola tribe and also an Americo-Liberian, won the presidency by a landslide. Twenty years earlier he had been an economics student at Bentley College. In the intervening years, he had served under the Doe government and then had fallen out of favor. Taylor had been leading an insurgency since 1990 and, now victorious, was serving as

Liberia's president.

The last time I had heard anything from my family in Liberia was in 1996 when Uncle Sam wrote to me. None of my subsequent letters were returned or responded to. Uncle Sam had indicated that they were at the Displaced and Refugees Center, but where were Mama and Papa and the rest of the family? Back in the village? Were they even alive? Was there no one who could answer these questions that haunted me? Was my brief telephone conversation with Mama in 1989 to be the last time that I would hear her precious voice? Would I never hear Papa's fatherly advice again? Would I never get the chance to hug them—and to thank them for the priceless childhood memories I got in the village? Would I be able to tell them about the travails of my journey and my determination to fulfill their dream for our family? Would they get to see their Gontor again; the little boy that they'd sent away with a massive plan and dream to rescue our family from poverty?

I prayed that God would be kind to me and grant me my deep desire to see Mama and Papa again.

* * *

In the summer of 1997, Valrie and her husband and child moved to Maryland. Although other individuals had joined the staff of the Children and Teens Ministry and the ministry was thriving, I was sad to see Valrie's involvement end. I was not in love with her—having kept myself from going there with a married woman—but she had a positive, calming effect on me. Furthermore, she was good with the children. She had an excellent and pleasant spirit who made the children love to attend church.

Carol had been elected president of the youth ministry in 1993 and she had worked tirelessly with the staff to build both the youth department, and the children and teens ministry. Although the youth department had existed for years, the ages for that department were not clearly defined. The teens' ministry started in 1996 when the first group of children from the children's ministry became teenagers. Carol was also able to skillfully and respectfully diffuse conflicts among the staff, as well as between parents and staff. She served two two-year terms as president of the youth department and left that office in the summer of 1997, but remained on as director of the children and teens ministry. I admired her devotion, creativity, and resourcefulness.

Carol had a knack for creating solidarity among the staff. She sought out and provided numerous training opportunities for the staff and field trips where the children, staff, and parents could bond. I don't know what fueled her tenacious commitment, but I could tell that she loved the Lord and she loved what she was doing. Along with all that she did in the church, Carol was a dynamic preacher who provided insight into biblical and theological truths. I loved to listen to her speak. She wasn't the prettiest sister in the church, but she was attractive and smart. She had a lot going for her, yet she was so humble and unassuming. I enjoyed working with her.

Chapter 19

Uncoupling

"My imperfections and failures are as much a blessing from God as my success and my talents and I lay them both at his feet."
— Mahatma Gandhi

The Russian novelist, Leo Tolstoy, makes a thought provoking statement in his novel *Anna Karenina* that *"Happy families are all alike; but every unhappy family is unhappy in its own way."* The factors that make a family happy are the same. They include the presence of care, love, support, time together, compassion for one another, the ability to cry together, the sharing of the good and the bad, and the ability of each member to be his or her own self. As a Christian, I must add that a reverent acknowledgment of the presence of God in our lives and the relationship family members have with God also are important factors in the creation and maintenance of a happy, joyful family.

Family means everything to me. It was my orientation to the world and my biological parents did well in loving me, caring for me, and ensuring that I was being prepared to meet the challenges of life. My sister, Tolema, died much too young, but she was so much fun to play with. My foster parents, Pastor Reuben Johnson and his wife, Edris, offered me the safety net, love, care, protection, and connection that I needed. During its first three years, my marriage gave me a brief glimpse of the joys that a fulfilling and loving marriage can offer. Our children released deep feelings of love in me that are beyond compare.

Laura and I had a golden opportunity to build the kind of marital relationship that is described in the Bible; a marriage where love, respect for each other, sexual fulfillment, friendship and togetherness reign. We raised our children in the same house but we missed so many opportunities to have fun and to create a healthier home for them. You see, people need people. We are all social beings and no matter how independent we become, we still can't shake the desire to be connected. Family fulfills the need for connection and it also provides, or has the potential to provide, invaluable support during times of hardship and distress.

As my family life became more complicated and demanding, I found myself on the verge of losing Mom. I visited her in the nursing home one evening and was moved to tears as I watched her looking so lifeless and helpless. She knew it was me who entered the room and her mouth moved as though she wanted to say something to me.

She called Dad's name. I was sure that's what she said; at least that's what I heard. Her attempt to say more was unclear, but I knew she was telling me to take care of Dad. Her tears were flowing.

"Mom, don't worry," I tried to console her. "Regardless of what happens, I will take care of Dad. He will be ok."

Mom's prolonged illness and her stay in the nursing home had taken a huge toll on Dad. He was naturally an introverted person; however, he seemed to have retreated further into himself. He still carried the weight of his demanding pastoral responsibilities and worked as a limousine chauffeur, even as he visited Mom daily. Dad was not one to complain, but I heard him say more than once that he wished more of the church members would take the time to visit Mom. For many years before her debilitating illness, Mom had been very involved in serving others but it appeared as if she was now forgotten. Out of sight, out of mind? She rarely had visitors. Our church had a nursing home ministry that facilitated members' visits to the nursing home where

Mom lived once a month. They would sing and share exhortations. I believe Mom was always thrilled to see us. She didn't speak to us but she looked so pleased that we had come to be with her.

Besides being a great sorrow and emotional drain for Dad, Mom's illness also exhausted the little savings that they had. Dad did not have a "big" job and he worked hard to take care of their needs since he had never been paid a salary by the church. Although some kind brothers and sisters would give him a gift every now and then, Dad struggled desperately to pay his bills, including his mortgage. He was a proud man, which was obvious from his elegant and impeccable attire, and his generally polite deportment. He loathed begging or asking others for favors and would do so only if he absolutely had no other choice. Knowing the great stresses Dad was under, I made it my duty to visit him at his house in the evenings to check up on him. Even then, he wouldn't ask me for anything. Not wanting to embarrass him, I would intermittently and discretely support him with words of encouragement and gifts.

After seven years in the nursing home, Mom succumbed to her condition in September 1997. She was 63 years old when she died. I had the good fortune to have visited her the day before she died. At her funeral, I sat in the church looking at her coffin, and feeling numb. The precious woman, who had rescued me from homelessness and an uncertain future, was now dead.

Mom, Mother Johnson, my "adopted" mother, my spiritual advisor and life coach, was dead and I missed her every day. I had promised her that I would take care of Dad so I continued to visit him almost daily after work or whenever he was home.

Laura and I were still living together, but our relationship was not getting any better. Our children had assumed first place in our marriage as we tried to raise them to know and revere God, and our marital relationship had become secondary. We kept knocking heads when it came to disciplining our children. She had a hard time getting the children to listen to her and obey her wishes, so I made a suggestion, which I thought would help us. Like her, I loved our children, but I also disciplined them. I disciplined them with love, not with a rod of anger.

"Babe, let's try to agree on how to discipline the children," I said to her one night when we were alone in our bedroom. "Why don't we do it like this: if you are disciplining them, I will support you, and if I am disciplining them, you will support me, so that the children know that we are together."

She stared at me as I spoke.

"I don't like to see that they are not listening to you when you speak to them," I continued. "They respond to me. They should also respond to you when you talk to them."

"Ok, let's try that," she agreed.

One evening after we made that agreement, our two older daughters were misbehaving.

"Girls, do you hear me talking to you?" She raised her voice, but they didn't answer. The girls continued to misbehave, and the younger children started laughing.

"Leah and Joy, I'm not going to speak to you girls again!"

She tried to speak sternly to them. She was now very flustered and angry so I decided to get involved to support her.

"Come on, girls! Stop it!" I said very sternly. "Didn't you hear your mother tell you to stop? Enough is enough."

The girls immediately stopped.

"Leah, go into the bedroom now. You, too, Joy," I directed. I went into the bedroom with the girls.

"Leah lie on the bed on your stomach," I told her. I cupped my right hand and slapped her on her bottom. Because I cupped my hand it made a loud sound although I didn't slap her hard. "Don't you ever talk to your mother like that, again got it? Have respect."

"Don't hit the children like that!" Laura shouted at me from the other side of the door. "It's not right!"

"Babe, remember what we agreed upon," I said. "Don't do that in front of the children."

"But you have no right to hit the children that hard," she continued. "That's not right. Come, Leah. Come, Joy."

The girls went to her, crying. She cuddled them in front of me.

"Sorry, girls. Your father didn't have to hit you so hard," she said to them.

"Babe you're not supposed to be doing that," I said. "Remember what we said.

The disagreement escalated in front of the children. The four children stood by looking confused as we argued about the broken agreement. This pattern of breaking agreements and arguing before the children was repeated many times. Discipline became a source of contention, with her pulling the children to her side by casting me as the bad guy. It became she and the children versus me. In this struggle for our children's loyalty, I believe she was the winner. Most children would be loyal to the parent that grants them favors and sides with them.

In retrospect, I realized that whenever she and I argued, I often allowed myself to enter the dynamics of our discord instead of maintaining restraint and a neutral stance. As the father of our children, I felt responsible for their proper upbringing. I felt the need to balance the immediate tasks of parenting with the long-term effects. I wanted them to learn to be good citizens who could take care of themselves, and not live wild and reckless lives. They might not love me in the end, but the greater risk was what might happen to them if they did not learn how to live as upright citizens.

I now see that arguing with her in front of our children was not helpful. It didn't solve the problems or bear the results that I desired. It didn't endear her to me, or make her want to work collaboratively with me to raise our children. Instead it created a greater wedge between us. I wish we had had the kind of relationship where either of us could pull the other into our bedroom or the bathroom and scold or challenge each other in private. Maybe we could have come to a consensus in the absence of the children. But our relationship was not like that. When I realized that I couldn't make her change her approach, that I could only change my own actions, it was too late to make a difference. We had a much bigger problem: a marriage that was embroiled in conflict and was on life support. We were at a breaking point.

* * *

Mom and Dad and the other church leaders were sincere and did the best they could with the knowledge and experience they had, but I feel sorry for them. On the one hand, they were very zealous and committed to the Lord's work. They emphasized preparing for the return of our Savior Jesus Christ and being a part of the restored Kingdom of God on earth. They also reinforced the practice of spiritual disciplines such as prayer, fasting, witnessing, and Bible studies. On the other hand, they were very repressed and they taught the young people to be repressed.

I've wondered many times why Dad did not refer us to an outside counselor. Undoubtedly, he thought it was unnecessary, due to our Christian commitment. Yet, I can't stop thinking that the outcome of our marriage would have been different if we had gotten more than pastoral counseling, and if we had been encouraged to spend the time to get to know each other better before marriage. Our troubled marriage was not the fault of the leaders. We were culpable. But I can't help thinking that the outcome would have been different if we were better prepared to meet the challenges of marriage.

I don't believe that we are the only ones whose marriage might have been negatively impacted by the lack of thorough premarital counsel and preparation. Couples in the church tended to be secretive about their marital problems, just as we later became. Not wanting to face gossip or rejection by the church leaders and members, some couples dropped out entirely, or left the church when their marriages began to fail and went to other churches. Sometimes, one member of the couple stayed with the church, whereas the other member left. Perhaps too many others remained together in dysfunctional and unhappy marriages. Those who continued in the church often referred to "following the teachings of the church." They believed that marriage is a covenant that could not be broken and so, once married, they were "bound to each other for life." Getting a divorce was therefore seen as a degenerate and irredeemable sin. From my observation, only a few of these married couples had marriages that were healthy, fun, and representative of godly marriage as defined in the Bible.

* * *

In the past, I would have sought advice from Mom, but since her death, I had longed for someone to play the role she played in my life. So, weighed by my failure to institute proper discipline for our children, in the fall of 1999, I decided to seek counsel from my wife's stepmother. She was Mom's best friend and she had always been very kind to me, and even regarded me as a son. I visited her house one evening after work, and she welcomed me in gladly. As soon as I sat down, I started pouring out my concern to her.

"We are not doing well," I began. "It's been that way for many years now. We keep arguing over every little thing."

"What are you saying?" she said. "What could you both be arguing about?"

"A lot of things," I replied. "For example, whenever we agree on goals and plans for the family, she diverts from them without my knowledge or consent. And when I bring it to her attention and ask why," I continued, "she refuses to answer, and when I insist on an answer, it turns into an argument."

"Is there any other thing that you both argue about?" she asked, looking worried.

"Another problem is regarding the discipline of the children," I answered. "The children take advantage of her and often didn't listen to her when she corrects them, but they respond when I correct them. So I talked with her in private and proposed that we work together in this area," I continued. "I suggested that we both support each other when either of us is disciplining them. And even if one of us didn't like the manner in which the discipline was done, we would still support each other, and discuss the disagreement in private, not before the children."

"That sounds like a good plan." Her stepmother was nodding. "How is that working?"

"That's the problem. It's not working," I said. "Laura diverts from it and sides with the children against me, then starts quarreling and reprimanding me in front of them. Then I retaliate. The whole plan disintegrates in front of them."

"My Lord!" she exclaimed. "In front of the children? That cannot be."

"That's what happens," I said. "I want to stop this behavior, because I see the look on the children's faces. They are confused."

"Sam, this is not good for the children," she said firmly. "They must not see you and their mother quarrelling like that. You both are going to hurt them."

"That's why I came to you," I said, with resignation. "We need help. Can you come and talk with us?"

"I don't really want to get involved," she said. "I don't think your wife would want me to get involved."

"Please, Mother," I pleaded. "We need you to get involved before things get any worse."

"I don't know, Sam," she said, her face filled with doubt. "I have to pray about it."

Estella did reach out to Laura. The day she spoke to her, Laura confronted me.

"Why did you have to go running to my mother with your complaints?" Laura faced me, clearly angry. "We are not children; we can solve our problems ourselves. We don't need her to get involved in our lives."

"Babe, I think we need help," I said. "If we can solve our problems ourselves, why haven't we? Why are things getting worse? We argue and fuss day and night. Is this the life you want? Well, I don't want this. I want some peace in my life."

* * *

While this home drama was going on, I was worrying about the disastrous civil war that had ravished my beloved Liberia. The long silences between letters kept me in a state of heightened anxiety. I often wondered whether my parents were alive or dead. How much were they suffering? Would the civil wars ever stop? Often there were no answers to my questions. History records that over 200,000 Liberians lost their lives and the lives of over two million others were shattered as they were displaced during the upheavals. Some escaped to neighboring countries such as the Ivory Coast, Guinea, Sierra Leone and Ghana as well as to America and other countries. The blood of the unfortunate people who died washed the landscape of our beautiful country.

Furthermore, rape was routinely used as a weapon of war. Not even young girls were exempted. Many innocents fought to save their lives and that of their families and neighbors, but there were too many who killed wantonly because of greed and misguided convictions and beliefs. The United Nations estimated that between 15,000 and 20,000 children between the ages of 9-15 years old participated in the conflict.[viii] It was as if my countrymen suffered from national insanity. I believe that the collective psyche of the Liberian people, including those of us in the diaspora, was traumatized during those years by the horrors that occurred in our land. What could have justified the deaths of so many people? What could have justified the loss of so much promise that these people might have offered to humanity?

In 1999, as if enough blood had not already been shed, a second civil war erupted in Liberia. This time, it was spawned by alleged corruption and intimidation by the Taylor government. This was a complex situation that involved fighters from our neighbors in Sierra Leone, Guinea, and Ivory Coast, as well as Liberians who opposed the Taylor regime. Again, this led to major disruption and instability in Liberia. Thousands more people were killed. In an effort to stem the tide of war in 2001, the UN imposed a weapons embargo against Liberia. However, this didn't stop the war.

Chapter 20

Dad's Turn

"I Will Rise"
— Chris Tomlin

In addition to my marriage difficulties and the stress of worrying about the safety of my family and my fellow Liberians, I was to encounter another factor that would shake my life to the core and bring me to a possible breaking point once again.

Sara Manning, author of *It Felt Like A Kiss*, makes a very thought provoking statement: *"Never complain, never explain"*, that makes me think of Dad. He did not have a pension from a corporation or from the church that he had served so faithfully for so many years. Yet, he never complained, in spite of his troubles.

One evening after returning home from work, I received a telephone call from BB, the church sister who had lived for years at the house with Mom and Dad. She had become a close friend of the family, and was also a close friend of mine.

"Have you spoken to your father lately?" she asked. I didn't like the sound of her voice.

"No. What's wrong?" I asked my heart beginning to race.

"Your father only has a few days to stay in his house before foreclosure. She spoke hesitantly, as though she was betraying his sacred trust.

"What!" I blurted out. "How could that be? Dad hasn't said anything to me."

"He didn't want to bother you," she said, "because of your family situation."

"This can't be," I said angrily. "Where is he going to live—on the street? That won't happen, not as long as I'm alive. Where is he?"

I was very angry at Dad for keeping this situation from me. Mom had told me to take care of him, but he wasn't giving me a chance to do so. I knew he was a private man and this must be an embarrassing situation for him. After all, he was one of the veteran pastors among the Church of God Seventh Day circles. There is a certain stigma that comes with not being able to take care of one's basic needs. I can see why he wouldn't want anyone to know about his plight. What depth of sadness, paralyzing shame, and desperation he must have felt!

Etched indelibly into the walls of that house on Eastchester Road were memories of yesterdays; good times spent with his wife and the youths and other members of the church who visited. The possibility of losing the home that had been a sanctuary to him and Mom must have stressed him to the point of numbness. But which would be worse, telling me, or being thrown out on the streets with nowhere to go? I know the feelings of desperation that accompany the reality that one is on the verge of homelessness. I no longer cared about embarrassing Dad. I decided to confront him the following day.

After talking with BB, I brought the matter to Laura's attention that night.

"Dad is in a bad situation and he is in desperate need of our help," I told her. "It would be good if we could help him refinance by co-signing for him."

"No. Not my name on that," Laura said emphatically.

"Babe, something has to be done," I urged. "We have to do something to help him.

"That's his problem; I don't want to have anything to do with that."

She spoke so coldly of the man she had known for decades. "Let him take care of his own business."

Looking at her, I realized that she was very serious about her position and she was not going to budge. I was deeply grieved by her lack of compassion for Dad and was immediately tormented by the possibility that he could become homeless.

"Ok, I will just have to do what I have to do," I said to myself, not wanting to waste time arguing with her.

Dad cast out on the streets while I sleep in my comfortable bed? No way! That night, I couldn't sleep. It was as if a million pins were sticking me all over my body. I told myself that I wouldn't allow it to happen. With or without Laura's assistance, I had to help him.

Early the following morning, I telephoned Dad.

"Hello," he said.

"Is everything ok?" I asked.

"...mmm, but..." he muttered then hesitated.

"...but what?" I asked impatiently. I could sense that Dad was holding back and didn't want to share his plight with me. "BB told me that things are very difficult with you," I rushed on, "and that by next week the bank will take back the house. Is this true?"

"Yea, she's right," he said reluctantly. "But I didn't want to bother you and your family."

"Dad, forget that," I said. "I told Mom that I would take care of you. What can be done to solve the problem?

"...mmm...you would have to talk with the lawyer. He can explain what has to be done," Dad said.

"Ok," I said. "Call the lawyer and ask him to come by the house to meet with us this evening."

"But Sam," he said. "Don't you think this will cause problems between you and your wife?"

"Dad, forget about that," I said. "We'll do what we have to do. Call the lawyer."

"Ok, Sam," he said sounding relieved.

We met with the lawyer as arranged, and we carved out a plan to save Dad's house. I was able to co-sign a new mortgage with Dad, making me co-proprietor, and thus, allowing him to keep it.

* * *

When I look back on this time in my life, it amazes me that I survived. Not only were the three prior crises weighing heavily on me, my health was a great stressor. I had started seeing a family doctor, who put me on Benadryl and Dilantin and gave me a report that all seemed fine. I took these medications for over three years and endured decreased muscle coordination, mental confusion, nervousness, and slurred speech. I learned later that prolonged use of Dilantin is linked to osteoporosis, significant bone loss, and experts recommend that more patients and doctors should be aware of this serious side effect. At first, the Dilantin helped to reduce the frequency of my seizures. However, my condition began to worsen again. There were times when I had seizures up to four times a week. Laura still called the ambulance and accompanied me to the hospital.

* * *

One evening while we were eating dinner, I had a headache. Instead of excusing myself from the table and going to the bedroom to rest, I did what I often do and pushed against my feelings. I remember my head feeling strange but the next thing I knew, I was opening my eyes and looking up at Laura and our four children. The children looked scared.

"What happened?" I remembered mumbling.

"You had a seizure," Laura said. "I didn't want the children to see that."

I agreed with her. It scared them. I also didn't want them to see me unable to speak. I felt confused as I tried to be strong before my family. It was impossible to get up off the floor by myself; I was too weak and dazed. She ordered the children to move away from me, where I lay. I usually have nocturnal seizures in my bedroom so this seizure at the dining table was a new development. It increased my fear of having seizures at work, or while driving.

In retrospect, I believe nocturnal seizures had played a major role in the demise of my marriage yet I can only speculate, because she never told me that they did. The medications caused me to be very drowsy during the day and restless at night. I started having terrifying nightmares. At various times in the nightmares someone was usually chasing me and trying to kill me. I would start "running" desperately, and screaming. Other times I would be engaged in fierce battles and was being badly beaten. When I awoke from these nightmares I was often bathed in sweat and felt very afraid. Laura did not say so, but I would not be surprised if my restlessness at nights contributed to her moving out of our bedroom.

"Dad, I need to talk with you," I said one day. I had decided to speak with Dad about my distress.

"About what?" Dad asked.

"Laura and I are not doing well," I said feeling despondent. "And my health is going down the drain. I didn't plan to say anything because she doesn't want us to talk with anyone."

"Sorry to hear this," he said.

"Dad, I want you to come to the house and pray with us." I didn't know what else to say. "She doesn't want you to come, but I want you to. I can't take it anymore."

"Sam, I can't come to your house if your wife doesn't want me to." He rubbed his head. "I will pray for you and your family but it wouldn't be right to go to your house when she doesn't want me there."

There I was again. Alone. Who would I talk to? I continued to pray on my own but I had become depressed and discouraged. During this time, I looked forward to attending church on Sabbaths (Saturdays), because I felt love among the brethren. They would greet me with warm smiles, words of encouragement, reassuring hugs, handshakes, and sometimes holy kisses on my cheeks. In spite of my illness, I prayed and fasted. I went to church every week and went to the altar for prayer. I kept going to work even after rough nights of seizures. I often drove Laura to work with one hand after frequent seizures weakened the ligaments in my shoulders causing them to slip out of the sockets. In spite of my utter unhappiness, I continued to care and provide for my wife and children, hoping every day that somewhere, somehow, Laura and I could reconcile our differences and live a peaceful, happy, and godly life.

But, I was not to receive a reprieve just yet, and was soon to suffer another major loss. Late in 2001, Dad became very ill and was admitted to the intensive care unit at Montefiore Hospital in the Bronx. He stayed in the intensive care unit there for over a week before the doctors informed BB and me that Dad was terminally ill. For some reason, my mind didn't fully process what the doctor told me, either that, or I was in denial.

Dad underwent major surgery to remove the cancer from his body. After the surgery, he was sent home, but there were complications and he returned to the hospital a few days later.

I was at the hospital along with some of the church brethren. As Dad lay motionless on the bed, I held his hand and talked with him. Just then, the machine he was hooked up to started beeping loudly. The doctors rushed into the room. I was listed as Dad's next of kin and so the doctor addressed me.

"Mr. Kamara, he doesn't have much time left," he said. "What do you want us to do? Should we try to resuscitate?"

"Yes," I said quickly my heart racing. "Do all you can to give him more time!"

The doctors asked me to step aside, and I could hear them trying to shock his heart into starting again. They failed. When I came back to his bed and held his hand, it was cold. I watched as he took his last breath. Dad died on Tuesday, January 15, 2002 of congestive heart failure. (It was Martin Luther King, Jr.'s birthday.) Even though I had seen him take his last breath and had seen that he was not breathing any more, it didn't register in my brain that he was dead. It wasn't until the day of the funeral in the church filled with people that my mind woke up.

I sat in the front row of the church, with Laura and our children in the row behind me. I stared at the coffin throughout the church service, dazed. When the funeral service manager re-opened the coffin for viewing I went up to look into it. Dad lay, there not moving. I held his hands then tried to hug him; actually my mind was telling me to lift him out of the coffin. I screamed and cried as loudly as I could. The people staring at me didn't register. In fact, I didn't care.

"He's not dead. He can't be dead," I told myself. "He can't leave me, not yet! Mom told me to take care of him. Furthermore, I have to take him to Liberia to introduce him to Papa and Mama. Mom is dead, but they have to meet Dad. They have to meet this saint who cared for me as his own son."

When I bent over the coffin, one of the ushers attempted to guide me away but one of the pastors told him to leave me alone. I'm glad he did because a strong surge of anger consumed me, and I wanted to grab the usher and throw him across the church.

Dad was buried at White Plains Rural Cemetery the next day. His coffin was placed on the upper level of Mom's grave. As I watched the attendants lower him into the grave, I felt numb and alone. As when Mom had died in 1997, a profound and abiding sense of doom and depression rested on me for months that turned into years. I was a grown man but I felt like a lost, abandoned child. There was no one to fill the gap, now that I had lost my second parents. The piercing pain I felt when I was separated from my biological parents returned. After Dad's death, to keep from breaking, I turned inward into myself, and began to stuff my feelings and worries down out of sight again.

My family and I continued to attend the same church and perhaps to others we seemed like a fine Christian family. But my marriage continued to crash violently against the rocks and my health got worse.

One of my worst seizure episodes occurred early one morning in the summer of 2002. For days before it happened, I had been feeling especially sad and depressed. I tried to shake those negative feelings by working harder on the job, playing basketball after work, and drinking an occasional beer. I cried and prayed to God for help but the negative feelings clung to me like wet clothes on a person who had walked into the ocean fully clothed.

Laura was apparently concerned about how she and the children would survive economically, if I were to die. She started to insist that I prepare my will. Under other circumstances, her suggestion would not only have been reasonable but also sensible. But amidst the stress of our marriage, I thought that she couldn't wait for me to die. I myself began to think that my own death was imminent.

When I went to bed the evening before this terrible seizure, I had difficulty falling asleep. I can't recall if she slept in our bedroom that night or whether she slept in the children's room so I don't know who discovered that I was having the seizures early that morning. She and the children stayed home that day. After coming out of the first seizure, I lay on the bed feeling very exhausted and exceptionally drowsy. My head was pounding. I had another seizure, and as I revived slowly, I could hardly move my legs, and my lower body felt paralyzed. I heard her speak my name.

I didn't answer or couldn't speak but I asked myself, "Why is she calling me? Does she want me to die?"

"Sam, can you hear me?" she asked again.

Whenever I have a seizure my speech and cognition are slow. I didn't have the strength to answer but I also didn't want to hear her voice. The more she called my name the more I wished I could die. I wanted to talk to my children. I don't know where in the house the girls were, but Junior was in the room. I remember thinking of calling to him maybe because he was the only other male in the family. I wanted to tell him to take care of the family when I was gone. Laura was talking, but I had stopped listening to her. Shortly afterward, I heard another voice.

"Sam! Sam!" it was a familiar female voice, a voice I wanted to hear. Yet it was so far off.

"Sam, don't leave us," the voice pleaded. "We love you, don't leave us."

I remember that the person was bending over me. She was touching me. It felt like someone had put a cool wet cloth on my burning forehead. I struggled to open my eyes.

"Sam, I love you," she said. Her voice was soothing. I felt as if I was being revived, as if someone was breathing life into me. I believe I was exiting this life when I heard her call me back. Her voice gave me the strength to turn back and open my eyes. I looked up at her worried face. It was Vashti, one of the sisters from church and a close friend of our family. She hugged me. I don't think she knew it, but when she hugged me, I felt rejuvenated, as if I mattered just for who I was.

That year, I turned again to Laura's stepmother in desperation.

"Mother, things are really bad," I told her. "I don't think I'm going to make it."

"I'm praying for you, and her, and the children," she said.

"Thanks, Mother," I said, feeling drained. "I don't know what else to do. I tried everything I can think of, but I can't do this by myself. I'm dying."

"Sam, you know that when I tried to talk with her, it didn't make a difference," she said. "She told me not to get involved. She said it was not my business."

There was no point, I realized, in her stepmother talking to Laura, but perhaps there was a point to her talking to me. I felt so alone and she was like a mother to me. Knowing that she genuinely cared was comforting.

"I'm especially worried about Junior and Loretta" she continued. "This kind of environment is not good for them."

"I know, my heart hurts for them," I said. "They're the reason why I've stayed in this marriage so long. I don't want to hurt my children, and I don't want any other man to care for them. They're mine."

My heart was aching and breaking.

Chapter 21

God Keeps Silence

"...My God, my God, why have you forsaken me?"
— (Mark 15:34)

In Liberia, the senseless and brutal civil war intensified in 2002, claiming even more lives. The US and British government and other nations began to pressure President Taylor to step down. As forces opposing Taylor and his government gained control of more of the country, and pressure from Liberian women and regional and other governments increased, Taylor agreed in 2003 to attend a peace conference in Accra, Ghana, to negotiate peace. The conference, sponsored by the Economic Community of West African States (ECOWAS) and chaired by John Kufuor of Ghana, began on June 4, 2003 and lasted for several weeks.

I have watched some very moving YouTube videos about the war. Those videos disturbed me greatly, to the point where I felt both angry and helpless. There was so much devastation and brokenness. How was it possible that our country could recover from such a deep national and personal wound? But two of the videos really were very uplifting: *Women of Liberia Fighting for Peace*[ix] and *Pray the Devil Back to Hell*.[x] Women and faith played a central role in the ending of Liberia's second civil war and a return to stability. The documentary *Pray the*

Devil Back to Hell speaks volumes about the bravery and importance of women in our nation. They stood up to power and spoke truth to power at the risk of losing their own lives. I really encourage all to watch this video, to get an insight into how the second civil war in Liberia came to an end, preventing even more destruction, misery, and death in Liberia.

* * *

In August 2003, under intense pressure from the world community, Charles Taylor resigned and went into exile in Nigeria. A provisional government was established.

Hearing that the second civil war had ended was a welcome answer to my prayers. I now wondered what was left in the wake of the war, and how soon would civilians be allowed to travel from the USA to Liberia. Which airlines would go to Liberia? I was eager to finally travel to my homeland to see Mama and Papa. By some miracle, I had finally gotten my birth certificate through the Liberian Consulate and had been able to process my application for citizenship in the USA. And yet, I still couldn't go. I didn't know where my family was, so I didn't know how to contact them.

* * *

While the civil war was over and technically, I could travel to Liberia, developments in my own home here in America hindered my search for my family in Liberia.

In the spring of 2004, several developments proved to me that things could indeed get worse. Laura left our church with her best friend and her best friend's husband to start a ministry. Our two older daughters went with her, whereas the two younger children continued to attend church with me. Conditions at home deteriorated further. In the past, in spite of our marital difficulties, Laura was supportive of me during my seizures. However, after she left the church with her friend, our marital relationship changed drastically. The chill was like an arctic blast. She was no longer responsive to me and often kept the children away from me. Our family no longer ate together, weekly family worship stopped, and we no longer went to church together. It was at this time that she finally moved permanently out of the marital bedroom to sleep in the younger children's room. Intimacy between us became a thing of the past.

I felt that life was about to break me.

My life continued to fall apart and so I longed for my biological mother's arms and for my biological father's words of encouragement. I longed for the wise Godly counsel and care that Mom and Dad had given me, but they, too, were gone.

In my distress, I cried and yelled before God and in the church. I needed Him to intervene. I needed Him to be a present help in the time of my troubles.

"Where is God in all of this?" I thought. *"I'm a believer."* I believed that God exists and that He rules in the affairs of humanity, yet I started questioning where God was in human suffering, in my suffering. Why did God stand on the sidelines and watch? Why didn't God intervene to end human suffering, to end my suffering? God is love. God is a caring God, who can be touched by humanity's infirmity. That's what the Bible says. But does God care?

Well, then, where the hell is God? I'd been a Christian for umpteen years, and yes, God had taken me through many breaking points in my life, when I could have easily descended into hopelessness, a psychotic breakdown, or complete insanity.

I remembered that, but how cruel was it for God to now stand by and watch my life unravel? Why would God stand idly by and watch my health deteriorate, my marriage totter on the precipice of doom, and why would God watch as I was about to lose all that I had worked slavishly for, over the past twenty-nine years? Why had God forsaken me? Knowing where God had taken me thus far, some may be thinking that I was most ungrateful. They might be saying that others went through worse than I, and that I should just have faith. But isn't that what Christianity does to us sometimes? We're afraid to talk straight to God and to ask God the tough questions? We hide our true feelings and pretend. Well, I was getting tired of pretending. Right then, I felt that God had given me more than I could handle.

* * *

My marriage continued to deteriorate and the seizures worsened. My life felt as if it was in freefall with no bottom in sight. Thoughts of all I stood to lose terrified me. I had worked so hard for all I had. Now, if things didn't turn around, I could lose so much: my family, living in the same house with my children, my house itself that had so much sentimental value, my money, and much more. The prevailing uncertainties in my life resurrected feelings of desperation that took me back to my life in Monrovia and to when I was thrown out by the Kamaras. In many ways, I felt as if I was on the verge of being homeless again. Where would I find the will and strength to start all over?

Because the seizures had begun to wear out the ligaments in my left shoulder, I was forced to wear a sling to protect it. One night my shoulder, which at this time was not fully healed, got dislocated again during a seizure. I was sleeping alone in our bedroom. Laura came in, turned on the light and asked, "Is everything alright? Is the shoulder dislocated?" I told her it was.

As she was about to leave the room to go to the bathroom, I asked her, "Do you know how the doctor put it back in place the last time?" She told me no, then left the bedroom. While still calling on Jesus' name and lying flat on my back, helpless and in pain, I prayed, "Lord, I don't want to go to the hospital again. Please do something for me."

In those moments of excruciating pain, the Holy Spirit said to me, "Hold your left hand down on the bed, squeeze your left fingers with right fingers in between, slowly lift left hand, close to the body."

When my right hand brought my left hand around my chest, the pain intensified. The Holy Spirit said, "No, lie more to your right side and pull slowly and steadily." When I did this, the pain shot up to the highest degree and the dislocated shoulder snapped back into place. Oh! Oh! What a relief that was. It was very painful, but victory was won! I shouted as loudly as I could "Hallelujah! Praise the Lord! God is real!" I kept shouting for several minutes, my eyes filled with tears of joy. Afterward, as I was going to the bathroom, I met Laura at the bathroom door and she asked if I had put my shoulder back in place.

"The Spirit of the Lord did it" I replied.

"Spirit of the Lord? Huh," she scoffed, and walked away while I continued praising the Lord. "Yes, truly hallelujah! I know the Lord for myself. He's real! His doings are still marvelous. He is the greatest of teachers. Bless the Lord, oh my soul, and all that is within me."

I went to see my orthopedist the following week and he told me that an MRI was necessary to find out whether my left shoulder was fractured or whether the weak ligaments were causing the pain I was experiencing in my neck, left shoulder, and arm.

Yes, indeed the affliction intensified. I slept only on my back with the left arm in a sling or on the right side of my body, for to sleep otherwise tormented me more and dislocated my shoulder more frequently. I praise the Lord that, in all this, I was always able to put back my dislocated shoulder, as instructed by my Great Master Teacher, Sweet Spirit of the Living God, whose son is Jesus.

"Oh, bless the Lord, my soul!"

A few times on the job, I spontaneously started praising God loudly. Not knowing what was happening; my boss and co-workers looked at me strangely. "Is everything ok?" they commented, "You look kind of jolly."

Nevertheless, my health condition to deteriorate. Early one Saturday morning, I had a seizure and fell off the bed onto the floor, down between the window and the bed. It was a tight spot and my left shoulder slipped out for the second time in one night. I was alone in the bedroom. The pain was so unbearable that I yelled for help at the highest pitch of my voice. No one in my family came to help me—neither Laura nor my children. Although my shoulder had slipped out before, I was in too much pain to think straight. God through the Holy Spirit came to my rescue again when I screamed out to Him.

I heard a still small voice instructing me what to do, once more. The voice said, "Sam, take it easy, move your right hand slowly. Lay flat on your back and slowly use your right hand to slowly lift your left hand."

I followed the instructions and moved inch by inch, second by second, then finally when I lifted my arm as high as it would go, I heard the voice say, "It will hurt a lot but now, move it quickly, ready, pull quick then snap it into place." I could feel the urine running down my legs as I snapped my shoulder in. The terrible pain raced through all parts of my body and I screamed with every fiber of my being. Relief came shortly afterward. I sat in my puddle of urine feeling empty and forgotten. That day, I went to church and shared my experience in a testimony with the congregation. It was then that most of the church members learned how bad things were at my home. I was ready to expose my family situation to the entire church.

Later that day, during the afternoon divine service, as the congregation sang, I fell to my knees.

"God of Abraham! God of Isaac! God of Jacob!" I yelled. "Have mercy on me!"

I don't remember what else I said but I remember repeatedly crying out to God. Before I left for home that day, Carol's cousin spoke with me. She asked me if I'd ever considered talking with a professional counselor. I told her no, so she suggested that it might be helpful to do so. I had not tried contacting a professional family and marriage counselor before, but at this point I was willing to do so. Maybe doing so would help.

My thought was to go to a counselor for my own sanity and well-being, to try to save myself. I was convinced that Laura would not attend with me; after all, she had refused every other outreach or offer of help. I was shocked when the counselor was able to persuade her, via a telephone call, to also attend the sessions with me. In the first session, she revealed that the reason she had diverted from our shared plans for our marriage was because she wanted to be in charge of her own life.

The counselor advised that in order for a relationship to work, both persons need to walk in agreement and be able to discuss and work through disagreements. The counselor further stated that even though things were bad between us, if we could forgive each other and resolve the issues, it was still possible to save the marriage.

I was very hopeful because she was attending the sessions, although we didn't say a word to each other about the sessions, after we returned home. It was as if we had never gone. After two sessions, Laura decided not to go back, and the attempt to get marital counseling collapsed. My hope for our marriage was ripped apart.

"I need my family," I said to myself. I had asked God for a wife that I would love and who would love me. What was happening was not what I had asked for, but I began to think that if she and I couldn't turn this marriage around, we would have to divorce. We were both Christian believers, and we believed in the biblical teaching that marriage between a man and a woman is a lifelong commitment, symbolic of the relationship between Christ and the church. But our relationship was not working; it had begun to wear me out physically, spiritually, and emotionally. We argued incessantly and more and more the resentment and animosity we felt for each other began to engulf our godly home. Our children were not untouched by the toxic environment, but they kept their feelings to themselves.

* * *

In my next visit to the orthopedic surgeon, I told him that my left shoulder kept slipping out of the socket. After he examined my left shoulder, he advised to me stop physical therapy, continue to sleep with my arm in a sling and take it out of the sling to work each day. He also warned me to be careful about lifting weights so that the weakened ligaments could heal. I told him that the pain in my left shoulder had decreased, but I felt insecure because it was always threatening to slip out. The doctor ordered another MRI to assess the situation. He informed me that the ligaments were worn, and if I continued to have seizures that resulted in more dislocations, I ran the risk of being crippled. He then recommended surgery to tighten the ligaments. It would be a delicate surgery and was scheduled for December 2004.

The surgery, which lasted for about four hours, was successful. I was grateful that, in spite of the icy state of our relationship, Laura stayed at the hospital until I came out of surgery. I believe she left while I was in recovery, but returned to the hospital later that evening. I was grinding my teeth in pain. She asked me if I was awake and I was able to answer yes. Her touch would have soothed me but she stayed away. The following day as I waited to be discharged, my gratefulness was chilled by her impatience at having to wait for me. The difficult recovery period lasted for about five months, during which, I couldn't work.

The prognosis for my seizure condition was not good. My doctors warned me of the grim consequences of uncontrolled seizures. Frequent prayer requests and regular visits to the altar at church for healing were not producing the results I greatly needed.

One evening, I came home from work feeling really depressed. I wanted someone to be happy to see me when I came home. I wanted to hear someone tell me that I mattered, that I was loved. I had money in my pocket, but the money was like trash and thoughts of jumping off a building to end it all kept racing in and out of my mind. Being in the house alone, I decided to take a shower, during which I had a fierce conversation with God.

"God, if you're not going to heal me and my marriage, please leave me alone!" I said. "Don't waste my time! Let me go, so I can enjoy the world. Why am I suffering so much when I'm trying to serve you? Why? Answer me, why?"

God did not answer.

"Enough is enough!" I yelled at God. "I have been serving you all these years with all my heart. I've made sacrifice after sacrifice! You have my life's report! I can't take it anymore!"

God did not respond.

"How many times must I ask you for help?" I continued to scream at God. "Where do I go from here? If you cannot answer my prayer, let me go. Don't waste my time! I would rather enjoy the pleasures of this world and go to hell than to make all these sacrifices and still go to hell because of hatred in my heart. I'm burdened and I'm dying!"

Shouting left me feeling emotionally drained. I stopped and waited for God to answer. There was total silence. A few minutes afterward, I felt a sensation and heard these words, as if someone had entered the bathroom and was standing behind me.

"Sam, why do people seek for gold? Where do you find gold?"

As the voice spoke, I bowed my head.

"Do you find gold on the seashore?" the voice continued. "No. Gold is found in the earth. You have to search for it, and when it is found, it has to be processed through refining fire. Why do you think the enemy is after you? It's because of your value—you're a gem. I am still working on you." After that, the voice stopped speaking, and I began to bawl and asked God for forgiveness for the irreverent and disorderly way I had approached Him. After this experience, no matter how bad things got I remembered these words. They always brought comfort to me.

PART FOUR:

THE SEARCH FOR NEW MEANING IN LIFE

Chapter 22

Looking for Answers

"The Wilderness holds answers to more questions than we have yet learned to ask."
— Nancy Wynne Newhall

When I read Biblical Scriptures such as the Book of Job, I couldn't help thinking that I knew exactly how Job had felt. Job had known the tension that often lives in the middle of our faith. He understood that faith and doubt are close companions. In Job Chapter 2:10 of the Christian Bible, he scolded his wife because she doubted God: "You are talking like a foolish woman," he said to her. "Shall we accept good from God, and not trouble?" Yet it was that same Job who in Chapters 3:1-3; 23-26 said:

> "…may the day of my birth perish and the night that said, 'a boy is conceived'…Why is life given to a man whose way is hidden, whom God has hedged in? For sighing has become my daily food; my groans pour out like water. What I feared has come upon me; what I dreaded has happened to me. I have no peace, no quietness; I have no rest, but only turmoil."

Despite being in the throes of my pain and trials, I dared myself to continue to believe that God was touched by my situation. Doing so was my only hope. In the midst of my theological questioning and the stiff challenges to my faith, I held on for dear life to Scriptures such as Romans 5:1-5:

> "Therefore, since we have been justified through faith, we have peace with God through our Lord Jesus Christ, through whom we have gained access by faith into his grace in which we now stand. And we boast in the hope of the glory of God. Not only so, but we also glory in our sufferings, because we know that sufferings produces perseverance; perseverance, character; and character, hope. And hope does not put us to shame, because God's love has been poured out into our heart through the Holy Spirit, who has been given to us."

And Hebrews 10:32-37:

> "Remember those earlier days after you had received the light, when you endured in a great conflict full of suffering. Sometimes you were publicly exposed to insult and persecution; at other times you stood side by side with those who were threatened. You suffered along with those in prison and joyfully accepted the confiscation of your property, because you knew that you yourselves had better and lasting possessions. So do not throw away your confidence; it will be richly rewarded. You need to persevere so that when you have done the will of God, you will receive what he has promised. For, 'in just a little while, he who is coming will come and will not delay.'"

* * *

To avoid quarreling with Laura after she left our church, I started withdrawing from interactions with her. This was for my sanity and survival because my frustration had fermented into anger and despair. Nevertheless, I still stuck to my commitment to care for her and our children. I still went to work, interacted with my children and attended to my religious commitments. During 2005, the untenable situation at home did not improve. Instead, our relationship continued to break down.

One Sabbath afternoon in December 2005, after teaching the intermediate class that I was responsible for, Carol asked, "Brother Sam, how are you today? How was your class?"

"The class was ok," I answered not wanting to share how I was doing.

"You have a big class," she said. "What if you and Andrew taught together, instead of alternating? Would that be helpful to you?"

"I'm ok. I can manage," I assured her. "If I need help, I'll let you know."

"Please do, because I can always adjust the schedule if necessary," she said. "Also if you need to take time off, please don't hesitate, just let me know so I can have someone cover for you."

"I don't need to take any time off," I said. "I'm okay."

"Okay, if you say so." Carol regarded me for a moment. "How's your shoulder, since the surgery?"

"So so," I said. "I'm still having pains in my shoulder and my neck."

"Sorry to hear that," she empathized. "What about the seizures?"

I described to her the agony and discomfort I endured at nights, because I had to wear a sling and be careful about how I slept. Fear and discomfort were my companions at night. I had to sleep on my back and I couldn't roll over on either side. I also worried about having seizures, falling off the bed, and dislocating my recently repaired left shoulder.

She gave me her full attention as I spoke.

The conversation seems to have stayed with Carol, kind woman that she is. In January 2006, she informed me about the Seizures & Epilepsy Education (S.E.E.) program, sponsored by *Finding a Cure for Epilepsy and Seizures (F.A.C.E.S.).* Carol was very resourceful and had a knack for researching useful information. She stated that she often approached problematic situations by asking, "What could be the cause? Why is this happening and how can it be resolved?" She did some research about seizures and it was then that she stumbled upon, or God led her to, the F.A.C.E.S. program at New York University. Carol encouraged me to follow up on the information and then wished me all the best.

F.A.C.E.S. is a non-profit organization affiliated with the NYU Comprehensive Epilepsy Center. The S.E.E. program is a two-day-long seminar. It was developed by Dr. Robert J. Mittan and includes video demonstrations, computer graphics, and stories of how real people overcame seizures. According to the S.E.E. website, the S.E.E. program helped to pioneer *Information Medicine in 1983*. This new science of Information Medicine recognizes that "...what a person knows of his or her disorder is every bit as important to a successful treatment outcome as any drug or surgery. Sometimes it is even more important!"

After learning more about the S.E.E. program's emphasis on providing help for people with seizures as well as for their family members, I was determined to attend the seminar. The program makes the claim that S.E.E. is for people who want to take control over their seizures, their treatment, and their day-to-day lives. The seminar was scheduled for a Saturday and Sunday. I asked Laura to accompany me to the seminar, but she stated that she couldn't, because it was being held on the Sabbath, the Lord's Day. That Saturday evening, after attending day one of the seminar, I brought home literature that explained factors that contributed to my seizure condition, what to avoid, and how to monitor the condition to prevent seizures. I was overjoyed and eager to share the information with her.

"Babe, I got some really important information about my seizures," I exclaimed. "You wouldn't believe how much I got from the seminar. Look at these information packets"

Breaking Point: A Journey to Self-Awareness and Finding Purpose in Pain

"Mmm…" was all she said, as I tried to hand the literature to her. She never took them from me. I had hoped that she would be happy for me and that when she looked at the literature I had received, she would have decided to come with me the following day. I was a person for whom the concept of family was powerful. Perhaps someone else, with a different past, would not have given Laura so much slack, but she and I were "family". Having her as family mattered in a way that someone who has not lost family, and wandered around in the wilderness of abuse and exploitation, could never understand.

That Sunday morning, Laura was preparing soup for her best friend's daughter, who was leaving for college, so she told me that she was too busy and couldn't attend. She asked me to give her a ride to her friend's house to deliver the soup. I gave her the ride she requested, and then I went alone to day two of the seminar.

The large lecture theatre was full of people. I wondered if all those people had seizures or if many just knew someone who did. The seminar was intriguing and eye-opening. Dr. Robert J. Mittan was the sole presenter; he seemed to know everything about seizures and epilepsy. The first day he had focused on getting the right diagnosis, because getting the right diagnosis means the difference between continuing to have seizures and becoming seizure free. Other areas covered included treatment approaches and practical suggestions about how to get better control over seizures. He also provided handouts with information on how to find an epilepsy specialist or treatment center. On this second day, Dr. Mittan talked about coping with fear, coping with the stigma of seizures or epilepsy, coping with feelings of guilt, and how and why to tell others about our condition.

When I saw Carol at church the Saturday following the seminar at NYU, I thanked her again for sharing what had turned out to be a life-changing resource. "Sister Carol, the seminar was great!" I concluded. "Thank you for finding that for me."

"You are welcome," she said with a beautiful smile. "I'm glad it was helpful. I don't think you should refer to your seizures as an attack from the devil anymore," she said calmly. "I think you have a medical condition, not a demonic condition. A seizure condition has a medical explanation."

I didn't respond to her statements. I had accepted, and then fought against, previous suggestions by Laura that I had a demon. I sensed there was probably some truth in Carol's statement, but I could not fully accept it. Nevertheless, I started making an effort to stop referring to my seizures as an "attack."

With the realization that my life could be different, I started feeling hopeful again. Attending that seminar was a significant turning point for me. Dr. Mittan made me realize that I was living what he called *"an epileptic life,"* meaning that I was living in fear of having the next seizure instead of enjoying my life. The list of neurologists who specialized in treating epilepsy and seizures that I had received at the seminar became precious to me. It was from that list that I chose the name of Dr. Sheryl Haut, a neurologist at Montefiore Medical Center in the Bronx. I wasted no time making an appointment with her.

Meeting with Dr. Haut inspired further hope. She was a slender lady who immediately put me at ease. After reviewing my seizure history, she told me that I had a rough road ahead, but that there was much hope for me. She told me about people with worse episodes than mine who were able to lead normal, successful lives. She named famous people with seizures such as: Alexander The Great, Theodore Roosevelt, Napoleon Bonaparte, Julius Caesar, and James Madison; musicians such as Elton John, Prince, and Susan Boyle; actors such as Danny Glover; athletes such as Olympic gold medalist, Florence Griffith Joyner, once the fastest woman in the world, Tiki Barber, former American football player; and Chief Justice of the United States Supreme Court, John Roberts.

Dr. Haut reiterated Dr. Mittan's list of things that I needed to avoid to prevent seizures. She suggested that I take my medication, avoid overwork, exhaustion, negative emotions, hatred, anger, depression and so on. She decided to keep me on Dilantin and monitor my blood levels every three months. However, she eventually decided to wean me off this medication, mainly because of the serious danger that long-term use of Dilantin would have on my bones. As a result, there was no more need to do blood work. Dilantin was replaced with Lamictal. Lamictal caused drowsiness, headaches, lack of balance, and shaking, but the seizures decreased to once a week.

While the frequency of my seizures was significantly reduced, early one morning, I had a seizure that caused me to fall off my bed once more. This was one of the worst things that could have happened. The seizure violently disrupted the healing of my left shoulder. After diagnostic examinations, the orthopedic surgeon delivered the dreaded news. He had to do a second surgery on the same left shoulder, this time; the situation was even more delicate and would require a lengthier surgery, about six hours. No, not again! I began to think the worst, but I knew I needed to go into the surgery with a positive attitude. I decided to trust God with the outcome. In October 2006, almost two years after the first surgery, I underwent six hours of surgical intervention to repair and tighten the ligaments in my left shoulder. I woke up hours afterward to excruciating pain, but the operation was successful.

As the frequency and intensity of my seizures continued to decrease significantly, my mood and temperament began to stabilize. I became even more amenable to working with Laura to reverse the damage to our relationship. Yet, she didn't seem to notice my reduced stress, now that I was being helped by the medication, or if she did, she didn't comment or make any change in her dealings with me. Nothing changed at home. This pained me and made me feel as if there was a hole in my heart. My thoughts were totally perplexed, what else could I do that I was not doing?

Looking in the mirror, I couldn't recognize the man who looked back at me. Who was I? Who had I become? The pain of the distance between Laura and me and between me and my children was so sharp that I didn't know what would bring me relief: revenge, suicide, or some miraculous intervention from God. Something within me had died. It was more than just the reality that my dream of an 'until-death-do-us-part' marriage was crumbling and that my four children, whom I loved with all my life, would inherit the legacy of a broken home; something that I had fought against with every ounce of strength in my body for the past twenty-five years. It was as if everyone and every situation had beaten me.

My prayers and tears went unanswered. I was spent. Could my marriage survive? I had no answers. I still desired sexual intimacy, but at this point all I really wanted was a warm hug and words of affirmation that I was loved and that I mattered. This was not what marriage was supposed to be. Was I so unlovable? Was I so terrible? Was I so undesirable and repulsive? Was there no good in me that she could find to love? To care about? Was I irredeemable as a person? As a husband? As a father? Was I no good? These thoughts left me feeling defective.

The Apostle Paul in I Corinthians 7:1-6 gives Christians some invaluable advice regarding how to prevent infidelity in marriage. As recorded in the Message translation of the Bible, Paul said:

> "Now, getting down to the questions you asked in your letter to me. First, is it a good thing to have sexual relations? Certainly, but only within a certain context. It's good for a man to have a wife, and for a woman to have a husband. Sexual drives are strong, but marriage is strong enough to contain them and provide for a balanced and fulfilling sexual life in a world of sexual disorder. The marriage bed must be a place of mutuality - the husband seeking to satisfy his wife, the wife seeking to satisfy her husband. Marriage is not a place to "stand up for your rights." Marriage is a decision to serve the other, whether in bed or out. Abstaining from sex is permissible for a period of time if you both agree to it, and if it's for the purposes of prayer and fasting - but only for such times. Then come back together

again. Satan has an ingenious way of tempting us when we least expect it. I'm not, understand, commanding these periods of abstinence - only providing my best counsel if you should choose them."

The preceding was really good advice. I wished Laura and I had been able to adhere to it, as it would have saved us so much pain and heartache. There are other areas of the Christian Bible that provide invaluable instructions for couples which, if heeded, would also help to build and enrich their marriages.

Laura doesn't bear all the responsibility for the troubles in our marriage. I bear my own share. In retrospect, it seems to me that seven factors led to the demise of our marriage, included in these factors is the breakdown of our spiritual lives. Others factors were shared between us: Four can be found on her side. They are: (1) her lack of love for me. (2) the negative influence of her biological mother; (3) the negative influence of her best friend; and (4) her unwillingness to forgive and reconcile.

On my side, there were two factors: (1) my anger that caused me to scream at her and the children and (2) my generalized epilepsy.

We both loved our children, and neither of us wanted to hurt them. As I have already said, we tried to raise them to know and reverence God and wanted them to commit their lives to God, as we had. I wanted our children to be independent thinkers who could make thoughtful and responsible decisions. I did what I could do to help them realize that I wasn't as bad as their mother portrayed me to be. I give God thanks that at the time of this writing, I still enjoy a good relationship with my son and daughters.

Considering divorce was torturous. It was as though I was reliving the wretched pain I felt when my sister Tolema died combined with the pain of all my other losses. I felt that I was going insane. I fought with myself daily. My first thought was about my children and the impact that divorce would have on them. My next worry was about the honor of Mom and Dad. Although I had engaged in further studies and dialogue that led me to a deeper understanding of the biblical doctrine of divorce, I knew that some in the church held on to the belief that if a person divorced for reasons other than adultery or desertion by an unsaved spouse, they were violating God's law. They also believed in the concept of "bound for life" and that a person could only be remarried if that person's spouse was dead or had committed adultery.

I also held these beliefs, but I had failed to save my marriage and needed God in the midst of my failures. I struggled daily with the question of whether my divorce would mar or dishonor the memory of Mom and Dad. Then there was my health. My body was tired. I didn't know how many more seizures or how much more medication it could tolerate. I thought my life would be shortened. I couldn't see myself living alone until one day it dawned on me that although I was married and had children, I was really still alone. Besides the religious and health factors, I wrestled also with the fact that I stood to lose a lot financially.

Based on my understanding of the Biblical teaching regarding marriage and divorce, I felt I had to seek reconciliation with Laura. Yet, I was fearful that if I tried to reconcile she might agree to do so but she would be insincere, and we would just go back to a dysfunctional relationship.

During these difficult days, arriving at work at The Garden provided solace for me. At lunchtime, I would often find a quiet place on the far side of the beautiful Peggy Rockefeller Rose Garden or walk along the trail road that leads to the waterfall of the Bronx River that flows from through The Garden into the Bronx Zoo. Whenever I viewed this scenery, I was always reminded of my early childhood in the Village of Teahplay where I learned to swim, fish and hunt for animals. Somehow, I could sense the presence of my parents and feel a warm sense of embrace there.

Sammy and Dr. Sheryl Haut, (Neurologist)

Chapter 23

The Death of a Marriage

"Ending a marriage is never easy, but sometimes it is for the best"
— WomansDivorce.com

Having done one final push to reconcile with Laura, I finally accepted the truth in the lyrics of the song sung by Bonnie Raitt:

> *"Cause I can't make you love me if you don't*
> *You can't make your heart feel something it won't*
> *Here in the dark, in these final hours*
> *I will lay down my heart and I'll feel the power*
> *But you won't, no you won't"*

I had not yet asked Laura for a divorce, and, because of my epilepsy, I was afraid to live alone. I began to survey the sisters in my church in search of a prospective wife. I identified two sisters at my church that would make a suitable wife for me, but unfortunately they were both married. I even visited various churches in our denomination in search of sisters whom I had grown up with in the church, as well as others who had joined later. I wanted a virtuous woman who would return my love. I wanted her to love me just as I loved her, no more or no less. I wanted a woman who was affectionate, friendly, and with whom I could pray, laugh, relax, communicate, and enjoy the rest of my life with.

I allowed myself to also wonder about Carol Mills. She had qualities that I had come to greatly admire, but I doubted if she would consider me, seeing as I had been married before. Would she love me? How would she respond to what some people might say? Over the years, I had started to adore her sweet, contagious smile, her friendliness, her ability to communicate, her trustworthiness, her readiness to forgive, her kindness, her graciousness, her respectful way of treating people (especially children), and her commitment and love for God. Furthermore, I saw that she was loving, down-to-earth, simply sophisticated, and had a keen ability to listen, so that a person felt that they were really being heard. She had all these qualities, but was she willing to be married? And could she handle the pressure?

She was a very educated and intelligent woman. Would her education make her feel that she was better than I? Would she look down on me? Because of these fears, I doubted that she was 'the one', so I continued surveying the churches for a suitable, virtuous woman.

I sought advice from some of the senior leaders in the church. I sought the Lord in prayer, and reminded him that I had asked him in my youth for a godly, virtuous wife, whom I would love all my days and who would also love and care for me.

"God, I'm coming back to you," I cried on many occasions when I prayed about my marriage to Laura. "This is not what I asked for. If this marriage is to refine me, then you have to help me bear this. If not, please release me."

Sometimes I felt as if I was merely talking to myself, but I continued praying.

"God, I want a wife who is trustworthy and quick to forgive," I begged. "God please help me or release me. Please!"

I spoke to Pastor Headley Deacon, the lead pastor of my church, about my decision to divorce my wife.

"Deacon Kamara, I don't agree that you should divorce her," he said firmly.

"Pastor Deacon, I can't take it anymore," I responded. "I have done all I could, but she doesn't love or care about me. If I remain in this relationship, I will not make it into the Kingdom of God."

"Hang in there some more, son," he said. "See what the Lord will do."

"Pastor Deacon, you know I've tried. I have even asked you to reach out to her and you, yourself, realize that she is not as easy as you see her."

"If you go through with the divorce," Pastor Deacon replied. "You know it is going to cost you. You can't be a deacon anymore. You know that?"

"Yes, I hear you, but according to the Scriptures, I don't see it like that," I replied.

"You know if you divorce, you can't remarry," he continued. "Remember what the Scripture says?"

"Pastor Deacon, I don't see it like that. I would like to have a study on the matter," I said. "When can I have a study on this with you?"

During the conversation, one of the recently ordained young pastors entered the office and overheard us.

"Brother Sam, that is what the Scriptures say, and there is no way around it," he chimed in without invitation.

"Well, let's have the study," I asked again. "When can we have the study?"

Neither of them suggested a time, and I got the impression that they were not interested in doing so. Time proved my hunch to be correct.

* * *

I will never forget the day, July 14, 2007 when I told Laura I was leaving. Looking back I wondered what I expected from her when I told her that I wanted a divorce. Would she wake up and realize how bad our relationship had become? Would she suddenly realize that, months before, I had started isolating myself from the family? Would she remember that most of the time, I was alone in our bedroom while she and the children were in the living room, or while she slept in the children's room? Would she beg me not to leave? Would the reality of divorce be the catalyst to redeem our marriage? Or would she cheer that the nightmare our marriage had become would finally be over? Those fantasies were dominated by the insistent thought that she wouldn't care if I left.

The months leading up to this day had been peaceful. I sometimes came home late and spent most of the time in our bedroom by myself. When I entered the house this day, she was in the living room combing Loretta's hair, and our children were watching TV. I went straight to our bedroom, changed my clothes, and then had something to eat. I sat on the bed with my head bowed; my thoughts were heavy. This was the moment to make a change, but my heart was racing. I tried to rehearse what I would say to her but never found the perfect words.

I stood up from the bed and opened the bedroom door. "Babe, can I talk with you please?" I asked hesitantly. She didn't answer but continued to talk with the children.

I went into the living room.

"Babe, can I talk with you please?" I repeated the request and went back into the bedroom. I realized I still called her *Babe,* but by then it was more out of habit than affection. Shortly after, she came and stood by the door. She didn't seem to be upset.

"Come on in," I invited her, and she entered the bedroom.

"What do you want now?" She spoke with resistance, but politely.

"I want to talk to you," I said.

"I'm here. Go ahead," she said. "What do you want to talk about?"

I was still formulating my words mentally and so I hesitated and took a deep breath, but did not speak.

"You said you want to talk to me, so go ahead," she said impatiently. "What is it?"

"Well, as you know, our relationship has not been going on well for a long time now. I called you in here to let you know that I can no longer live like this," I said slowly. "I want a divorce."

"What!" she said in disbelief. "You want a divorce?"

"Yes," I replied calmly. "I want a divorce."

"Do you know what you're saying?" she asked, then sighed heavily. "You know what the Bible says about divorce?"

I kept silent.

"You know what the church teaches about divorce?" she continued.

"Yes," I replied.

"If you divorce me, you won't get any more cream," she said with a slight sneer, in reference to sexual intercourse.

I said nothing.

"How about the children?" she said.

I remained quiet.

She looked at me and gave a sarcastic smirk, and then she left the room. She went back into the living room, but she didn't share the news with the children.

That night I took forever to fall asleep and had difficulty sleeping. Scenes from my life kept racing through my head. I felt burdened and sad. I was the one who had asked for the divorce, yet I felt uncertain about the outcome. I was especially worried about the children's response to the news of the divorce.

The following morning, I told her that I would be informing the children of my decision.

"Okay, go ahead, if that's what you want," she said with an I-don't-care attitude.

I called the children into the living room.

"I would like to share some information with you," I said.

Laura sat impassively while the children stared at me.

"As you know, life between your mother and me has not been easy."

There was total silence.

"Last night, I told your mother that I've decided to move on with my life," I continued. No one spoke. "I told your mother last night that I want a divorce."

"I knew this was coming!" Leah, my oldest daughter screamed, and started bawling. "I knew it would eventually happen." Junior and Loretta started crying, too. Laura bowed her head.

"You know something—I've been watching this for a while," Joy, our second daughter, faced her mother and spoke sternly. "I'm not surprised. The way you have been treating Dad has not been fair."

"Do you know who you are talking to?" Laura snapped at Joy.

"Yes, Mom. I'm talking to you," she continued boldly. "You have not been treating him right. The way you guys have been living together has not been right."

She tried to stop our daughter from speaking, but Joy persisted and was very outspoken. That was a very sad day. It was a day that I had dreaded and did not wish upon anyone. But with my unstable health condition and without reconciliation, I could not go on any longer in the marriage.

The following Saturday, I asked Pastor Deacon, for the opportunity to announce my decision to the church. This was a defining moment, because no one had ever done this in our church. I wanted to make the announcement myself because I wanted people to hear it from me. I had been tortured by indecision for years, including my fears about how much I would lose if I divorced Laura. Now, I felt embolden by the God-given affirmation. God, through His loving will, gave me permission to proceed with the divorce so that my failure in marriage could be used as an object lesson to others.

The message was not that everyone who has problems in their marriages should follow me and divorce their husbands or wives; it was that husbands and wives should do all they could to work together, to be accountable to God and each other, to maintain their marital relationships, and to make every effort to reconcile differences, in order to preserve their marriages. Furthermore, it was to send the message that the primary marital relationship between the man and the woman should be nurtured so that it could sustain the secondary relationship with the children.

The news that I was getting a divorce sent shock waves throughout the sanctuary. Divorce just doesn't happen in our church, and if a couple gets divorced, it's never announced in the church. So when I announced my divorce, some people thought I planned to leave the church. Some empathized and sympathized with me, whereas others cried with me. The news spurred the lead pastor and the pastoral team to start a coordinated series of sermons and teachings about marriage and divorce. They emphasized that marriage is God's idea. God's intent is for marriage to be a lifetime commitment between one man and one woman. As such, the married couple is bound for life as long as the couple is alive.

In the weeks that followed my announcement, during which the pastors preached, I had mixed feelings about what they were doing. On the one hand, I was glad that they were finally giving meaningful attention to this very critical area of life. Maybe their new, focused attention would provide much needed help for others who were struggling in their marriages. Maybe other marriages could be saved. Yet, on the other hand, I was disturbed. The teachings and the sermons were more warnings to others against violating God's ideal for marriage, the way I was about to do. I didn't get a sense that there was any compassion for people like me, whose marriages were ailing or had suffered a fatal crash. I had suspected that this would be their approach: the pastors would turn my situation into a public taboo. Notwithstanding, I told myself that I had to remain strong and not allow myself to be shaken. My hope was that eventually the need to care and maintain marital relationships would be emphasized and practiced among us.

For months after I shared my decision with the family and the church, I was torn and distressed. I continued to cry out daily to God for further direction, because I wanted to make sure that I had done the right thing in the sight of God and my "Church family". How could I go on alone? I had no family here in America other than my children. Mom and Dad were gone, and their adopted children hadn't stayed in contact with me. Although my seizures had improved, I was still having them periodically.

I was troubled by the thought of living alone. These thoughts followed me day and night. Through all of this, I was still living at the house with Laura and the children, but I knew we would eventually part ways. The atmosphere at the house was very tense. We communicated only when it was absolutely necessary. I was isolated, as she and the children stayed away from me. It was clear that they had already divorced me.

One day, while lost in deep thoughts, the Spirit of God said to me:

"Sam, before she came into your life, who was there? After your parents left you in Monrovia with your uncle who was there? When your uncle gave you to his friend, who was there? When the Kamaras brought you to New York and abandoned you on the street, who was there? Before the Johnsons took you in who was there?" At that point, I began to answer, "It was the Lord."

"It was the same God that has kept you all along," the Spirit continued. "This same God is able to keep you for the rest of your life, so rest upon His words." After this encounter, I felt relieved and comforted that I would not be alone, in spite of my fears and the uncertain road ahead.

My lawyer served Laura the notice of divorce at the end of July 2007.

When I think of my marriage to Laura, I don't regret loving her. God gave us a great opportunity, and we blew it. If given a "do-over" with her, I would still do my best to express my complete love to her and treat her well. I would not be too big or too proud to say "I'm sorry" to her when I hurt her. I often did so in the marriage, even kneeling at her feet in tears, and begging for her forgiveness. But eventually I realized that I was only humiliating and degrading myself before her. And I know now that I would seek help for myself.

Here is what I would not do again; I would not try so many different and humiliating ways to save the marriage. I would not be so co-dependent that I felt I had to be at her mercy, or the mercy of others. I would not waste so many precious years of my life in a dysfunctional marriage with a woman who didn't love me and distanced herself from me, refused to forgive me, and refused to reconcile our differences. I would only give seven years of my one life. Seven years because I believe seven is God's prefect number. In that time, perhaps God would work a miracle on our behalf and save our marriage.

Chapter 24

New Day

"The best is yet to be"
— Robert Browning

"Until death do us part" is a phrase from the marriage liturgy. This phrase is equivalent to the "bound for life" concept of marriage in the biblical teachings of the church. "Until death do us part" or "Whom God joins together let no man put asunder" are idealized concepts, which I also embrace. However, reality doesn't always measure up to the ideal. Very often there is a gap. In this case, an important question to ponder is: when does the death of a marriage really occur? Is it only when one member of the couple dies? Or is it also when the relationship dies? Isn't divorce a natural corollary of the death of a marital relationship?

Laura did not contest the divorce petition in any way. In fact, she seemed eager to hasten the process. In some part of me, I agreed with her haste. I wanted to start over with someone who truly loved and cared for me. One-sided love is painful. Yet, another part of me wanted her to contest the divorce. If she had done so, it would have at least indicated that I mattered to her, that she needed me, and that I was of more value to her than the material possessions I afforded her and our children. But I can't think of one thing she did to try to save our marriage or stop the divorce. I was disappointed but not surprised.

In the summer of 2008, we appeared in Bronx Family Court to finalize our divorce. The divorce Stipulation of Settlement and Agreement represented the final step in our uncoupling. The judge granted the divorce on the grounds of constructive abandonment. The terms of the divorce were decided; the specifics of how this was to be done rested with the lawyers and the court clerk. We were given joint legal custody of our two younger children, Junior now 15 years old and Loretta, 13. She had residential custody and I was given unlimited right of liberal visitation with the children at their house, or at my house at another location. These visits were to be mutually arranged and agreed to by us.

Laura and I walked out of the Bronx County Court House that July day in 2008 as two strangers—not exchanging a word about the tragedy that had just ended in the Court House. The death of our twenty-seven year old marriage had happened long before and on this day, it was merely being declared official by the State.

When the specifics were worked out I was to receive the car, while all our other assets were divided equally. In order to do this, we had to sell the house in which we had lived and raised our children for over twenty years. The full impact of this sale would not strike me until later. I was not satisfied with the terms of the divorce because I lost a significant amount of money, as well, the cushion of savings I had put aside for my retirement years. I also felt terrible about not living with my children, but I felt relieved that the burden of having Laura in my life was now lifted.

The house held much sentiment for me, as it had previously been owned by Mom and Dad, and I had lived there during my teen years. It also bore witness to the intimate details of my life with Laura. We had laughed together, prayed together there; she had conceived Joy, Junior and Loretta in that house. We had raised our four children there. But relational termites had slowly but surely eaten away the emotional beams that held our home together. The house was still standing, but our home had collapsed.

That summer after the divorce, I found it difficult to sell the house; it held so many memories for me. That house was one of the few solid links to my past. I did own a tie that had been Dad's and that served as a link to him, but the house was a much stronger connection. Every room summoned a memory of him and was full of vivid links to my children, as well. Nevertheless, due to my inability to secure funding on my own, I was forced to sell the house I cherished.

I moved out of the house in the fall of 2008 and into a small studio apartment—it had once been a garage—near Boston Road in the Bronx. I was now fifty years old, and this was the very first time in my entire life that I had lived by myself. My bed was a little cot that I had bought through a magazine ad. Joy, Junior, Loretta, and BB came on different occasions to see where I was living. They thought my bed was inadequate for a man my size. What if I had a seizure? I had increasingly pushed that fear to the back of my mind but I secretly dreaded having a seizure while I lived by myself.

Shortly after I moved out, Laura and the children eventually moved to another residence.

I wasn't sure which way my life would turn, but I knew I didn't want to live alone. It wasn't the domestic chores that I was worried about. I could cook and clean better than most women. My biggest fear was my health. Although the frequency of my seizures had drastically decreased, I was still not seizure-free. Furthermore, I longed for companionship. I longed for intimacy. I longed for passion and love.

During this time, every night before I went to bed, thoughts of my children occupied my mind. How were they coping? I was concerned about Leah and Joy, but I was admittedly more worried about Junior and Loretta. Had they not been born, I believe I would have had the courage to leave my unhappy and irreconcilable marriage earlier. Leah was now 25; Joy, 21; Sam, Jr., 15; and Loretta 14 years old. During and after the divorce, Junior and Loretta's academic performance had fallen off, which was troubling, as they were smart children with bright futures. It wasn't them I had divorced. I would always love and cherish them, no matter what. I promised myself that I would do all I could, not only to help them survive the family breakup but to overcome the odds against them that the divorce had created.

The other thing that weighed on my mind was how to find a suitable partner. My search in other churches had been unfruitful. Surely, there were many unmarried sisters at my church and the other churches, sisters with whom I could share the rest of my life. My desire was strong but the fear of choosing the wrong person was even stronger. I didn't want to marry a stranger and I didn't want to make a mistake. As the saying goes, "once bitten, twice shy." I wanted to play it safe by exploring a relationship with someone whom I knew. Since the first two sisters I would have asked were still married, I decided to approach someone who was not. That person was Carol. She had so many fine qualities that I admired. She had grown up in the church and had been serving God and the church steadfastly for many years. Having spent my life taking care of others, I did not want to have any more children. I also knew her family.

Although I had known Carol for over fifteen years and had worked closely with her in the children and teens ministry, I felt shy and hesitant to approach her. My greatest fear was that she would reject me. What if she considered me her brother in Christ, only? What if she thought that I was not educated enough for her? I wanted to assure her that it was not her education that mattered to me, that I was drawn to her because of the person she was.

One Saturday night in December 2008, after a service, we stood outside the church talking about the ministry and church. We chatted about the future of the youths in the church and how to help them stay in it. We also talked about current challenges that the leadership faced and possible actions that were necessary. It was a very innocent conversation. I didn't enter that conversation with any ulterior or carnal motive. Carol also confessed that neither had she. In fact, Carol had earlier said that she would not marry a divorced man because she felt he would bring too much "baggage" to the marriage. At the end of the conversation, I attempted to kiss her good night on the cheek. It was a confused moment. I can't even remember specifically how it happened and Carol later told me that the moment was a blur to her, as well. Whatever it was, when I attempted to kiss her on her cheek my lips touched hers. When this happened, it was as though a bolt of electricity ran through every nerve in my body. Our eyes met, and, although Carol didn't say anything, I was convinced that she felt it, too. She quickly said goodnight and ran to her car.

Oh, my God, was she mad at me? Was that why she had run? I hoped she realized that I hadn't tried to violate her in any way. That night, I couldn't get thoughts of Carol out of my mind. I had honestly doubted her capacity for romantic feelings. Of course, she was a woman and anything was possible, but she rarely allowed her emotions to show. Unbeknownst to her, I had often watched her smile and enjoyed her cheerful laughter. I had watched her being playful with others and noticed her sensitive sense of humor. All the things that I had admired about her over the years, but had really paid no attention to, became magnified now. I felt magnetized by her. I lay in bed, wondering if she was also thinking of me. What would I say to her when I saw her next? Should I pretend that nothing happened between us? Maybe I should let her bring it up, rather than do so myself.

When I saw her on the following Saturday at church, she greeted me just as she normally would, in a friendly but unaffected way.

"Good afternoon, Brother Sam," she said, avoiding my eyes.

"Good afternoon," I replied and stretched out my hand to shake hers. She didn't extend her hand. I was not surprised. Carol usually presents herself as being completely composed and in control. I suspect she feared that touching me would disturb her emotional equilibrium. I felt embarrassed, but I understood.

That was the extent of her interaction with me before the divine service started at 1 p.m. After the service, we normally ate lunch at the same dining table in the church's fellowship hall. This time, Carol didn't come to the lunch table right away. It seemed as if she was deliberately talking with as many people as she could, to avoid coming to the table while I was still there. When she finally came, most of the people at the table had already finished their lunches. I lingered at the table, but she barely looked at me. She was obviously trying to control the situation, so that it would not get out of hand. I had planned to leave my seat to sit directly beside her but I changed my mind and decided to leave her alone. I would talk with her in private, or wait until she approached me. Of course, she did not approach me, so at the end of the evening service, I decided to approach her.

"How are you?" I asked her. As I stood before her, I could feel the magnetism between us once more.

"I guess I'm ok," she said softly and smiled as she looked up at me. When we looked into each other's eyes, a sweet feeling flooded my body. I wanted to touch her face, to hug her and to kiss her passionately. Thankfully, we were at church, and I was able to control myself.

"I would like to talk with you in private," I said, holding her gaze. She didn't look away, and in that precious moment, without her saying a word, I knew that she shared the same special feeling I felt.

"What do you want to talk about?" she asked, still looking at me. "I don't want to walk into a trap."

When she said the word "trap," she gave a sweet smile. It was a smile that I had seen many times before, but this time it captivated me. I wanted to keep her smiling. I think I felt both happy and relieved because I had feared that she would think that I didn't measure up to her standards.

"It's not a trap," I said, returning her smile. "I'm not good at setting traps."

"So what is it?" she asked again.

"Something private," I answered. "I want to ask your opinion in private."

"My opinion?" she echoed. "I can give you my opinion in the public, too."

I could tell that she was teasing me, yet I wasn't upset with her. The ball was in her court, and I had to wait until she decided to play it.

"So what is your answer?" I asked.

"Can we talk on the phone?" she asked. "You can give me a call tomorrow, because by the time I reach Brooklyn tonight, you might be fast asleep."

Yes! I know that she was playing it safe by choosing to talk with me via phone but that was ok. In fact, that was better for both of us.

As planned, Carol and I spoke on the phone the next day. Neither of us mentioned the magnetism that had been activated. Instead, we talked about general things including about my desire to return to Liberia and the challenges that continued to prevent me. I also told her that I wanted to write a book about my life. She thought it was a great idea to write a book and said that she would do some research to find out how other displaced Liberians in the USA were finding their relatives in Liberia.

I wanted to tell her that I thought she was a beautiful person but I didn't. The magnetism between us was like a baby elephant, in a closet, that was growing bigger and bigger every day.

There really is no formula for "falling" for someone. Nature doesn't like a vacuum and usually fills it with something – good or bad.

As I began to have feelings for Carol, it was perhaps natural that I asked myself many times, "When did our uncoupling begin? When did Laura vacate my heart?" This seemed important to know, if I was to prevent the same thing from happening again.

I still don't have a definitive answer, but I've concluded that marriage, like a plant or any living organism, needs to be maintained in order to remain alive. Apathy coupled with entropy will kill any marriage. The blame for the downfall of our marriage rests at both our feet, as I've said before. But I feel a sense of redemption when I consider the efforts I made to try to save the marriage, with all its flaws and troubles. At one point, I could only see Laura as "the problem." *If only she would change. If only she would stop doing this and start doing that*. Then I started focusing on me, on *my* contribution to our problems. I still have my flaws. I still struggle with the effects of the trauma and they trigger strong, angry emotions in me. But I sought help and all I wanted was for us to find some common ground to work together. That would be the starting point for our reconciliation, but we just couldn't find that point

In the end, I had to place some value on myself. I had to rebuild my self-esteem. I had to learn to believe that I too deserved care and happiness and that being a Christian didn't exempt me from those basic necessities of life. I expected to encounter difficulties, sickness, even poverty in life. We had acknowledged life's uncertainties in our marriage vows.

But, as the years rolled on, the uncoupling process between Laura and I had covertly progressed. The special love and desire I had for her dissipated like the air escaping from a balloon. In the end, I still cared about her. I would help her if she was in need, but I no longer had tender loving feelings for her. I guess I could have done what some persons in my church have suggested. As they said, "Stay and let the Lord work it out." I actually agree with the concept of staying and waiting on God. After all, that is what I did for twenty-seven years. I stayed, and struggled, and hurt, and tried to do what I could to get help. I only moved when God gave me the release. Otherwise, to this day, I would still be in a dysfunctional marriage that was greatly contributing to the deterioration of my health and the demolition of my faith. I wasn't becoming a better person. I was too beaten down to see the good in me and to realize my potential. I was merely surviving. And I don't blame Laura for all of this. I blame myself for not being able to place more value on myself. I blame myself for tolerating some of the indignities that I endured.

Now, the encounter between Carol and I had begun to produce feelings that started to fill the vacuum in my heart, the space that Laura had vacated. The people who say that I left Laura for Carol are wrong. That was not what happened. Carol filled a space that was empty. She entered a new relationship with me after Laura had left. Laura's departure from my heart was not a sudden event; it was a slow, torturous process. So I cannot give a date, but by 2005, I had to admit to myself that the romantic and tender feelings I had for Laura had been gone for a long time. Those feelings were replaced at first by nonsexual and brotherly feelings; later even those feelings faded away and I began to look forward to being separated from her.

Chapter 25

Serious Conversations

"All along this love was right in front of me! ...Now I understand what love is, love is for the first time."
— James Newton Howard & Jud Joseph

As the summer of my divorce turned into winter and the divorce decree would become final in February, I decided not to wait any longer to explore a relationship with Carol. At this stage of my life, I felt that there was no sense in delaying. I began to see Carol as God's answer to my many tear-soaked prayers. She was a woman of God and she would help to make me a better person. I could see us making a life together. I could see us sharing a passionate love affair in marriage.

So, when the divorce was finalized in early 2009, I decided to remarry soon.

We met one evening after work in late February, and I decided to "pop the question."

"Carol, I've been thinking about us," I said shyly. "And there is something that I want to ask you."

She didn't look at me, and she didn't say anything.

"Did you hear me?" I asked.

"Yes, I heard you," she said with her usual sweet smile. "Go ahead and ask me."

"Well, I have been observing your fine qualities," I continued. "I like what I see."

She didn't comment so I went on.

"I admire you greatly," I said and paused. I really wanted a reaction from her.

"Thank you," she said, and smiled again. "What is there to admire about me?"

"A lot." I said grinning. "For example, I love the way you smile."

This made her laugh. This was going well, I thought, so I proceeded right to the question.

"Carol, would you like to be my wife?" I asked. This time, she looked at me and we held each other's' eyes for a few seconds. Though there were people talking and moving about in the restaurant, it was as if time stood still, and no one else was around. Knowing Carol, she would not be glib about it. She took some time before responding.

"Are you asking me to be your wife?" she asked finally, again teasing me, "or just asking me if I like the idea?"

"Yes, I'm asking you to be my wife." I held my breath.

She paused again. Obviously, she was in deep thought.

"Well, I don't know," she answered.

"What do you mean you don't know?" How could she not know?

"Sam, what would the church people say?" she asked. "And how would your children respond to me?"

"The issue is neither the church nor the children," I said. "It's about the decision that I have to make to move on with my life."

"I understand that," she said. "But can you deal with what the church people and your children will say and their behavior toward you?"

"If God is for me, I can make it," I assured her. "I didn't make the decision to leave my marriage lightly. I played my role well. Furthermore, I sought God's counsel about it and He was the one who gave me the go ahead."

Carol still seemed concerned and deep in thought.

"I don't know if *I* can handle it," she said finally. "You know people will blame me for the breakup between you and your ex-wife, that's just the nature of people."

"You're right. You can raise the dead and heal the sick and people would still find something negative to say about you," I said. "You just can't worry too much about what people will say."

"Sam, if I say yes, I'm not going to run away from here." She looked uncertain. "I still feel called to serve at our church."

"I'm not rushing you," I assured her. "Think about it and let's pray and fast for guidance. Let's see what God will do."

That evening, I hugged and kissed her lightly on her lips. Carol seemed worried and didn't say much more.

* * *

At the end of March 2009, I approached her again, as I needed to know if she had made her decision. We met at the New York Botanical Garden where I still worked. Although it was winter, that day was not particularly cold. I had picked her up at the #2 Train station at Pelham Parkway in the Bronx and driven her to the Garden. We held hands as we walked to the Conservatory building. This building is a glass greenhouse comprised of eleven smaller greenhouses, each with its own climate zone for various species of plants. We continued to hold hands as we walked about the Conservatory, observing the scene as we talked about what life would be like if we were to be married to each other. We considered the positives as well as the negatives. We also talked about whether we would want to have children or not. All this talk was enlightening but it was hypothetical, because Carol still had not told me her decision. "Carol, have you made your decision?" I finally decided to ask her directly.

"To be or not to be, that is the question." She smiled as we exited the Conservatory and walked back toward my car. Once inside, I turned to her and looked in her eyes. Her eyes tend to reveal more than she is usually willing to say.

"Carol, I need to know," I urged. "Is your answer *yes*?"

She smiled shyly and turned her head away. My heart started pounding. Had she turned away because her answer was *no*? There was silence in the car, and I noticed that Carol wasn't smiling any more. She stared straight ahead of her, stone-faced. I just couldn't read her expression well. A wave of uncertainty crept over me, and I started imagining the worst. She was going to say *no*, I just knew it. I guess she just didn't know how to break the bad news to me. If her answer was *no*, why had she led me on? Why hadn't she just told me from the start that she wasn't interested? The familiar and painful sense of rejection began to fill me.

"Yes," she said slowly, still staring straight ahead of her. "Yes, my answer is *yes*. I will marry you."

"Are you sure?" I asked in disbelief. "Did you think about it enough? Can you deal with what people might say?"

I don't know what was wrong with me. This is what I wanted to hear, and now I was the one who was worried about others. I was worried for Carol. Did she know what she was getting into? I knew I would love and cherish her, but I was worried about how others might respond to her.

"I don't know if I can deal with what people will do or say," she said, still not looking at me. "But I had to answer to God and my conscience first. I had to go down my checklist of non-negotiables."

"List of non-negotiables? What's that?" I asked.

"Well, I had to be sure that I was not the reason you left her," she replied. "When I considered what you have shared with me and the efforts you made to remain married, I was satisfied that it was not me. I could never live with myself if I thought I had broken up someone's marriage. Furthermore, I could never live happily with you," she continued, "if I knew you had left her for me. I've always told myself that I would rather be happily unmarried than unhappily married."

"You were not the reason," I assured her.

"I think divorce is such a sad thing," she said. She sounded as if she was about to cry. "I want to believe that every marriage can work, but I know that in reality every marriage doesn't work. I prayed for yours to work out."

"I don't think you prayed more than I did," I said. "I not only prayed. I tried to do something about the situation."

"I also had to think about our ministry in the church," she said, still in deep thought. "I'm not sure how this decision will affect our service. I know God has called us to work with children, youths, and families, but not everyone may understand."

"We just have to trust God and leave the rest to Him," I tried to assure her. "If we trust God, then we don't need to worry about people."

"Sam, it's not that easy," she said. "But I agree the most important thing is that this is God's will for us. If it is God's will, then we will survive. If not, our marriage is dead before it even starts."

* * *

I wanted my children to be the first ones to know of my decision. Then I planned to inform the church leadership and the church in general.

My children's responses were intense and emotional. I expected the emotional response; their lives were changing in ways that they had no control over. Notwithstanding, I didn't expect them to be so intensely negative about Carol. She had taught them in the youth ministry, and they had liked her. They loved the way that she ran the ministry and the activities and experiences she provided for the children and youths. Now they said that they hated Carol and claimed that she was the reason why I had left their mother. Although they had lived in the house and knew the life their mother and I had lived, their mother was able to convince them that Carol had been the reason for the demise of our marriage, not her.

My oldest daughter Leah was the angriest.

"Why so soon?" She scowled at me. "Why so soon? This is what

Mom was talking about! Why not someone else, prettier and outside the church?" she continued without letting me answer her question. "If I see her in the street, I will attack her. I will not love you anymore!"

"Carol is not the reason why I left your mother," I said. "You know that."

"I don't know anything," she said. "I don't even want to see her. You didn't have to do this."

I called my second daughter, Joy, on the phone to inform her about my decision to marry Carol. At first, she seemed to understand.

"Why so soon?" she also asked. "Is Carol pregnant?"

"No, she's not," I replied. "She's not pregnant. That's not why I've asked her to marry me."

"Why?" she asked. "Why are you going to marry her?"

"I love her and she loves me," I said calmly. "I believe she will take care of me. I don't want to live alone."

Joy and I spoke again a few weeks after this conversation. This time she was very angry. I suspected that she had spoken to her mother and older sister.

"Mom said you were leaving her for this woman," she blurted out. "How can you live with Carol in the same house that you lived in with us? This is despicable!" she continued. "Carol will not be invited to our birthday parties, and the family will not love you anymore!"

"I don't know what your mother told you," I said. "But I wish she had told you the truth. When you made your decision to marry, you made it on your own. I respected your decision. All I ask of you is to respect my decision."

I told Junior and Loretta at the same time. They were both angry at me. I had called Vashti, who had been a close friend of our family and confidante to me, and shared with her before I told my children about my decision. I did so because she was very close to Junior and Loretta. She had been their babysitter and caretaker when they were younger. Vashti's son, Jimmy, was Junior's best friend, and she was always there to help our family. Unfortunately, Jimmy overheard me telling his mother about my decision to marry. He quickly telephoned Junior and shared the information with him before I got the chance to do so. Junior was furious when I tried to tell him myself.

"This is what Mom has been saying," he said. "Why did you betray us?

"I told you that I did not make any plans to marry," I responded. "I told you that I would see what God wanted for me.

"…and why did Jimmy know this before me?" Junior continued as if he didn't hear my response. "I will not love you again."

Loretta was in tears.

"Why not someone else?" she said. "The church does not believe in divorce and remarriage. I will not love you anymore."

"I am sorry that you guys have to be hurt by this," I said. "But I couldn't live with your mother anymore. I have to take care of myself. I was taking care of everybody else. Who was talking care of me?"

I told friends before I informed the general church and their responses were very strong, but mixed.

"I have nothing against it," the acting senior pastor, assured me. "I have been studying about this. If Carol loves you and you love her, ok."

The acting president of our church joyfully approved.

"I'm glad for you and Carol," she said, looking very pleased. "If you intend to go through with this, I will prepare my wedding dress."

My good friend, BB, as we affectionately called her, expressed strong reservations. She was a confidante and had had inside information about my life with Laura.

"Why so soon and not later when things are calm?" she said. "You know what people will say, and the impact it will have on the children."

"BB, I can't stop Laura and people from talking," I said. "People will gossip and say whatever they feel like saying."

"You will lose your deaconship, and I will not be there when you make your open declaration," she continued. "Carol can stay home, or outside of the sanctuary and it is best that I do the same. I know how people will react."

"BB, I have to go on with my life," I said.

"You know she will not be accepted by the family," she said.

Laura's stepmother, who had strongly supported me during some very difficult times in the marriage, also had reservations.

"Sam, why not wait until later?" Estella asked. "You know people will say that you left Laura because of this."

"I know," I said, but I hope that they will see my situation and understand."

"You know the effect it will have on the children," she continued. "I know you love them very much but you must know this will hurt them a lot."

"I know," I said, feeling sad about that reality.

"Anyway, I love you very much and desire the best for you," she assured me. "Who is this girl?"

"She goes to our church," I said. "She has been at the church for years."

"Have you gotten the Lord's approval?" She sounded concerned. "Knowing that you have no relatives here, you need to screen her carefully and watch your finances."

"Yes, Mother, I have sought the Lord and prayed about it," I replied. "She is the one God intends for me."

"I was praying that things wouldn't come to this, but I'm with you," Estella assured me. "You have my blessings." In the past, Estella had often commented to me that she admired my commitment to God and my devotion to my family. She was a very loving and kindhearted grandmother to our children.

Vashti also thought I was getting remarried hastily.

"Take it easy for a while before proceeding with Carol," she advised. "I love Carol and you even more."

"Well, as you can see, I had to make a decision to preserve my health," I said. "I can't live by myself, because of my seizures. Who would be there to help me in case of an emergency?"

"Oh no! Goodness, the children." She sighed with concern. "Do you know the impact of this on the children, especially the young ones?"

"Yes, I know," I responded. "I've agonized over that for years and that is why I stayed with Laura until now. It will still hurt, but they are bigger now. Junior is 15 years old and Loretta is 14. I did my best for them. But someone has to take care of me, too."

"I understand, and I know it's not easy," she said. "I'm prepared to work with Junior and Loretta."

I also shared the news of my remarriage with Dorothy, a relative of Mother Johnson. She always expressed love and kindness toward me.

"I'm all for you, if you both love each other," she said. "You deserve a caring woman in your life."

"Thank you so much," I said, feeling grateful for her support.

"How are the children responding to it?"

"They took it really hard," I said. "But I'm supporting them as best as I can."

Muriel was another dear, elderly church sister who always expressed love toward me. I worked with her son, Aaron, and her daughter, Natasha, for years in the children's ministry. Her children are now adults, and married, with children of their own.

"Oh, dear," she said joyfully, when she heard the news. "It was pressed on my heart, about you and Carol. I have wondered whether the two of you could be together. You have my blessings."

Chapter 26

Engagement

"I will never compromise Truth for the sake of getting along with people who can only get along when we agree."
— D.R. Silva

On Saturday, April 11, 2009, at the end of the main service, with only members present, the acting senior pastor gave me permission to inform the church that my divorce was final. As I stood to tell them about the finalization of my divorce, I thought it best that I also share with them that I had decided to remarry. Some members of the church had disagreed with my divorce but even more had sympathized with me and expressed their sadness.

"Good afternoon, brethren," I greeted them as I stood in front of the church. For some reason I didn't feel nervous. "About two years ago, I shared with you my decision to ask Laura for a divorce. I would like you to know that the divorce is now final."

There was total silence. All eyes were fixed on me.

"I thought it best that I share the news with you personally because I didn't want you to hear it through the grapevine," I continued. "The Spirit of God bids me to do this for the edification of the church, because there are so many people who are hurting in marriages and there's an urgent need for maintenance and accountability in marriage."

Still, there was still total silence.

"So if you have any questions," I said. "Please ask me now. I will answer as best I can."

No one asked a question, so I continued.

"I would also like you to know that, since my divorce is final and I am free of my marital bonds, I have decided to remarry."

The atmosphere was full of suspense. I saw signs of disbelief in some people's faces. People started whispering and looking at each other, clearly wondering who the lucky—or unlucky—female was. Was she from this church?

"My new wife-to-be is...," I said beaming with joy "...Carol Mills!"

As soon as I called her name, about ninety percent of the members who were present, erupted in shouts and cheers, clapping, jumping, and screaming. It was as though the church had won the toughest Bible-quiz competition ever. They were delighted. I'm not sure what had ignited their excitement. Were they glad for me or was it for Carol, who, they also knew, was a faithful servant in the church? Or were they glad that both of us could find happiness together? I didn't want to know. I was overjoyed myself, that my world knew that I found someone with whom I could truly share a lifetime of reciprocal love.

I invited Carol to stand beside me. This was a big moment for her. She looked shocked, as though she couldn't believe her eyes and ears.

"Come on, Carol," I said, grinning widely. "Please join me."

Carol is very unassuming and didn't like the limelight. She hesitated, and then walked from the back of the church to join me. I hugged her and could feel how tense she was.

"Please allow me to say something very important," I said. The people looked at me eagerly. "I know that there will be some speculation. But, please know that Carol was not the reason why I divorced Laura. My marriage to Laura failed because of her abandonment of me and because of her lack of desire to reconcile. If you have any questions, please ask me."

That day, most of our church brothers and sisters greeted us excitedly, hugged us, and expressed love and good wishes for us. Voices of dissent were low and in the minority. Nevertheless, although the voices of dissent were in the minority, most of the owners of the dissenting voices were considered to be spiritual giants in the church. They were the "morality police." They were the power brokers, with clout among the congregation. Some of these people had loved and supported me in the past. They had prayed for me during my time of sickness and pain. Nevertheless, as time passed, Carol and I learned that religious dogma would take priority over love and the redeeming Grace of Christ.

Some have accused me of being selfish, of not considering the ramifications of my decision and how it would affect the church—especially the children and young people that I had worked with. These statements could not have been further from the truth. I had been married for twenty-seven years. The first three years were great, but the remaining twenty-four years were filled with trouble and pain. Throughout those years I sought help from my foster parents, Pastor and Sister Johnson. I sought help from Laura's own stepmother. I sought help from church leadership. I sought help from an experienced Christian Marriage and Family Therapist. I begged Laura to forgive me for any offense I had caused her. I begged her to the point where I humiliated myself, kneeling before her, and literally crying for forgiveness. I made a fool of myself, thinking that I could make her love me when she didn't love me. It really is a cognitive distortion, an idiotic thought, that one can change another or make another offer the gift of love when they don't want to.

I was unhappy for years. I was depressed for years. I was tortured by pain – emotional and physical – for years. I fought for my marriage as much as I could. I loved Laura and my children with all my heart. I abandoned myself, gave up my right to be loved, so that they could be comfortably cared for. Instead of seeking my own care, I worked hard to ensure theirs. Instead of abandoning the home when my children were young, I bore my unhappiness; I wore a mask and withstood the storms of my marriage because I wanted to be there for them.

Yes, I thought about the church and the impact my decision could have. I also thought about the memory and legacy of my foster parents, my father, Pastor Reuben Johnson, and my mother, Edris Johnson. I agonized for years and I didn't make a move until the Spirit of God gave me the release. Without that release, I was prepared to suffer to the end. For if I wasn't sure that God was with me, I would be miserable. I wouldn't have left if I wasn't convinced that God was with me. You see, I live my life to please God first and everyone else comes second.

No, I was not selfish; as some people accused me of being. Instead, I cared for everyone *but* myself. I practiced self-denigration, self-hate, self-humiliation, and co-dependency. I was afraid to be me. I was afraid to disagree with others. I was afraid to value my own thoughts. I was afraid to ask for the care I desired and needed. Instead, I offered care and help to others. They accepted my help and my sacrifices gladly. How many realized that I was living in pain? How many looked beyond the mask that hid my pain? If they only knew, they would be glad for my release.

* * *

Carol and I planned to get married on Sunday, July 26, 2009 at 2 p.m. The date of our marriage was announced in church in May 2009. We had the blessings of the acting senior pastor, the acting president, and the senior assistant pastor. On Sunday, May 3, 2009, we picked out our wedding rings and the next day we started premarital counseling with an experienced Christian Marriage and Family Counselor. We met with our wedding coordinator, Carol's aunt, Barbara.

When Carol had introduced me to Barbara, Barbara immediately put me at ease with her witty sense of humor. Her questions indicated that she loved and cared about Carol. For example, Barbara wanted to know if my ex-wife was planning to come back for me and if I planned to take care of her niece.

Barbara was our guide in the dark. Her knowledge and experience helped to keep our stress levels under control. She helped us decide on a color scheme, took Carol and the bridesmaids to select their dresses, and the groomsmen and me to select our suits. Every aspect of our wedding was meticulously planned and executed by her with some input by us.

* * *

My proposal of marriage to Carol had occurred during a critical time in the history of our church. In the fall of 2007, the leadership of our church had been shaken up when Pastor Deacon, who had succeeded Dad as lead pastor in 2002 after Dad died, abruptly resigned as lead pastor due to a personal matter. The church's executive board had appointed the vice president to the temporary position of acting president so that the president of the church could serve as acting senior pastor. Dad had been one of the pioneer members of the church, its first pastor, and had served as senior pastor for over thirty-six years. Pastor Deacon had served about six years as senior pastor when he resigned. The sudden change in leadership in 2007 created chaos and a host of issues that impacted the church in general and now threatened to impact us directly.

As the date of our wedding approached, the voices of the dissenting minority members and power brokers in the church became louder. Carol and I didn't learn that there was also dissension among the leadership until sometime in June. The acting senior pastor invited us to a meeting with the pastoral team. The senior assistant pastor and two of the three younger pastors, who had been ordained as pastors in May 2006, were in attendance. The third young pastor was out of the country.

In that meeting, the pastors were given the opportunity to ask us, especially me, questions about my former marriage and other questions, in order to give them more insight into my situation. I believe they were trying to ascertain whether I had gotten divorced on "Biblical Grounds". It was a cordial meeting, and I felt that the pastors demonstrated some sensitivity to my situation. They also had concerns about whether I would be allowed to remain in office as deacon. No decision was made on this matter. The acting senior pastor advised us to "keep a low profile for awhile." He didn't suggest that my office as a deacon would be rescinded or that Carol and I would be excluded from ministry within the church.

I don't remember the exact questions posed to me in the meeting, but I believe that one of the younger pastors also asked "Why so soon?" Another young pastor stated, "We didn't even get time for buy-in", meaning that we didn't consult with them to seek their input or agreement before we made our decision. When the suggestion was made that I should have waited longer before getting remarried, I asked, "How long should I have waited?" No one knew the "right" waiting time, but choosing not to delay my remarriage really upset the young pastors as well as others. They held very strong feelings about my divorce and remarriage, but had no guidelines to offer. To some extent, I can understand their point of view, but it is a theoretical one that is not connected to the realities of life. I wish they had tried to see things from the point of view of a person who had lived an unloving and unconnected marital life for many years with a spouse who had no desire for mutual reconciliation. If they had lived the life that I had lived, and finally had a chance at reciprocal love, would they want to wait any longer?

If they had suggested that I delay my remarriage to allow them, as pastors, to deliberate about how to "prepare" the congregation for my remarriage, I would have listened to the counsel. I would still have been willing to participate in any congregational discussion or study aimed at helping the congregation to resolve their concerns about my divorce and remarriage.

After this meeting, the pastors met, but did not ask me to sit with them. Of course, I couldn't tell what was being said behind closed doors. However, I learned later that the three younger pastors had strong reservations about our marriage and were probably not going to support us. This was a significant warning to Carol and me that there could be difficult days ahead.

In June, about five weeks before our wedding, we learned that the acting senior pastor, who had recently retired and was living in Florida, had returned to New York and would conduct a congregational study on the subject of divorce and remarriage. In his presentation, he referred to the Scripture's exposition on God's intent for marriage and the conditions that might lead to divorce. He elaborated on the Apostle Paul's teaching regarding the married couple's sexual obligations to each other. One of the main points of his exposition was rooted in 1 Corinthians 7 where Paul was responding to marital questions posed by the Church of God in Corinth. In verse 15, Paul states: *"But if the unbelieving depart, let him depart. A brother or a sister is not under bondage in such cases: but God hath called us to peace."* As soon as he read that verse, a sister who was staunchly against our marriage interrupted him and shouted:

"Unbeliever! Paul is talking about the unbeliever, not two believers."

The acting senior pastor asked the congregation to hold comments and questions until the end of his presentation. Most members listened attentively; others mumbled to each other. He continued to make the point that Paul was responding to a question that had been posed by the church at Corinth. He noted that if an unbeliever has neglected or abandoned the obligations and responsibilities of the marriage covenant, and is determined not to reconcile and abide by the covenant, then that believer had become a heathen or an unbeliever. The biblical principles outlined in Matthew 18:15-18 NKJV are applicable to my situation: *"Moreover if your brother sins against you, go and tell him his fault between you and him alone. If he hears you, you have gained your brother. But if he will not hear, take with you one or two more, that 'by the mouth of two or three witnesses every word may be established.'*

And if he refuses to hear them, tell it to the church. But if he refuses even to hear the church, let him be to you like a heathen and a tax collector. Assuredly, I say to you, whatever you bind on earth will be bound in heaven, and whatever you loose on earth will be loosed in heaven."

He concluded that, in a case like this, the principle of Paul's response in 1 Corinthians 7:15 also apply to two believers.

Members started asking various questions after the presentation.

"So is this the new teaching of the church?" one sister asked.

"Are you saying that it is ok for Brother Sam and Sister Carol to get married?" another sister demanded to know.

"I am just presenting the study," he stated. "I cannot unilaterally say whether this is a new teaching of the church."

It was obvious that the acting senior pastor was hesitant to speak definitively about the teachings of the church on the subject. Reference to "the church" was really a reference to the unchallenged, possibly unexamined, view point of the forefathers of the church. The church leaders were not theologically trained, they were simply men who had felt the calling and had responded. They were diligent students of the Bible, but there was no larger ecclesiastical body to reexamine church doctrines, or to which I could have made an appeal. The same pastors who were in conflict with me were the ones who were also judging matters related to me. I was at the mercy of the limited dimensions of their knowledge and interpretations and their unwillingness to engage in studies with me. Notwithstanding, I believe it would have helped a lot if these pastors, some of whom had had limited life experiences, had received seminary training in sound practices for heading a church before they were thrust into the role of leading a church of over two hundred souls.

I was very grateful for the limited support of the acting senior pastor but I was disappointed that he didn't deal with the matter with more authority and straightforwardness. At the end of the session, one of the young pastors came to us and told us why he and his wife would not be attending our wedding. The three young pastors and some of the members also declined an invitation to our wedding. One of the young pastors was Carol's cousin. She was very hurt when he called her on July 1 to inform her that he had decided not to attend the wedding. Instead of rejoicing with us, they chose to stick to dogma, rather than respect our humanity. Their response paved the road that led to other strong negative reactions and rejections of our wedding invitation. It was clear that this minority was determined to launch a campaign to exclude us from full church membership.

I often wonder why the acting senior pastor did not support us more fully. Did he think that he could not have supported us in this controversy because he was merely acting as lead pastor? Was there some other unstated reason? He was living in Florida, but he still flew back to visit our church and attend to church business occasionally. It was on one of those visits that he presented his study on divorce and remarriage, late one Saturday evening. The following morning, he was scheduled to fly back to Florida. There was no way he could answer the questions that the congregants had on the subject, nor could he greatly influence their opinions.

His visits to New York were infrequent and seemed to be confined to very special occasions. As a result, there was a critical leadership vacuum. Our church is an autonomous entity, without a diocese or headquarters to hold leadership accountable. The fate of the church was in the hands of the Executive Board and the pastoral team. An articulate and domineering young pastor was the acting chairman of the Executive Board and the spokesman for the pastoral team. This was a problematic arrangement. In the absence of senior leadership, it created a concentration of power in this one individual with very little accountability to the Board and his pastoral colleagues. It was as though no decision could be made without him, and his *modus operandi* was to block and sideline anyone he didn't like or agree with. This set-up understandably placed congregants in one of two groups, "insiders" or "outsiders."

On July 18, 2009, eight days before our wedding, this extroverted young spokesman of the pastoral team preached on the topic *"Bring Back the Glory."* He urged the congregants to overcome obstacles because every obstacle happens to give God the glory. "Children of God don't back away!" he urged. "Let's see the good in our imperfect spouses." He went on to urge couples to hold on when "there's no peace or no joy." Then he declared that God had given him the assignment to deal with the issue of marriage in this church.

In spite of those who decided not to attend our wedding, Carol and I decided to proceed. As the day of the wedding approached, I became even more convinced that it was God's will for Carol to be my wife. Due to my beliefs, I understood that God's perfect will was for us to keep our covenant of marriage sacred and alive for a lifetime. This is so, because God's intent for marriage is that it be a monogamous, committed relationship between one man and one woman, for life. I believe that God cried when my first marriage failed. But God hadn't failed. Laura and I had failed to keep our part of the marital covenant but, thankfully, God gives second chances and Grace.

Chapter 27

Learning to be Married

"Well I never had a place that I could call my very own but that's all right my love 'cause you're my home"
— Billy Joel

July 26, 2009, was one of the happiest days of my life. It eclipsed many memories of pain, depression, sadness, and loss that had dogged my life for years. I could hardly wait for the ceremony. The wedding was scheduled to begin at 2 p.m. but I was ready by 12 p.m. My best man, who was also a member of our church, came to pick me up before 1 p.m. I couldn't believe that the day had finally arrived. I was disappointed that the young assistant pastors, their families, and a few of our brethren chose not to attend the wedding. They were a minority in the church, so our wedding could be held there with the blessing of the majority. Even so, it hurt to be rejected, even by the minority. In spite of that, I felt free and fresh. It was as if a cooling breeze had blown over my soul. I felt assured and strong. Hope had been restored and life was worth living again. God had assured me that He was with me and I could feel His presence.

Carol hadn't believed that we would actually get married. Now our wedding day had arrived. We had handpicked the songs for the ceremony because they were a part of our testimony. The church hymns were: *"He Leadeth Me"* and *"There is a Redeemer".*

* * *

The church was beautifully decorated in gold and ivory. Large candelabras lined the aisle leading to the altar where we would exchange solemn vows. The lights were dimmed so the lighted candles added to the ambiance of the church. As the music began to play, my best man and I turned to face the door where each attractive bridesmaid, dressed in a hand-stitched, embroidered gold grown walked down the aisle. Each of them was met in the middle of the aisle by an elegantly dressed groomsman. The groomsmen, who wore black suits with gold satin vests, Ascot ties, and white shirts, escorted the bridesmaids to the altar where I stood with my best man. I could feel the excitement building. The atmosphere was filled with expectancy as I stared steadfastly at the main door, eagerly awaiting Carol's entrance.

The wedding attendants rolled out a purple velvet runner for Carol to walk on. She was indeed royalty as the color purple signified. There was silence, and then *"When God Made You"* by Natalie Grant & New Song started to play.

My mouth suddenly felt very dry. There she was, dressed in a very sophisticated white wedding gown with latticed, laced sleeves. She was being escorted by her brother, Andrew. As she walked slowly up the aisle she smiled at our guests. Oh, how radiant she looked! I wanted her to look at me but I believe I was the last one she looked at. When our eyes met, I could tell that she felt the same electricity I felt. I smiled nervously as I walked to meet her in the middle of the aisle. As we faced each other, her sweet smile warmed my heart. Carol looked so beautiful and appealing. I felt so proud that she was my woman. Gently, I led her to the altar and we stood before the officiating minister, one of the marriage ministers at our church, and the assistant, who was one of Carol's friends. I felt a sense of deep joy. In all the time we had spent preparing our wedding ceremony, I had never imagined how beautiful Carol would look, or how deep my feelings for her would be.

After the wedding ceremony, we travelled in a 1964 Rolls Royce to The New York Botanical Garden to take pictures with the bridal party. Bob Heinisch, the then vice-president of operations, was very helpful in facilitating this photo session in the famous Rockefeller Rose Garden. Carol caught me on a few occasions, staring at her. She responded with her usual sweet smile. She didn't know how much she contributed to my joy. Carol had told me that she didn't want a part of me. She wanted all of me or none of me. I hope she realized that I had given her all of me.

Our reception was held at Glen Terrence in Brooklyn, New York. It was a very celebratory atmosphere. There were so many people there who loved both of us. Some of Carol's family members had travelled from Canada, Jamaica, and various parts of the USA to celebrate with us. Many of our beloved church brothers and sisters also embraced us and told us how much they loved us. I was amazed at the number of children and youths who were there. Many, if not all of them, were children that we had taught in the children and teens ministry throughout their childhood and teenage years. Five of the female guests, Cheri, Danielle, Dominique, Jalesia, Kay, and Teresa, added to the flavor of the evening by dancing to a lively African song. Carol and I danced to two special songs. At the reception, we danced to Rod Stewart's song, *"For the First Time"* and Billy Joel's, *"You're My Home"*. As we danced, I was filled with even more rapturous delight.

* * *

At the end of the reception, I noticed that Carol looked exhausted. I hadn't slept well, so I should have been even more exhausted than she, and yet I felt wide awake.

We had planned a honeymoon night at the renowned—and luxurious—Waldorf Astoria Hotel located on Park Avenue in

Manhattan to rest and begin our life as husband and wife. After travelling to the Waldorf-Astoria by cab, we entered an exquisite lobby where a whole new world opened up to us. From the onset, the service was flawless. Up in our room, the bed was the most comfortable I had ever slept in, in my entire life. The linens were of the finest quality. The hotel knew that we had just gotten married, and they added a dash of extra attention to make our stay even more memorable. This experience was a gift from Carol's cousin, John, who was also one of my groomsmen.

* * *

For weeks after our wedding, the pastors kept their swords raised against our marriage. On August 8, 2009, one of the introverted young pastors preached on the topic, "The Anatomy of Deception." He gave six strategies of the devil, one of which was twisting the Scripture to suit one's condition. He stressed that this is deception. He even declared that some people decide to twist the Scripture, then turn around and call others hypocritical. "Do not violate your conscience to compromise the truth," he emphasized. Their sermons contained truths, some of which I even embraced. However, the timing and focus of their teachings and sermons were like barbs aimed at us. It was as though they had seized the opportunity to use the pulpit to throw stones at me; just as they would have stoned adulterers, long ago.

The pastors still weren't sure how to deal with me. Should I be held up as the poster boy for the violation of God's sacred Scripture, a rogue member of the church who had wantonly violated the *"Bound for Life"* rule of marriage? Should they protect other marriages in the church, by doing all they could to isolate and exclude me? After all, if they were to rejoice with me or offer any support to facilitate my healing, wouldn't that set a dangerous precedent for other congregants, who might be struggling in their marital relationships? Supporting us would be like giving a license to others to rush to divorce court and then follow our "bad" example by getting married. Furthermore, it was evident that they believed the acting senior pastor had acted recklessly and unilaterally by giving Carol and me the ok to proceed with our marriage. They seemed to believe he should have gotten their agreement to support my remarriage or joined them in opposing the remarriage.

* * *

Florence and Fred Littauer wrote a book entitled: *"After Every Wedding Comes a Marriage."* Everyone who dreams of getting married should read this book. It covers topics such as *"When Reality Sets In"*, *"How To Be A Pleasing Wife"*, *"How To Be A Pleasing Husband"*, *"How Can I Check My Ability To Communicate,"* and *"Build Up Relationships And Tear Down Walls."* Carol and I were quickly reminded that indeed, a marriage comes after the glitter and glamor of a wedding. Reality can set in hard, and quite swiftly.

The first dose of reality came when on August 20, 2009, less than one month after our marriage; I had my first seizure. We couldn't afford an extended honeymoon immediately after our wedding day so we had planned to tour New York City via one of the tour operators. The package we purchased included a ride throughout Manhattan, lunch in Little Italy, also in Manhattan, and an insightful journey around the New York Harbor on the circle liner boat for a close up view of Ellis Island and the Statue of Liberty. Everything was planned. I had come such a long way since I started seeing Dr. Haut, and my seizures had become infrequent under her care. But early that fateful morning, I had a seizure.

As I recovered, I noticed the panicked expression on Carol's face. This was the first time she had seen me in this condition. I began to think that she must now be sorry that she had married me. I was determined that I would not disappoint her; we would still go on the trip.

"Darling," she said. "How do you feel?"

"I'm ok," I said sleepily. "I'm ok. Don't worry."

"Are you sure?" she asked. "Do you think we should still go?"

"Of, course," I said, although I really wanted to sleep. I had to work to get myself together. Carol was really looking forward to this trip; she had put so much thought and effort into planning it. Furthermore, I didn't want to waste the money we had already paid for it.

"Darling, I'm depending on you to tell me how you really feel," she said with concern. "We don't have to go today. I can always call them to tell them we have an emergency. I'm sure they would give us back our money."

"Sweet, it's okay," I said. "I'm going to take a shower. We can still go."

"Ok, I'll fix some porridge for breakfast," she said and went to the kitchen.

I remember going into the bathtub and turning on the shower. The last thing I remembered was stooping to pick up the soap I had dropped. I don't know how long I was in the bathtub before Carol discovered me with the shower beating on top of my head. When she pulled the bathroom curtain I was seated in the bathtub with my back against the pipes. She said I was in a daze and stared unknowingly at her when she came into the bathroom. I can only speculate that I had had a seizure in the tub. Only God prevented me from fatally injuring myself. This time Carol ran out of the bathroom. I later learned that she went to call our marriage counselor for advice. When she came back, she held me and tried to lift me out of the bathtub. I was able to muster enough strength to lift myself. I felt lifeless and extremely tired. Carol wrapped me with a towel and guided me to our bedroom.

"Sam," she said. "We're not going."

It was clear that she had made the decision, and I slept until late in the evening. I visited Dr. Haut the next day, and she decided to change my medication. She placed me on 1000 mg of Kepra. I took this medication for a few months but I felt very drowsy and low in energy every day. I could barely make it through the day at work. At home, I was too exhausted to be with Carol; as soon as I sat down to relax, I would fall asleep. One evening, Carol said to me: "I want my husband back."

"I'm going to go back to Dr. Haut," I said, holding her to assure her that all would be well.

Dr. Haut said that the required dosage was 1000 mg daily. She was reluctant to reduce the dosage, but after a few months, she agreed to do so. She prescribed 500 mg of the medication and after taking the reduced dose, I started feeling more like myself. Dr. Haut required me to see her monthly for medication management. Flashbacks of the misery caused by past seizures frightened me. I prayed earnestly again for God to heal me completely of generalized epilepsy. I didn't want seizures to ruin my relationship with Carol.

Chapter 28

Dreams and Plans

"All that is gold does not glitter, not all those who wander are lost"
— J.R.R. Tolkien

Early in 2010, we started planning to reconnect to our roots, the countries where we were born. Carol had not visited Jamaica for over fifteen years so we decided that we would finally have our delayed honeymoon there at the end of June 2010. We settled on an exotic, all-inclusive resort in Ochi Rios, St. Anns, Jamaica. Following this, we planned to visit Liberia in the spring of 2012 even if we hadn't yet located my family. My co-worker, Andrew, who was also born in Liberia, was in contact with his family there. Andrew informed me that the country was developing, and that President Ellen Sirleaf-Johnson was doing her best to bring improvements. He also informed me that many Liberians were returning home and buying land, so if I were interested I should also buy land. I informed him that I didn't know where my family was and I didn't have the slightest idea how to go about buying land in Liberia. He assured me that the country was safe, and that I should visit. As he encouraged me, I started feeling more confident about visiting.

In spite of my prayers, on May 25, 2010, I had a near death encounter with seizures. The evening before the seizures, I had played a rigorous game of street basketball with Junior, and some of his friends. My relationship with him had greatly improved and we often played basketball or spent time talking with each other. Complete exhaustion coupled with two days of missed medication resulted in my having two seizures at home early the following morning. Carol called 911, and I was rushed by ambulance to the hospital.

While waiting to be seen by the doctor, I started seizing violently on the stretcher. Carol informed me that a female doctor jumped on the stretcher and skillfully injected me. Shortly afterwards, I fell into a deep sleep which lasted from 8 a.m. to way into the evening. The attending doctor spoke to Dr. Haut who advised the staff to admit me if I had a fourth seizure. Thankfully, I did not so they allowed me to return home that night. I don't know what afflicted me but, for days following, I just sat in our living room, staring. I only spoke to Carol if it was absolutely necessary; I had no appetite and had no interest in making necessary decisions. My anger became inverted.

The pressure at church was another matter. It strained our marriage and posed an even greater threat to its stability and future. The interpersonal challenges we faced as newlyweds, were merely irritating pebbles in our shoes; but the issues that we took home from church were as if mountain lions had jumped on our backs and we couldn't shake them off.

Those leaders and the few members who did not embrace our marriage, because they felt we had violated the teachings of the Church still seemed to view us as irredeemable sinners. This state of affairs began to resurrect feelings of exclusion and hurt, humiliation and dehumanization from my past. In retrospect, I see that the resistance and rejection I experienced had begun to deteriorate my mental and emotional health. Being at church was a constant and disturbing reminder of my painful previous marriage, of my life with the Kamaras, and of life in Liberia. And yet, I refused to be forced out of the church that had given me spiritual birth and a large, nurturing Christian family there.

Our marriage counselor repeatedly advised us to take a sabbatical from church.

"Go somewhere where your spirits can be refreshed, restored, and revived," she advised. "Sometimes we need the outworking of Psalm 23 and we need to know when the Lord wants us to lie down in green pastures so that he can restore our soul, our mind, our will, and our emotions. He wants to lead you beside still waters. Sometimes people come to appreciate you more, after a while. Stop torturing yourselves unless, of course, you feel that you are being taught some lessons through the fire."

Yes, we—Carol and I and the church—were being taught lessons through the fire. I strongly believed that the lives Carol and I were living at this point were meant to provide much needed edification to the church, regarding marriage, divorce, and remarriage. In light of this, I refused to run away.

During this time, Carol and I had some very heated arguments. Church was really rough for us during 2010 and 2011, and the issues began to spill over into our relationship and home. As time went on, I had begun to mistrust the leaders and became increasingly angry at them for ignoring and excluding us. Their treatment of us resurrected past thoughts and feelings that Uncle Henry had implanted in me. I saw their treatment of me as callous injustice. Initially, I was not aware of the depth of my reaction to what I perceived as a violent dismissal from the church that I had loved and served faithfully and sacrificially for over thirty years.

I became more convinced that I couldn't run away to another church. I had to confront unfairness, biases, rejection, and injustices at my church. I was tired of pleasing people. All my life, I have striven to please people: Uncle Henry, my ex-wife, my children, the church and others, while ignoring myself. All I got in return for my faithfulness to them were "whippings", wounds, and scars. I finally concluded that, from henceforth, I would please God only.

Carol is not a pacifist. I've seen her go to battle on a number of issues over the years that I've known her, but she didn't quite see eye to eye with me on several occasions. I appreciated her respect and regard for me in public. She never tried to humiliate me in front of others and, rather than express disagreement, she would remain silent. When we got home, that was another matter. We have never had a physical fight but we have had several serious verbal altercations. Carol is very skillful with words. She has given me some sharp verbal jabs that shook me up, but I've verbally slammed her, myself. In my anger, I've said things that hurt her. I've been belligerent and have repeatedly accused her of siding with the church people who had ganged up on me. She hated it, whenever I accused her of this. But sometimes when she spoke, it was as if she was pointing the same finger that the naysayers at the church were pointing at me. They accused me of having angry outbursts at inappropriate times, such as when the church was filled with visitors.

Tension kept building at home and at church as the conflict between me and the church festered. Having been "beaten up" for too long in my life, I decided, almost unconsciously, that I would now stand up for myself. I began to view the young assistant pastors as my persecutors, especially the spokesman among them. They had the power of the mic to come at us from the pulpit in their sermons and we just had to sit quietly and take it. On several occasions, I spoke out openly and strongly against unfair and undeserved treatment in the church.

Prior to our marriage, we had agreed to attend post-marital counseling with our marriage counselor. For us, going to see her was equivalent to going to see our medical doctor for routine checkups or to the dentist for a cleaning. These checkups with our counselor were often a lifesaver for our marriage. She was a prayerful Christian woman with a healthy sense of humor. She advised us to select a place in our home where we would argue, but not to let our marriage become an argument or a quarrel. She would listen to our disputes and speak the truth to us. Both Carol and I admired and respected her greatly; she had earned the right to rebuke us, call us out, embrace us, cry with us, and pray with us. We loved her. Her godly counsel, our prayers, and those of others, as well as our willingness to forgive each other, preserved our marriage. We instituted a "no-pretense rule" for our marriage, and we embraced principles of effective communication, prompt forgiveness, love, and tenderness.

Looking back, I ask myself, why did my marriage to Carol not fail? It got its share of vicious punches. What contributed to its survival during those difficult times? Various factors come to mind. Firstly, the Spirit of God and the Word of God are cornerstones of our marriage. Carol and I love and revere God. We are conscious of the grace and mercy of God and were determined not to take them for granted. Also we prayed for each other; privately, and in each other's presence. We were miserable when we felt that we were outside of the will and counsel of God.

The "no-pretense rule" that we had laid down for our marriage was also a stabilizer. We both knew that, in the privacy of our marriage, we could reveal the good, bad, and ugly parts of ourselves to the searing heat of scrutiny. We were able to journey to this point because we discovered that the only true way to genuine and passionate love is through being vulnerable with each other. This belief is supported by the Biblical statement in the Book of 1 John 4:18:

> "There is no fear in love; but perfect love casts out fear: because fear has torment.
> He that fears is not made perfect in love."

At first, being our unpretentious selves before each other was very intimidating. I was afraid of being rejected or taken advantage of. We were both afraid of the other's dislike. Nevertheless, we decided to take the chance to trust and believe in each other. The journey led us to a place of freedom from fear, and the knowledge that our love is deep and wide enough to cope with our imperfections. My imperfections are not greater than hers, and vice versa. This "no pretense rule" is a powerful formula for longevity in a relationship. For this formula to work, we realized that we had to strive to be our best selves. This demanded humility, the willingness to yield to each other, and to be willing, ready, and able to forgive each other's transgressions and failings.

Other factors that have contributed to the growth and stability of our relationship include: shared dreams, a shared mission, a shared calling to children, youth, and family ministry, shared leisure activities, attending events together, eating meals together (sometimes from the same plate), and shared bible study and discourse. Intimacy and lovemaking have a sacred place in our relationship. We make time for cuddling; we hold hands when we walk, laugh at and with each other, and call one another by special, endearing names. Also very important is our shared love for people, and our willingness to lend a helping hand wherever and whenever we can.

My advice to other couples is: love and please God and take the risk to be open, honest, and vulnerable with your mate. This is what breaks down walls and builds trust and intimacy with each other.

* * *

Carol and I intensified our search for my family. I remembered that Uncle Sam had stated that they were in a displacement center. Carol suggested that we try contacting the International Red Cross. We contacted the Red Cross in New York City, and they assigned me to a social worker. Her name was Bridgette Ames. I met with Bridgette in June 2011, to provide information for the search. She was very pleasant and supportive. Three days later, she sent me the following letter:

> Good Morning, Mr. Kamara,
>
> I have attached both of the tracing requests we completed on Tuesday for your review. I have submitted the case for

your uncle Samuel Wongan to our National Headquarters in Washington, D.C. who will then review the request and forward it on to the respective Red Cross or Red Crescent Society internationally. I will keep you updated as I receive further information in regards to this tracing request.

In regards to the trace for your uncle Philip Diah, I will keep the paperwork and submit it when tracing becomes available in the Ivory Coast. In the meantime, please contact me to let me know what the names of Philip's mother and father were (your maternal grandmother and grandfather). I had missed this detail in our conversation.

I again thank you very much for your time and truly hope we are able to assist in the search for your relatives. Upon reviewing the attached documents if you have any questions, concerns, or further additions please let me know.

Sincerely,

Bridgette Ames

Caseworker, Service Programs

Disaster Planning & Response

ì American Red Cross in Greater New York

Carol started browsing the internet daily, for hours. She searched various Liberian connections, websites, and magazines as well as establishing a Facebook page and email address for me. None of these efforts paid any dividends. I was beginning to think that the reason we couldn't locate my family was because they were among the over 200,000 Liberians who had died in the civil wars. There just could be no other explanation. After all, my coworker Andrew had been able to reconnect with his family. Then one fateful morning, Carol called me at work to say she thought she was onto something. In the course of our conversation the previous day, I had mentioned a radio station in Liberia called *Eternal Love Winning Africa* (ELWA). She had a strong feeling that if ELWA had been a popular radio station when I was a child in Liberia, it was possible that the radio station had survived the war, since it was located in the capital city. She followed that lead. Her internet search produced the name and telephone number of the radio station manager, Moses Nyantee.

When we arrived home from work that evening, we decided to call Mr. Nyantee. It didn't cross our minds that Liberia was in another time zone. Liberia is four hours ahead of New York City. When we called at 9 PM/EST, we didn't connect with anyone. The following morning when Carol called the number—Bingo!—she was connected to Mr. Nyantee. She introduced herself and related my story to him. He told her that there was peace in Liberia, and it was safe to travel to the country. Mr. Nyantee couldn't advise us where to look for my family but he offered to give me the chance to make an appeal on his radio station, to ask for information about my family. He gave us his email address to facilitate communication. I was ecstatic and could hardly stop shouting, "Praise the Lord!"

We considered traveling to Liberia in October 2011, but were warned by friends against doing so, since Liberia was in the midst of political campaigns. President Sirleaf-Johnson seemed to be successful in handling the reins of government and striving to promote economic growth. She was now in the middle of a very competitive campaign for a second term as president. Carol and I began to earnestly pray that the elections would be peaceful. The political climate in the country was very heated, and opposition parties had made several accusations of election fraud. However, the election commissioner and observers insisted that the elections were free and fair. When the run-off election was held on November 8, 2011, most people were confident that President Sirleaf-Johnson would be re-elected as president. This was confirmed on November 11, 2011.

I was preoccupied with thoughts of returning to Liberia. Each day I awoke with a special feeling of excitement, as if I had won a multi-million dollar jackpot. Our major concern was where we would stay. Although the war and elections were over, we had no idea how to find our way around the country. We didn't know which areas were most secure. Carol chose the Mamber Point Hotel, which was considered to be renowned. It cost more than other hotels, but we hoped that the cost meant that the hotel was secure. At last, the date was set; we would leave New York on Delta airlines on Thursday, April 5, 2012, and arrive in Monrovia, Liberia on Friday, April 6, 2012.

Chapter 29

The Road to Teahplay

"To get through the hardest journey we need take only one step at a time but we must keep stepping"
— Chinese Proverbs

Papa and Mama had set me on what turned into a very long and perilous journey. When I left the village of Teahplay at the tender age of seven, I carried with me their "half-baked" dream of escape from a life of abject poverty to find a better life for the family. They really had no idea of which path led to where. I carried their dream like the Olympic torch that travels from city to city before it reaches its final destination, but instead of leading me to a spectacular finish line, this journey became a maze through which I wandered for a long time.

The journey back to Liberia would be much like finding my way out of this maze. The day had finally arrived when I would travel back to where my life began. I hoped that I would find Papa and Mama again. The night before our flight across the Atlantic Ocean, I couldn't sleep.

"Sam, you need to sleep," Carol said sleepily. She had obviously felt me tossing and turning on the bed. I didn't respond to her because I wanted her to go back to sleep. She did, but in spite of wanting to, I hardly slept a wink that night. When Carol awoke, I was still wide awake.

"Sam, did you sleep?" She looked worried.

"Sort of," I said smiling. "I feel so excited. I can't believe that we're traveling to Liberia today. Remember to pack the camera and camcorder in our carry-on luggage."

"Believe it or not, we are on our way," she said as she got out of the bed. "We need to double check to make sure that we have packed everything."

"The most important things are our passports, the camera and camcorder," I said. "We can leave everything else, but we can't go anywhere without our passports."

"The passports are in my bag." She double-checked. "Let me go over the checklist." Carol has a habit of making checklists and to-do lists, although she has such a good memory. I sometimes wonder why she bothers to make those lists at all.

I was taking some money with us for Papa, Mama, and my brothers. We had decided that both of us would have an allotted amount to spend, without asking the permission of the other as to how to spend it. I was allotted more money than Carol, because I was hoping to find my family in Liberia and give them monetary gifts. The exchange rate in Liberian dollars increased our purchasing power.

We were scheduled to fly out of John F. Kennedy Airport at about 7:45 P.M. on Delta Airlines to Hartsfield-Jackson airport in Atlanta, Georgia. From there, also on Delta Airlines, we were to fly to Accra, Ghana, then on to Monrovia, Liberia. I was very eager to leave for the airport.

"Darling, are you ok?" Carol asked. "Why are you pacing up and down the apartment?"

"I guess I am nervous," I said. "You should start getting ready. We have to be at the airport by 5 p.m."

"Do you know the time?" I could hear the humor in her voice.

"It's 12 noon," I replied. "But you never know if we'll have traffic going to the airport. We don't want to miss our flight."

"We are not going to miss the flight," she said. "I think you should take a nap."

"You must be joking," I said. "Please start getting ready. I don't want us to be late."

"Sam, you're driving me crazy," she protested. "It's way too early for us to get ready for the airport. I don't want to go there and sit for hours."

I could sense an argument brewing so I decided to leave her alone. I had come to realize that Carol doesn't like to be rushed. Whenever I hurry her, she seems to move much more slowly.

Finally, at 4 PM, we left the house. Luckily, the traffic to JFK was light. When we arrived at the airport at 4:45 PM, we learned that our flight to Georgia had been delayed. The plane left JFK about 9 PM and we were on our way to Africa. All I carried with me were vague memories of street names and images of buildings from my childhood. I planned to use these clues to track down Uncle Samuel in the city of Monrovia.

My thoughts returned to memories of my trip from Liberia to the USA in 1972. At that time, my tears were tears of sadness and hopelessness. This time, my tears were tears of joy and great anticipation. I was going back to Liberia with the woman I deeply loved. She looked at me and squeezed my hand, as if she had read my thoughts and was assuring me that everything would be okay. I leaned over and kissed her.

After we left Atlanta, it took us about twelve hours to cross the Atlantic Ocean. The airline attendants fed us very well. We got dinner, snacks, breakfast, and lunch. I got up a few times to stretch and to go to the bathroom. The travel neck pillow that Carol had brought eased my discomfort and allowed me to sleep most of the night. When I awoke, we were approaching Accra, Ghana. After landing in Ghana, we were not allowed to disembark the plane, as we were continuing passengers. Looking out the window, I could see Africa, Africa where I was born; Africa which I had not seen in 40 years! We stayed there on the tarmac Ghana for almost two hours before flying the last leg of our journey to Monrovia, Liberia.

The travel time from Ghana to Liberia was only two hours, but how impatient I was to step off the plane and touch the ground in Africa, to set foot once more on the soil of my beloved Liberia. At last, on Friday, April 6, 2012, at about 4 P.M. Monrovia time, we arrived in the capital city. When the plane landed on the tarmac, my heart started racing. Finally! As we disembarked, Carol and I stopped on the steps, when one of the ground crew offered to take our photos. I was so thrilled that all I could do was grin like a Cheshire cat. I felt like leaping and shouting Hallelujah, but I managed to keep from making a spectacle of myself. A shuttle bus picked us up on the tarmac and drove us to the airport building.

The airport building was small and plain-looking compared to the large, sophisticated terminals at modern airports in the USA. After we cleared Liberian immigration, we were picked up by the hotel shuttle bus and taken to the Mamber Point Hotel. When we arrived, we found security at the gate, which justified the higher cost of staying there for us. After we checked in, hotel attendants took our bags and led us to our rooms. It was late in the evening and since we had been advised that it was unsafe to walk around the city alone at nights, we decided to watch TV in bed.

After eating breakfast the following morning, which was a Saturday, we contacted Mr. Nyantee by telephone. A very pleasant man who laughed a lot, he invited us to meet him at the ELWA radio station compound. When we got there, he greeted us as if we were his long-lost relatives. Then, he led us into his office. He told us that a young man who worked in the radio station was also from the Gio tribe. This young man was from a village near Teahplay. The young man entered the office as Mr. Nyantee was speaking.

"Hi, Manker," Mr. Nyantee said. "Meet Sam and Carol. These are the people I was telling you about."

"Hi. Nice to meet you," he responded with a very thick Liberian accent. A Gio brother! Though his accent was thick, I was thrilled to hear it.

"I was telling them that you're from the Gio tribe," Mr. Nyantee continued. "I told Sam that I would let him go on the airwaves and make an appeal to find his family."

No one spoke. All eyes were focused on Mr. Nyantee.

"But as I discussed with you," he continued. "I told them that you might be willing to take them to Teahplay."

"Yeah, I'm from the Gio tribe," Manker said. "My village is near Teahplay, but I have not been to Teahplay in years."

"Can you take us to Teahplay?" I asked quickly. This was a unique opportunity. We had only been in Liberia for a few hours and already things seemed to be falling into place.

"Yes, I can take you," he replied. It had been so long since I had heard the Liberian accent that I had to listen carefully in order to understand him, and realized that I had lost nearly all of my own accent. "I have a jeep so you won't have to pay me," he told us. "You just have to buy the gas."

Of course, we agreed and made arrangements to leave Monrovia very early the following Monday morning.

Manker connected us with his friend, who operated a taxi service. He was a native of Liberia, so he was very familiar with the streets and areas that I wanted to visit. Our first stop after leaving ELWA was a Seventh-Day Adventist Church where we visited their children's ministry service and later attended the adult worship. We were given a warm welcome and an invitation to return.

The Adventist Church where I had attended school as a child looked very different now. It was a bigger more modern building. I pulled out my list of places and streets that I wanted to visit, eager to share this part of my past with my darling wife. But we couldn't locate the house where I had lived with Uncle Henry; neither could we locate the grade school that I had attended. The Ducor International Hotel, which was once one of the most spectacular buildings in Monrovia, was now a burnt out shell, riddled with bullet holes. The Executive Mansion, meant to be the home of the President of Liberia, was still there, but it was not being occupied by President Sirleaf-Johnson due to a fire that had gutted the building in July 2006. The Liberian Supreme Court was still standing. Bullet holes and dilapidated buildings still gave testimony to the civil wars that had ravaged the country.

We got out of the car and strolled along various streets, such as Broad Street, Water Street, Gurley Street, and Tubman Boulevard. The names were familiar but everything looked different. The roads were much better than when I left in 1972. Our next mission was to search for Uncle Sam, who had been a solider in the Liberian Army. When we arrived at the army barracks, we were told that he was no longer in the army. The personnel at the retirement home for retired soldiers, to which we were directed, informed me that my uncle had returned to Teahplay.

* * *

"Darling, this is it," Carol said to me on Monday morning as she closed the small "carry-on" suitcase with the clothes and toiletries we would need for our journey to Teahplay.

"I'm so excited." I was beaming. "I've longed for the opportunity to return to Teahplay since I left Liberia in 1972 but I can't believe it's finally happening, that I will see Papa and Mama and the rest of my family again."

"Well, we've come this far and we are not turning back," Carol said, smiling mischievously.

"I'm taking some money with me for my parents," I told her. "I also have the camera and camcorder with me. We have to get some great shots!"

"That's fine with me," she said. "Just make sure that we have enough left to pay for this expensive hotel, buy our meals, and take a cab back to the airport."

"We have enough," I assured her as I placed our travel documents and other valuables in the hotel's safe. "Don't worry about that. I won't leave us stranded."

The thought of seeing Papa and Mama again made me feel tense.

"Sweet, make sure we have all we need for the two next days," I said. "I don't think we will find shops in the village."

"Don't worry," she assured me as she guided me toward the door.

Manker, our driver, was leaning against his white Ford Explorer as he waited patiently for us in the parking lot.

"Good morning," he greeted us as we approached his vehicle.

"Good morning," we replied. A cool breeze from the Atlantic Ocean was blowing. "Thanks for this big favor," I said as I shook his hand. "We really appreciate it."

"You're welcome," Manker replied, as he helped us with our bags. "I'll need to stop for gas. We need to fill the tank and these two plastic bottles." He had two large five-gallon plastic bottles in the back of his vehicle.

"Why do we need to buy extra gas?" Carol asked. "Can't we just buy it at a gas station on the way?"

"That would be a good idea." Manker laughed. "But the next gas station after this one is hours and hours away. We would run out of gas before we reached it."

After filling up and buying bottled water, we were on our way. We carried crackers and canned tuna that we had brought with us from the USA. Knowing that Liberians often eat large snails and bush meat such as deer, monkeys, porcupines, chimpanzees, groundhog, large field rats, and other animals that Carol is afraid of, she had decided that we should take our own food. If we ran out of the food we carried, she was prepared to fast until we got back to Monrovia. Growing up in Liberia, I had eaten some of these meats. It is no different than eating the meat of goats, pigs, sheep, and cows.

We drove from Monrovia, which is in Monserrado County, to Bong County. Along the way, we saw shabbily dressed children, often only partially clothed and walking barefoot or in flip-flops. Some adults were selling coal, fruit, drinking water in plastic bags, or roasted corn. We stopped to buy roasted corn, mainly to satisfy my desire to patronize those small business people and Carol's desire to try the roasted corn. She claimed it reminded her of her childhood in the island of Jamaica. The landscape was littered with broken down or unfinished concrete and zinc houses. We saw water stations where people with large plastic bottles waited to buy water. At the borders of each county there were checkpoints, manned by soldiers dressed in green.

Manker drove in silence and mainly spoke when we chatted with him. I kept asking him questions about our country, and he readily supplied answers. After traveling for about seven hours, Manker drove into a small town that was crowded with vendors and buyers. He informed us that we were in Scalepea, one of the six districts in Nimba County. Manker suggested that we get out of the car to stretch our legs. While we were walking around in the market, he left us, and went to find one of his relatives who lived nearby.

I decided that I would buy some items for Mama.

"How much does this cost?" I asked holding a bottle of lotion. The vendor gave me a price, and I bought three of them, a comb, and other items.

"Carol, smell this," I said giving her one of the lotions. "Do you think Mama will like the scent?"

"Yes, it smells nice," Carol said. "I think she will like it."

Just as the vendor was putting the items in a bag, Manker returned.

"Did you buy something?" he asked.

"Yes, I got some items for my mother," I replied. "I can't wait to see the look on her face when she sees me."

"She will be happy," Manker said, smiling.

"Did you find your relative?" Carol asked.

"Yes, I saw him," he replied. "I also found a place for you to sleep tonight. The roads to the village are very bad, and it's getting dark, so it's best to rest until early in the morning. Then, we'll travel again."

"Ok, we will do whatever you say," I agreed. "You're our angel."

"Come with me," he said. We got back into the vehicle and he drove for a few minutes and then parked outside a gate.

"This is a guest house," Manker informed us. "They have a room available for the night. It's US$25. They have security and a generator."

"Where will you sleep?" Carol asked. "Are you staying with us?"

"Yes, but I will be sleeping in my car," he replied. His car was parked in the yard. He helped take our belongings to the front room of the house.

The house was made of concrete and had a verandah and a main door that opened to a hallway. On either side of the hallway were doors. Our room was the first door nearest to the entrance. When we entered the room, we noticed the modest furniture—a bare mattress on a wooden box frame, a small table, and a chair. A bathroom adjoined our bedroom. In it were a toilet bowl and a three-by-four-foot concrete area for bathing. There was no running water. Instead, there was a large plastic barrel filled with water, which we were expected to use for our baths, and to flush the toilet. Carol started inspecting the rooms and became quite alarmed when she saw the door lock.

"My God, Sam, what is this!" She pointed to a bent nail that, twisted in place, would serve as our lock. "This is not a lock! A child could open this door by pushing gently against it."

"Well, this is all that's available," I replied. "We'll be ok. Furthermore remember that Manker said they have security."

"Security? Where is the security?" Carol looked worried. "Sam, please, ask Manker where the security is, because I didn't see any security guard and they definitely don't have an alarm system here."

Carol was very disturbed. I knew she wouldn't be able to sleep if she was this worried, so I went outside to tell Manker about our concerns. Manker came into our bedroom to assure Carol that the place was safe.

"You'll be ok," he said. "You don't have to worry. No one will bother you. The security is on the verandah."

Carol didn't seem convinced. "Is he there now?"

"Yes," Manker replied. "He will be sleeping outside on the floor, across the entrance of the main door."

"Thanks, Manker," I said. "See you in the morning."

Manker went back to his vehicle. I pulled the door closed and used the large nail to latch it. Although she said nothing, I could tell that Carol was still nervous.

"Sweet, everything will be ok." I tried to assure her once more. "Let's pray and leave our protection in the hands of God."

The sheet on the bed didn't meet Carol's standard of cleanliness. Since we hadn't brought a sheet or pillow cases with us, Carol spread her clothes on one side of the bed and advised me to do the same. I told her that I was fine and lay down on the sheet that was provided.

"You're going to catch germs," Carol warned me. "Here use this to put your head on."

"I'm fine," I said refusing the T-shirt she offered me as a pillow cover.

We brushed our teeth, and just as we were about to get into bed, the light went out and the place was in total darkness. It was apparent that the generator that was running had been turned off to save fuel. There would be no light until morning.

"Jesus, what is this?" Carol said in a low, frightened voice. "Darling, do you know where our flashlights are?"

"Yes, stay where you are," I instructed her. "I'll get them."

I knew exactly where the flashlights were and was able to retrieve one quickly. Carol positioned herself on the small section of the bed where she had spread her clothes. I took the other side. In our prayers, we thanked the Lord for taking us safely, thus far, on our search to find my family. We also asked for protection for us and Manker through the night. After praying, Carol and I chatted about the part of our trip that we would face the next day. Manker had said the roads were too bad for us to travel at night, and we wondered how bad they were. We would soon discover that our image of potholes was nothing compared to what we would see in daylight.

Carol must have been very tired because she fell asleep in the middle of one of her sentences. I lay on the bed staring into the darkness. Sleep once more eluded me. Carol kept turning on the bed. The box frame was made of boards with no coil springs and the springs in the mattress seemed to be worn. It was dark, but I bet that Carol rolled onto the sheet she was afraid would touch her skin. I smiled at the thought, but didn't wake her. Sleeping on the sheet was not going to kill her.

Taking my seizure medication and getting adequate sleep is important to help me keep my seizures under control. But, I just couldn't sleep. Thoughts of reaching Teahplay and seeing Papa, Mama, George, and Mark kept flooding my mind. I found myself wondering what they looked like. Would I even recognize them? Would they recognize me? Had the village changed? I hadn't found Uncle Sam in the city. Would I see him in the village? What was the village like now? Did people still live in mud houses with thatched roofs? How bad could the road be? Was Manker exaggerating? Were there streetlights? How long would it take for us to reach Teahplay? Would Manker, in fact, be able to find Teahplay? He had said that he had not been there for many years. Would we be lost?

I couldn't wait to hold Mama in my arms and to hug Papa. I wanted them to know how much I still loved them. I wanted them to be proud of me. I had done it! I had learned to read and write and I had graduated from high school in the USA. Their lives would no longer be full of unmet needs and sickness. Their dream was finally about to come true. They wouldn't have to die in abject poverty, as Papa had feared they would. I had not discussed my thoughts with Carol, nevertheless, I was thinking of building a house for them in Liberia and providing for their care.

The dawn finally began to lift the heavy darkness of the night. Since I couldn't sleep, I decided to get dressed and sit on the lone chair to wait for the sunlight to stream into the room. Carol would be awake by then, since there were no black out shades here. As I waited for the sun to shine into the window, I started feeling profoundly sad. My efforts to withhold my tears failed, and I started to sob. Carol was awakened by my sobbing.

"Darling," she called to me. "Where are you?" As her eyes adjusted to the dim light she noticed that I was sitting on the chair and came over to me.

"Darling, what's wrong?" she asked with concern. "Are you okay?"

I didn't answer. I feared that the reservoir of my tears would break and I wouldn't be able to stop crying. She stooped and held my hands.

"Sweetheart," she said softly. "We're in this together. You're not alone."

"I want my mother," I said. "I want my mother."

I got up and stood in a corner of the room. Carol joined me and hugged me around my waist. She didn't speak.

"Oh, God!" I cried. "Oh, God!" I felt I was screaming. Carol held me closer. Again she said nothing.

"Sweet, I want Mama," I said, looking at Carol with my tear-drenched face. "I long to see Mama."

"I know," Carol said, trying to soothe me. "I know. We're going to Teahplay to see her. Thank God we've come this far."

I rested my head on Carol's and allowed the tears to roll down my face onto her head. Having her there with me brought me such comfort. At home, she often told me that whenever I hurt—even though I often hid it and didn't tell her about it—she hurt, and whenever I was happy, she was happy. At that moment, we were thousands of miles away, in Africa, but those words still rang true. I sensed that Carol understood that the pain I was feeling was raw. I don't know if she also sensed that I was also somewhat afraid—afraid of what I might find in the village. Were my folks back in Teahplay? Had my parents and I lost too many years? Mama had often been sick. What was the state of her health now?

We heard a knock on our bedroom door. At first, we didn't answer.

Then we heard Manker's voice.

"Sam, are you up?" he asked.

I quickly wiped my tears and answered, trying to hide any evidence that I was crying.

"Yes, we're up," I replied. "We'll soon be ready."

Carol looked at me with worry in her eyes.

"Darling, did you sleep?" she asked. I think she knew that I hadn't slept.

"I tried," I said. "I believe I got a little sleep. There was so much on my mind."

"How are you going to get through the day?" she asked. "Manker said we still have far to go, especially with the potholes in the roads."

"I have to make it, Sweet," I answered. "Let's get ready."

"Darling, eat something, please," she begged me. "No sleep and no food is not a good combination."

"I don't feel like eating," I told her. "It's as if my appetite flew away."

"I'm worried about you," she said. "I think you are existing on adrenaline."

"I'm glad that you're with me," I said as I embraced her. "I'm glad that you're by my side."

"I wouldn't want to be anywhere else," she said with that sweet smile that I love so much.

We packed our belongings. Carol placed the clothes she had slept on in a plastic bag—I wondered if she would ever wear them again—and we left the guest house at sunrise. As we travelled on the main road, we soon realized why Manker didn't want to drive at night. There were no street lights, and the narrow roads were filled with deep craters, not the little potholes that we sometimes see in the USA. Manker veered the vehicle this way and that to avoid getting stuck in one of the deep holes that gutted the roadway. I felt sorry for his vehicle. As we drove, I began to doze off but staying asleep was very difficult because of the rough terrain. Notwithstanding, my body kept trying to get some sleep. Manker had been wise to stop for the night.

We drove for about three hours before Manker stopped in a village named Blarley. The landscape that separated the villages we passed was forested, with a few zinc houses along the roadside. He got out of the car and called to a teenage boy, dressed in long pants, T-shirt, and slippers, who was carrying a notebook in his hand, as if he was on his way to school.

"Come here, youth," Manker said. "Do you live around here?"

"Yes," he replied.

Carol and I also came out of the vehicle and stood beside Manker.

"Do you know a village by the name of Teahplay?" I asked the youth.

"Yes," he answered. "I have family there, too."

"Wait a minute," I said eagerly, "Do you know a family by the name of Wongan?"

"Yes, I'm a member of that family," he said with a puzzled look.

"Wait a minute," I repeated my excitement mounting. "Do you know a man by the name of George?"

"Yes," he answered again. "That's my cousin."

"Your cousin?" I asked in disbelief. Was this really happening? "Does he have brothers?"

"Yes, he had two brothers," the boy replied. "The younger one died and the older brother is gone to America, but we don't know if he's dead or alive."

I couldn't keep quiet any longer.

"Well, this is he that you have heard about all these years," I said, grinning.

"Huh!" The youth was clearly shocked. There was no time for delay. I wanted to see George.

"Can you take me to see my brother, George?" I asked.

"Certainly," the boy said. "Let me ask my cousin to come along with us."

When he came back with his cousin—our cousin—I asked them about my parents. I hadn't asked about them before because I hadn't wanted to hear any bad news. Now that everything was going surprisingly well, I felt confident enough to ask.

"Are my parents still alive?" I asked slowly. "Are they in Teahplay?"

"Oh, yes. Your parents are still in the village," they said, looking at each other instead of at me.

My heartbeat was racing even faster. I couldn't believe my ears. How had Manker known to stop this young man? Why hadn't he stopped the people we had seen earlier? This must have been a divine intervention. We hurried back to the vehicle, joined by the youths. The one we had first seen was named Nelson and I can't recall our older cousin's name. Guided by Nelson and our older cousin, Manker resumed our journey to Teahplay.

The rough roads continued to be a major obstacle. After dodging numerous craters, Manker's vehicle fell into a deep hole in the road. This time the vehicle was stuck in wet mud, and the wheels merely spun. We tried putting rocks and wood under the wheels to gain traction but that didn't work. Manker put the vehicle in neutral and we pushed, but the vehicle refused to budge. Nelson took off his flip flops and went into the deep mud to put additional rocks and tree limbs under the wheels. Some men who were passing stopped to help us while Manker steered the vehicle side to side. With the extra manpower and favor from God, the vehicle finally lurched forward.

I felt happy. My dream of seeing Papa, Mama, and my brother again was about to come true. I felt sad that my little brother Mark was dead, but I had not been close to him, since I had left the village before he was born. I was more familiar with George, although time had also robbed us of the precious brotherly moments that we would have spent with each other.

"I can't wait to see Mama," I said grinning. "I can't believe I will see her again."

No one else spoke so I continued.

"I'm going to lie in her lap like I used to when I was a child," I said still grinning. "I'm not going to let her out of my sight again. I've waited so long to see her once more."

Should I let her and Papa stay in Liberia or should I bring them back to America with us? I wasn't sure, since I hadn't discussed it with Carol, but if I could, I would want to take them back with me.

When I stopped speaking, Manker and the young men started speaking in Gio. I couldn't decipher what they were saying to each other but I didn't think that was something that I needed to worry about. My dearest dream was about to come true. I would finally get to see Mama, Papa and George again.

Then Manker stopped the vehicle.

"What's wrong?" I asked. "Is everything ok?"

"Sam," Manker said slowly. "I have something to tell you."

"What?" I asked, not liking the seriousness in his voice.

"Are you a man?" Manker asked.

"Yes, I'm a man," I answered.

"Can you take shock?" he continued.

"Yes," I said slowly. "Why?"

"The brothers just told me what they told you," Manker said. He called them brothers because of our close tribal connections.

"What?" I said feeling confused and beginning to get upset with Manker.

"Won wo beah, won deh kon," he said in Gio.

"What's that?" I asked, now totally shocked and confused.

"It means 'what they say is not so'," he explained.

I was stunned. There was total silence in the vehicle. Manker was sitting in the driver seat, and I in the front passenger seat. I stared at him fiercely.

"Your parents..." he said without flinching, "...your parents are no longer alive. They're gone."

No words came out of my mouth at first. I felt dazed and figured that Manker and the boys were just playing with me.

"You're joking," I said sternly. "You got to be serious, man."

"No, Sam," Manker said. "I'm not joking. The brothers said they told you your parents were alive because they didn't want you to feel bad."

There was something unreal about Manker's announcement. I heard what he said but it was as if I wasn't there. I felt as if my thoughts were not mine, as though I was floating outside of myself. I was in the vehicle, yet I felt I was not there.

I wouldn't believe a word that Manker or those boys said. *"They're all lying and playing with my emotions,"* I told myself. *"This is a serious matter. Don't they realize how important this is to me?"* So far, Manker had proven himself to be an honest and serious person. I had no reason to doubt what he was saying, but I just couldn't believe or accept what he told me. I couldn't see Carol's face because she was sitting behind me, but I knew she didn't believe them either. We hadn't come this far to hear this.

Chapter 30

Heartbreaking News

"We all want to do something to mitigate the pain of loss or to turn grief into something positive, to find a silver lining in the clouds. But I believe there is real value in just standing there, being still, being sad."
— John Green

I sat in silence as Manker resumed driving to the village. He had barely started when we saw a motorcycle coming toward us.

"There is George!" Nelson shouted. "That's George coming. That's George on the bike!"

Hearing George's name woke me up and lifted my mood. I immediately became excited again.

"Oh my God!" I exclaimed. "Oh my goodness! Guys, please, please don't identify me. Let me see if George still remembers me."

Manker stopped the vehicle, and we got out. I went to the back of the vehicle where George had parked his motorcycle.

"Excuse me, sir," I said. "What's your name?"

"George," he replied.

"George?" I echoed. "Do you have brothers?"

"Yes. My younger brother is dead," he said looking at me. "My older brother left Liberia many years ago. He is in America someplace, but we've not heard from him for many years. We think he's dead or has forgotten about us."

"Do you have parents?" I asked eagerly. He was my brother so I figured he would know for sure if our parents were alive.

"Yes, but my parents are dead," he said.

"Papa and Mama are dead?" George's words hit me like a brick. Manker had been right. George stared at me curiously.

At that point, I couldn't hold back any longer. I thought of their years of labor and the part that they had invested in me. The drive of my heart was to give them a hug, and to let them know how much I appreciated their investment. I wanted them to know that their dreams were about to come true.

But now they were dead?

"Are there other relatives in the village?" I asked.

"Yes," he answered hesitantly, obviously wondering who this stranger was, asking him all these questions.

"You don't have to give me any more details of your family," I said. "It seems as if you don't know who you're talking to but this is Sam from New York, who came to look for you."

He stared at me and yelled, "No!" then said something in Gio.

"Yes!" I insisted. "This is Sam that came to look for you."

George looked confused and continued to speak loudly in Gio. He grabbed my arms and stared in my face, then fell to his knees and hugged my knees. Then he jumped up and hugged me so tightly that I could hardly breathe. After that, he ran and fell prostrate on the ground— his body stretched out so that his hands were flat against the ground. He seemed to be conveying news of my return to our dead parents and giving God thanks. As much as he was trying to hold back tears, George started bawling. He just couldn't believe that this dream could come true.

"Take me to the village," I mumbled. George was at a loss for words. The other guys around us said nothing. Carol was in tears.

"Take me to the village," I said more loudly. "I want to see my parents."

I didn't wait for his answer. I returned to sit in the vehicle. Carol and my two cousins climbed in, also. George, who was still shocked and overjoyed, squeezed himself into the backseat with the others and allowed someone else to ride his motorcycle back to the village. We drove for about thirty minutes more in silence. A feeling of heaviness pressed down on me. This was not how it was supposed to be.

"We're now entering Teahplay," Manker broke the silence

The rising sun had just chased the cool away. As Manker drove into the village, men, women, and children stood staring at our vehicle. Manker stopped and George and my cousins jumped out and started to excitedly share the news of my arrival. Some of the men had machetes in their hands as though they were going to the farm, women were busy getting ready for the farm, or were taking care of their families. Scantily dressed children and youths were sitting around. The word of my arrival spread like wildfire. The villagers didn't have access to social media, telephones, or radio, yet, Manker's vehicle was quickly surrounded by people who had heard that we were there. By the time we parked near the houses a crowd of people had gathered. Some of these houses were mud walled with thatched roofs, like the ones I remembered from my childhood. The others were more modern houses, made of cement with zinc roofs.

As Carol and I exited the vehicle, we were surrounded by the large crowd of people. The chief of the village gave the signal and men started beating drums, women joined in chanting and dancing. The beating of the drums was the villagers' way of sending signals of good news and celebration to nearby villages.

George spoke excitedly in Gio. We learned later that he was a quarter chief in the village, so he commanded the respect of the villagers. They formed a circle around Carol and me. It was then that I saw Uncle Sam for the first time. When he saw me he grabbed my hand and hugged me tightly.

"Welcome home!" he said. "Welcome home, my son!"

Uncle's words opened the reservoir of my tears. Carol hugged me in silence as the tears rushed out. I was oblivious to the crowd around me.

"Don't cry," Uncle Sam tried in vain to turn the reservoir off.

"I wish Papa and Mama were here to welcome me home," I said as I tried in vain to hold back the tears.

"Don't cry, son," Uncle repeated. "I am your father now. We are your family."

Uncle couldn't understand how hurtful his words were to me. He meant well but his words didn't console me, instead they pierced me.

"Let him cry," Carol responded to Uncle. "It's ok to let him cry."

Growing up in Liberia, I saw boys cry, not men. Now here I was a grown man bawling before this crowd of people. It didn't matter to me that they might have felt helpless or embarrassed by my tears.

"Please take me to their graves," I begged.

George uttered words in Gio, and then led the way to Mama's grave first. She was buried in the middle of the village close to the Wongan family house, whereas Papa was buried in a corner of the village, about a ten-minutes' walk away. The crowd stood in silence as George informed me that Mama had spent the years crying daily for me, she wanting desperately to see her eldest son again. Her happiest days were when she received news that a letter from me had been received, assuring her that I was okay. George informed me that they had never received any money from me to help Mama. That report hurt me to the core because I had sent money numerous times to our blood relatives to help her. She also never got money to buy the mattress she had asked me for.

"She would do anything to get to see you again," George explained in English. "Our mother talked about you to everyone she met. Everybody knows you."

My grief was too heavy for me to speak.

"We had little money, and no way to take her to doctor when she was sick," George continued passionately. "There was no way!"

It was as if I became mute, still no words came. George kept talking.

"Once Mama was so sick, and we had no means to take her to the nearest clinic," he continued to explain. "No means. You know what we had to do? Our brother Mark and me put her in a wheel barrow," he answered his question. "We went far, far to find a doctor for the old lady."

"Naar, couldn't take the sickness no more." George bowed his head as though he was now sharing my heavy grief. "Our mother died in 2004, just after the second civil war ended."

"When did Papa die?" I asked, still weeping.

"Our father died later," George replied. "Papa died from sickness and lack of proper care in 2008. Our brother Mark died during the war."

I felt ashamed and guilt-ridden that Mama and Papa had died in want and that they were not buried beside each other. If I had returned sooner, I would have been able to provide for them, and perhaps help them reconcile. Although Papa had returned to the village during the war, George told me that he did not, or wasn't allowed to, resume his honored position as head of the Wongan family. Whoever made the decision to bury Papa away from Mama obviously chose to underscore his estrangement from her.

I had returned with my hands full of gifts for my mother but I was too late. And my father never got to see the man I had become. A feeling of helplessness besieged me as I stood by the unmarked graveside of the man that had given me life. He would never know how hard I had tried. I did my best to carry the torch of his ambitious dream of a better life. But I couldn't make it back in time to help them escape the abject poverty that they had so desperately wanted to leave behind. Our expectations had crumbled and our dreams lay buried in the rubble. I had done my best, but my best had not been good enough.

"Mama talked about you all the time," George said gloomily. "Everybody knows about you."

"Did she?" I said eagerly. "What else did she say about me?"

"She cried every day for you," he said. "She said she wanted to hug you and hold you."

I stared at George, waiting eagerly to hear everything that Mama said about me.

"She said she wanted very much to see you again," he continued. "She said that if she died without seeing you again her belly would swell."

Life can be so cruel. Why couldn't my poor mother have had her greatest wish come true? Why didn't she get the chance to hold me, her first born son, in her arms again? Now that I was better able to help her live her dreams, why was she not here to enjoy it?

The warm welcome and excitement of the villagers made me temporarily forget my profound sadness. Since Papa and Mama weren't there, I planned to return to Monrovia later the same day. However, George and the other villagers refused to let us leave.

"You know you cannot leave," George said. "You have to spend the night with us."

"George, we have to return to the city," I replied.

"We're not letting you leave," George insisted. "You have to stay at least a night with us."

I consulted with Carol and she agreed that we should stay.

"Okay, George," I said. "We will stay the night."

When George communicated my response to the villagers in Gio, they let out loud cheers. They were smiling and jumping. I didn't know most of them but they "knew" me, because Mama had kept my name alive.

That evening we stayed at George's house. It was made out of concrete, with a zinc roof. There were still a large number of mud houses in the village, but George's house and others like it indicated that the villagers had experienced some "upward mobility". Other improvements to the village included a large space used as a soccer field and a dilapidated school building which had been built by the villagers. The school had no doors or windows, and the zinc roof had loose and missing sheets. From inside the school building, you could look up and see the sky. The inside had a dirt floor, with no chairs for the children to sit on, and a broken board to serve as a chalkboard. There wasn't a book or colorful poster in sight. This wasn't a place that inspired learning.

Since we had been persuaded to stay overnight, Carol and I decided to tour the village. The village still did not have running water or electricity. Notwithstanding, the presence of a water well with a hand pump in the center of the village and outdoor wooden latrines were more signs of upward mobility. When I was a child, we had to carry water from nearby rivers or streams, leaves were our toilet paper, and the bushes were our toilet. Two houses in the village now had generators; everyone else used lanterns or flashlights.

Throughout our day in Teahplay, the villagers gathered around us as if we were celebrities. Many of them did not understand English and so the few who did translated for them. I watched as George, Uncle Sam, and Uncle Sam's son, George, "overdosed" themselves with alcohol. My brother's eyes were red, and he kept staring at me as if he was seeing a ghost. I don't know if they were alcoholics, but they reeked of alcohol and they spoke excessively both in English and Gio.

The people either stared or grinned at us. I observed that the children's clothes were more modern. Many of the boys had on T-shirts, shirts, shorts, long trousers or briefs. None of them wore the *bombor* or loincloth that I had worn as a child. The girls wore dresses, although some of the older girls wore *lappas*. Most of the children wore flip flops, although others wore nothing on their feet. When I was a child in the village, no children wore slippers or shoes.

As evening approached, the women of the village set water in basins in the outdoor "shower room" for us to bathe. They also began to worry about what they would offer us to eat. They brought us a chicken and a goat. Carol and I couldn't decide what we wanted to eat so the women decided to kill both. Carol is used to her spicy and well-seasoned Jamaican food, and was afraid to eat the food prepared by the villagers.

"Darling, what kind of seasoning do they use here?" she asked me.

"I don't know, Sweet," I replied. "You'll know when they feed us, later."

"I don't think I want any," she said.

"Why not?" I asked. "Nothing is wrong with it. You can eat it."

"I don't know how they will prepare it," she said. "Will they wash their hands?"

"Stop worrying," I tried to assure her. "You'll not die. If you don't eat it, they will feel insulted."

Carol didn't answer, but I could tell that she was trying to think of a way to decline the villagers' meal without insulting them. When the dinner was ready, George's wife, Dorois, called us inside their dimly lit living room which was sparsely furnished with an unvarnished wooden table, two rough wooden stools and some photos on the walls. It had a dirt floor. George's wife uncovered the food that had been covered by a white lace cloth. There was a large bowl of white rice and two bowls of meat.

"Darling, you have to eat some," I whispered to Carol. "Just eat a little."

"Ok, I'll try," she whispered back to me.

Carol is so particular about what she eats and who she accepts food from, that I knew this was a difficult experience for her. She was probably thinking about the bun and cheese and crackers that we had brought with us. I watched as she put a spoon of rice and a small piece of chicken on the plastic plate. Both the goat meat and the chicken looked white. Like Carol, I relish the smell and taste of Jamaican curried goat and curried chicken. But the villagers were my people—this is where I was born and I would not be hindered from bonding again with them. As we ate, villagers crowded the room as though they were watching television.

"I am full," Carol announced aloud. I looked at her quizzically. She was obviously lying because she had only eaten the spoonful of rice and the chicken was still on her plate.

"The food was very tasty," she said to George's wife. This was obviously her effort not to insult the villagers. I just prayed that they didn't realize that she was lying.

"Yes, the food tastes very good." I joined Carol. "Dorois, you and the other ladies can really cook."

Just as I finished my comment, one of the women brought in another bowl. I had no idea what it was, since they had already given us the goat meat and chicken. Carol grabbed my arm.

"Sam, I just saw something move in the bowl," she whispered. I looked at her wondering what she was talking about.

"Don't eat it!" she continued to whisper with urgency. "What is it?"

"I don't know," I whispered back to her. Uncle Sam was sitting the closest to me so I decided to ask him what was in the bowl.

"Uncle, what is that?" I asked pointing to the bowl with the "new" meat.

"Oh, that," Uncle Sam responded loudly so that everyone could realize that I was asking about the meat. "It's snails. Eat it. Taste good. You liked it as a child."

Carol's eyes widened. Fearing that she would bolt out of the room, I held onto her thigh and whispered, "Don't move." She has an irrational fear of snails, lizards, and other reptiles. Whenever she comes in contact with these creatures, her behavior is unpredictable: she might either start running or screaming. I had to control the situation so that she didn't frighten or embarrass these poor people. I had to think quickly.

"Thanks," I said to the woman who brought the large snails. Then turning to Uncle Sam I said, "Uncle, I can't eat this, because I changed my diet."

Carol still looked frightened but she relaxed a little when I declined to eat the snails. As soon as we got up from the table, some of the villagers swarmed the table and started eating the food we had left behind.

We went back outside and sat on the make-shift bench in the

middle of the village. Again the villagers gathered around us. One of the elder tribal leaders addressed the gathering. He thanked me for remembering my people and for bringing Carol with me. The villagers sat on the ground or stood quietly. When the elder paused, they cheered. Other villagers expressed their delight with our visit. They listened attentively as I shared my story of life in the city in America, and the translator retold it in Gio. When I was finished, many of them shook my hand, hugged us both, and thanked us for remembering Teahplay. They kept thanking Carol for allowing me to come back to the village. According to one villager, other men from the village who had gone to America had married white women and never returned. Those who hadn't thought I was dead thought that I had married a white American woman who didn't want me to return to the village.

Shortly afterward, we heard the beating of drums and chanting. A group of dancers entered the middle of the gathering with palm leaves in their hands. I was fascinated by the creativity and energy of the dancers. A soothing feeling swept over my soul. It felt good to be with my people, again. I played with some of the children who gathered around and gave them candies. They were excited to get the treats. When I spoke to them, they mostly smiled but said nothing—presumably because they didn't speak English. It was way into the night, about midnight, when George finally asked the people to go home. We apologized to them and reminded them that we would see them before we leave in the morning.

I don't know where George and his wife slept but Carol and I had their bedroom. We used our flashlights to find our way in the room. Carol was concerned about the "lock" on the door. I told her that when I was in the village, the doors to the mud houses did not have locks and we were not concerned about break-ins or being hurt by anyone. Trust had obviously weakened in the village. Most of the houses had locks. The lock on George's door was a very small padlock. There was no way that that feeble lock could have deterred a prowler. The thief just needed to lean on the door and it would fall in.

The "bed" was a large, king-size wooden frame with wooden rails, no head or footboard, no mattress, and no pillows. We had a small bottle for Carol to use if she needed to use the toilet during the night. She was terrified of going to the outside latrine during the night, mainly because she was afraid of encountering a lizard or some other nocturnal creature. That night, Carol woke frequently; she kept turning over, as if she was searching in vain for a comfortable spot. I barely slept myself; I was itching all over and kept scratching myself feverishly. We decided that it wasn't the bed that made me itch but I might be having an allergic reaction to something I had eaten that evening. We both must have dozed off out of sheer exhaustion, because the next thing we knew light had begun to stream through the little window in the bedroom. We also heard voices outside. I peeked through the window and saw a group of people gathered there.

"Sweet, lots of people are outside the house," I informed Carol. "It seems that they are waiting to see us."

"Are you serious?" Carol peeked through the window. "Oh my God! Sam, you're right."

"I guess they didn't want to miss us," I said. "They came to say goodbye to us. Let's get dressed."

We really didn't have to get dressed because we had slept in our jeans instead of in night clothes. When we went outside, we were greeted by a crisp, cool breeze and a crowd of people who hugged us. Some people wished us well and asked us to come back. Others stuffed money (Liberian dollars) in our pockets, some brought us plantains, chickens, and even a goat. At first we tried to refuse the gifts although I knew that, by refusing their gifts, we were insulting and embarrassing them.

"Thank you, thank you," I said. "But we can't take these on the plane." The people refused to listen and kept pushing the gifts unto us.

"Take them," Manker whispered to us. "Take them. They will not be happy if you refuse their gifts. It is how we do it around here."

"But…" I tried to protest.

"...take them," Manker insisted. "You are insulting them; also they think life will be better for them if you accept their gifts."

I remembered that the giving of gifts to visitors was a part of the culture, but I also knew I had nowhere to put the plantains, the chicken, and the goats. Carol and I were staying at a classy hotel and Delta Airlines would not allow us to take these things with us even if we had wanted to take them with us.

"Manker, we can't take them with us," I insisted.

"Take them and when we leave, you can give them to me," he suggested. "I'll take them with me when we get to the city."

"Ok," I said with relief. "Thank you, thank you." I turned to the villagers, smiling. "Let me take that. Let's put it in the back of the vehicle."

The villagers who gave us the gifts were delighted that we took them. They kept saying "God bless you. Remember us." Some even asked Carol and me to take their children with us back to America, so that their children could give them a better life. We had to repeatedly explain that it was not possible. Some villagers gave me African gowns and Carol was given *lappas*. George gave me a gown that had once belonged to our father. Because I was our father's first son, George felt that it rightfully belonged to me. I immediately put it on. Having something that belonged to Papa was a priceless treasure. I wanted to wear it back to the city but decided against it. Carol suggested that I needed to wash it before wearing it.

Before we left, I asked to be taken to my parents' graves once more. Mama's grave was close to George's home. Her grave didn't have a tombstone. I stooped and touched the hardened dirt in silence. No words would be good enough. Everyone around me was also silent. My grief was profound, I can't describe the pain—it was so deep. I could feel Carol's arms around my waist when I stood up. She didn't speak. It was as though everyone was responding to an unspoken edict not to speak because this was a sacred moment—everyone except for Uncle Sam who broke the silence.

"Don't cry again," he said. "Don't cry. We are all here. We are your parents. I am your dad."

"Let him cry," Carol said to Uncle Sam. "If he wants to cry let him cry." Carol spoke softly but firmly and directly. Uncle Sam listened to her.

"Take me to Papa's grave again," I said.

We walked to Papa's grave near the jungle. They had barely buried him in the village. It appeared that my family had not fully forgiven my father for leaving the family when he did. I loved my father, and if I had been there when he died, I think I would have buried him beside Mama. I didn't cry at Papa's grave, but my sadness was as deep as it had been for Mama. I loved them both and will never forget them.

We got into the vehicle and Manker slowly drove out of the village. Many of the villagers would normally have gone to their farms early in the morning, and some children would have gone to the dilapidated school building, but on this morning many of them ran behind Manker's vehicle as it drove away from the village. I had surprised them with my unannounced, unexpected visit and now, within a day, I was gone again as suddenly as I had arrived. I gave the lotion and other items I brought for Mama to Aunt Mary, Mama's sister. The money I had brought for my parents I secretly distributed among George and other members of the family.

Due to the terrible state of the roads, the ride back to the city of Monrovia was rough and treacherous. Manker stopped at a small city to buy gas, and we drove for most of the day. There were no fast food or deli restaurants and no rest stops. The bushes were the only toilet until we got closer to the city and were able to stop at a market near the side of the road. The so-called toilet was made of zinc. Carol used it, and one of the ladies from the market had to hold the zinc door to keep it closed.

We arrived in the city at about 2 AM. that Thursday morning. The ride back had been exhausting, and we were starved. The hotel restaurant was closed, so a good meal was not an option. We decided to feast on bun and the cheese and crackers with water before preparing ourselves for bed. When we awoke, we lay in bed cuddling for a while before Carol sprang up to get the small video camcorder we had brought with us.

"Darling, this is so exciting!" she exclaimed. "I can't wait to see the photos and the videos we took when we were in Teahplay." She jumped back in the bed with the camcorder. "Do you want to see them?" she asked as she turned the camcorder on.

"How could you ask that question?" I leaned forward eagerly. "Of course, I want to see them.

We sat up in the bed and started looking at the videos. The videos were those we had taken before we left for the village. Carol started searching for the video chip with the scenes of me meeting George for the first time, our entry into the village and our time spent there. She searched the carrying bag. Then she jumped off the bed and started searching frantically.

"Sam, I can't find it," she said with a very frightened look on her face. "I can't find it!"

"What are you looking for?"

"I can't find the chip with you and George and the villagers."

"Are you sure you looked everywhere?" I said as I joined the search. "There is no way that we could have lost that chip. It had too much irreplaceable memory on it."

"Well, if you can find it, find it." Carol sounded a bit irritated with either herself or with me.

We turned the hotel room upside down but could not find the chip. Concluding that it was lost forever, and not wanting to pour my frustration, anger, and despair out on Carol, I went into the bathroom and started weeping. Life could be so mean to me at times. I finally had the joyous and long anticipated opportunity to return to Teahplay, now the only memories I would have would be the ones in my head. Now that the chip was lost, I had nothing else to remind me of the moment that George and I had embraced for the first time after forty years, nothing else to remind me of the good times I had had in the village, and of my trip to my parents' graves.

"Darling, please let me in," Carol said softly as she tried to open the bathroom door. I had locked the door because I had wanted to be alone with my grief.

I didn't answer her. Maybe I was angry at her for being so careless with something so important.

"Darling, I'm sorry," she said. "Please let me in."

She sounded as if she was crying, too. I know she didn't mean to lose the chip. After all, she had been so involved in helping me find my family and sharing the realization of my dream. She and Manker had dutifully videotaped everything and taken some photos. Of course she didn't mean to lose it. I opened the door.

"Darling, forgive me, please," she said, looking up at me with tear-filled eyes. Not knowing what else to do, we hugged each other and cried.

The pain of losing the chip cast a shadow on us for the rest of the day. Carol called Manker to ask if he had seen the chip. She remembered that he was the one who took the chip out of the camcorder because it was full. Manker told Carol that he had given the chip to her and she had wrapped it in a piece of tissue. Carol remembered putting the chip into the pocket of her jeans instead of putting it in the camcorder's carrying bag. She stated that she was trying to protect it and ensure that it wouldn't get lost, even if someone stole the camcorder.

We tried to put our profound lost out of our minds as our driver arrived to take us around the city. We wanted to buy some African fabrics and gifts for family and friends in the USA. I also wanted to visit more places that I remembered from my boyhood days in Liberia. We didn't see any fast food restaurants or diners in the city so we returned to our hotel to eat Jamaican cheese and crackers. Lunch at the hotel restaurant was too expensive and we were running out of money.

That Thursday evening, we had dinner with Moses Nyantee at the hotel restaurant. During dinner we thanked Moses again for helping us find my family. We chatted about life in the city, our trip to Teahplay, even politics and religion. Since we were scheduled to leave Monrovia the next day, Friday, April 13, for the USA, we started packing after we returned to our room from dinner. Our flight was scheduled to arrive at LaGuardia airport in New York on the evening of Saturday, April 14.

On the morning of our scheduled departure, we decided to visit a place called Paynesville, in Monrovia. Since our flight was leaving at 6 PM, I figured that we would have enough time if we arrived at the airport by 4 PM. William, our taxi driver, knew better and at 12 noon suggested that we leave Paynesville to return to our hotel. He suggested that we should arrive at the airport by 2 PM because that is when Delta started checking in passengers. William's suggestion sounded unbelievable. How could they start checking in at 2 PM for a 6 PM flight? I asked him how long it would take from our hotel to the airport and he stated that we needed an hour. I then assured him that we would have enough time. But I was wrong.

We arrived at the airport at 4 p.m. and were told that the flight was already closed. We were now stranded with no money and nowhere to eat or sleep.

"That can't be," I said as I approached the door to speak with the police officer at the door. The officer didn't wait to hear what I had to say before he answered my unspoken question.

"Check-in is closed, sir," he said. "No one else will be let in."

"But we have to leave today," I insisted. "We are on time, how can you close a flight at 4 PM when it is supposed to leave at 6 PM?"

"Excuse me," the officer said and closed the door in my face.

An uproar from other disappointed and angry passengers ensued. This forced one of the airline personnel to come outside to address us. He reiterated that the flight was closed and that we would have to go to the airline office in the next building to reschedule with Delta or buy a ticket from Air France. Since Air France had seats on their flight, which was scheduled to leave later that day, Carol suggested that we travel on Air France through Europe, and back to the USA. I agreed.

"What? $3,000!" Carol was in utter shock at the price quoted by the Air France personnel. "$3000 for one-way tickets? Forget it! We can't afford that."

We went back to the Delta counter to plead with the agent. She was a native Liberian working with Delta. She advised us that the next Delta flight out of Liberia would be on Sunday, April 15, 2012 and that we would have to purchase new tickets to reserve a seat on it.

"Sorry, but you have to buy new tickets," she advised. I dreaded what the price would be.

"How much is it?" Carol asked.

"It will be a total of $1000," she replied. "Do you want the tickets?"

"What choice do we have?" Carol handed her our American Express credit card.

The agent took the credit card without responding.

"The card is declined," she said shortly afterward.

Carol and I looked at each other in utter disbelief. The airline only accepted American Express cards. We had no money here. What would we do?

"What do you mean the card was declined?" Carol voiced our disbelief. "We used it a few days ago, here in Liberia, and it went through."

"I will try again," the agent said, not yet frustrated with our insistence.

I could read the look on her face after she tried again.

"I tried," she said. "The card was denied again. Do you have cash?"

Cash? I wished we had cash because we now had a desperate need. Where would we sleep the two nights that we would be stranded in the country? What would we eat? Most of the food we had bought from the USA was gone and we had left the rest in the hotel room. Without cash or a credit card that worked, we were desperate.

"May I use your phone to call American Express?" Carol asked the agent. That was the very least that Delta could do. The agent allowed us to use the phone. Carol was able to speak with an agent of American Express in the USA. She argued with the agent who confirmed that the card was declined because we had exceeded our credit limit. During our visit we had gone to the bank and taken US$1000 cash, on the credit card. We had to answer many security questions to verify that we were indeed the rightful owner of the card.

"What are we supposed to do?" Carol asked the agent. "We have been faithful customers of American Express for nine years. We are desperate! Can't you help us?"

The agent must have told Carol that in order to help us we had to make a payment on the account.

"I just explained that we are stranded in Liberia," Carol raised her voice. "All our resources are in the USA. We will pay when we return."

There was silence.

"You have to help us," Carol insisted. "We have to return to work in the USA on Tuesday, April 17. If not, we're going to be fired and we won't be able to pay any of the money we owe you."

Carol's last comments pushed the agent to action.

"Thank you so much," Carol said with relief. "We really appreciate your help."

The credit card agent agreed to allow us to charge $1000 on the card – the exact amount we needed for the tickets. She advised us to visit the Delta office on Saturday to confirm our flight and pick up our tickets. Now, the million dollar question was, where would we stay until Sunday? We were practically homeless in Liberia. I came up with a plan.

"We have to call William and borrow the US$200 we just paid him to take us to the airport," I said. "Then we can sleep in Manker's car in the the ELWA compound."

"Sam, I am not sleeping in Manker's car," Carol said sternly. "It is not safe; furthermore, I'm afraid of those big croaking lizards in that compound."

"Where are we going stay then?" I asked, irritated. "Those little lizards won't harm you. This is not the time for fear of lizards."

"You are so insensitive." She glared at me. "You have no regard for my feelings."

"Carol, put away that silly fear," I rebutted. "The lizards are running from you. They're not going to bite you. We have bigger problems."

"That's exactly what I'm talking about," Carol was getting increasingly upset. "I have a phobia, and you don't understand it."

"Carol I'm sorry about…" I started to say but she interrupted.

"A phobia is an irrational fear," she explained. "It may seem silly to you but it's real. When I see a croaking lizard, my reactions are automatic; I am gripped by fear. Can you try to understand that?"

"Ok, we won't sleep in Manker's car," I relented. "Now let's call William before he gets too far from the airport and doesn't want to drive back."

Luckily, we had not given away the cell phone we bought in Liberia. We had decided to keep it so that we would always have a phone to use when we visited.

"Hi William," I greeted him on the phone. "We have a big problem and desperately need a favor from you."

I explained our predicament to William but I didn't tell him that we needed to borrow the money we had just paid him to drive us to the airport. He quickly returned to the airport to pick us up. I wasn't sure what our destination would be. Only God knew. Anyway, I had to first tell William that we needed to borrow the money from him.

"William, we need to ask you a big favor," I said to him as he came out of his car. "We need to borrow the money that we just paid you."

For a moment I thought he was going to say "no". I think he was shocked by my request. He just stared at me without uttering a word. I figured he must be wondering how these rich foreigners could be borrowing money from him.

"We will pay you back when we return home," I tried to assure him. "I will send your money to Manker via Western Union. I will even add something extra to it."

William reluctantly agreed to lend me the money. He must have had plans for it. Furthermore, he didn't really know us. How could he be sure that he would get his money back?

We drove in silence. Then, I realized that I had not called Manker to ask him for help. I also needed to borrow money from Manker. We needed a divine intervention because I had paid Manker on Thursday for taking us on our trip and had also given him money to fix his battered vehicle. What if he had used the money and couldn't help us? Uncle Philip, who lived in Monrovia did not have the conveniences to accommodate us. I uttered a prayer beseeching God to help us.

"Hi, Manker," I greeted him on the phone. "We have a big problem."

"What happened?" Manker asked concerned. "Why are you not on the flight?"

"We missed the flight," I replied. "We arrived at the airport at 4 p.m. but they told us the flight was closed."

"Oh, sorry," Manker said.

"We need somewhere to stay," I said. "…somewhere safe, with security."

Manker stated that he knew of a few visitors' lodges but he was concerned about security. Finding a place was one thing, having the money to pay was the other.

"I need to borrow the money I paid you," I said. "Our money was finished so I had to borrow back the money I paid William. I told William that I would pay him back when we return home. I would do the same for you."

Manker didn't hesitate to lend us US$200 so now we had US$400. Before we left the USA for Liberia, Carol had identified other safe and reputable hotels besides Mamber Point Hotel. That night we decided to stay at the Bella Casa Hotel. The price of a single room, single bed was $200 plus a fifty per cent surplus if two persons occupied the room. We didn't have enough money so we decided to beg the hotel agent for mercy. We explained our predicament and desperation. God was on our side, the agent took pity on us. Claiming that it was the only room she had left, she gave us what seemed to be the smallest single room in the hotel. Nevertheless, it was clean; we had a TV and a shower and a toilet with running water.

By this time, we were ravenously hungry. The hotel had a restaurant downstairs so we decided to go in search of food with the US$10 that we had left. When the waitress seated us and presented us with the menu, we realized that we didn't have enough money for a meal. We needed another favor. I explained our predicament again and emphasized how hungry we were. She said she would ask her boss to help us and asked us to wait. Carol and I whispered a prayer.

"I spoke with my boss," the waitress informed us. "He is going to help you. Give us what you have."

"Thank you so much," we said with relief. "Thank you so much, we will never forget your kindness."

I don't know if it's because we were so hungry, but the chicken and rice with vegetables tasted delicious. It was the best food we had eaten since we landed in Liberia. We had no money for breakfast so we asked if it was ok for us to come back for breakfast. It was either that or fast until we boarded the plane on Sunday and received some food from Delta. The waitress didn't seem to be someone with money but she offered to pay for our breakfast if her boss said no.

That Friday night, after saying a prayer of thanksgiving, we slept well in each other's arms. We went for breakfast at the hotel restaurant as planned, and received generous portions of scrambled eggs, toast, and fruit, with tea and orange juice. This time we were not taking any chances on missing our flight. We were the first ones to arrive at Delta's office, before they were even open for business. After receiving our tickets we went back to the hotel and decided to rest before going to walk around the city. We went to bed early that night and got up early. This time it was Manker who took us to the airport, driving his brother's vehicle. His Ford Explorer was still in the mechanic shop for repairs. We arrived at the airport at 12 noon, checked in and waited to board the flight.

Breaking Point: A Journey to Self-Awareness and Finding Purpose in Pain

Forty years ago, when I had boarded the plane with the Kamaras, I had been taken away against my will. This time, I was leaving my native land by choice. In fact, by this time, I was very homesick—for New York. I had been happy that I could return to Liberia and reconnect with my family there but I longed to return to the conveniences of life in the USA. I longed for the cozy bed I shared with Carol and the life we had there. Often in life, we imagine a connection with something in our past and then, when we reconnect, we realize that the connection is long gone and that our newer life is where we belong.

The reality of my parents' death still seemed unreal to me. Although George was the only sibling left, he was like a stranger to me. So much time had passed and we never did have the time together to develop a brotherly relationship. We had missed the opportunity to play together, to laugh together. We were strangers and needed time to build a trusting, brotherly relationship, to bond.

The decision to spend only one day in Teahplay had been made long before we had arrived there. I would have loved to walk around more, visit the farm where I had worked with my parents, visit my sister's grave, swim in the Nuon River where I had bathed as a boy, and enjoyed more of life in the village. But we didn't know whether we would find my family or what we might encounter. So, we had only arranged to spend a week in Liberia.

Carol and I decided that we would return to Liberia to offer a helping hand to the children and families who are living in the abject poverty that my parents tried in vain to escape. We will never forget the desperation we saw in Liberia. In this moment I felt reassured that the rest of my life would be spent with Carol and our marriage, which was already dedicated to God, and would be our sanctuary.

The flight over the Atlantic Ocean was long but welcomed. Carol and I held hands most of the time. It was as if words were inadequate to communicate our thoughts and feelings. Touching each other was our way of expressing our deep feelings for each other. The journey and experiences we had shared on this trip had already begun to deepen our love for each other, and strengthen the bond that we shared. Our bodies surrendered to our emotional and physical exhaustion and so we slept for most of the flight.

We arrived at LaGuardia airport in Queens, New York, the afternoon of Monday, April 16, 2012 and took a cab to our apartment – home sweet home!

(**Update:** A few months after we returned to NY Manker called to inform us that the video chip was miraculously found by someone in Teahplay! When we received it in the mail, it was not damaged.)

Sammy, Carol, George {brother} at family reunion in the Village of Teahplay

EPILOGUE

"The gem cannot be polished without friction,
nor man perfected without trials."
— Chinese proverb

December 12, 2012, I was honored for 35 years of exemplary service as an employee of the New York Botanical Garden. The ceremony was held at the famous Arthur and Janet Ross Lecture Hall at the Garden. As I sat in the lecture theatre with the other honorees, dignitaries of the Garden, other employees, and well-wishers, I reflected on all that had passed since the day I first started working at the Garden as a summer intern. I was now a senior maintainer in the Operations Department of The Garden.

The New York Botanical Garden played a critical role in my development from youth into adulthood. My abilities and talents were valued by the Garden and I took pride in doing quality work. I was also able to set an exemplary work standard and developed a reputation as a Christian with integrity.

How did I make it? How did I overcome the many obstacles in my life?

I believe that it was God who protected and preserved me. God provided this nurturing job environment for me with its security. Mark Cupkovic, current vice president of the Operations Department is a friendly, God fearing man who has been very supportive of me. When I shared my vision of starting a non-profit organization to help children and teens in Liberia who are affected by poverty and violence, he gave me constructive tips and advised me to consult with Mr. J.V. Cossaboom, Vice President of The Garden and Mr. Gregory Long, President of The Garden. Both Mr. Long and Mr. Cossaboom gave me great insight and continue to support the development of *Reaching Out to Children with Kindness* (R.O.C.K), www.RockReachesOut.org the non-profit that Carol and I started in September 2012.

Earlier in this book I quoted Soren Kierkegaard, the Danish philosopher and theologian who made an insightful commentary about awareness when he said: *"We live life forward, but we only understand it backward"*. We live our lives from birth to death yet it is only in hindsight, after the fact, that we see what we *should* have done, the stupid mistakes we made, the heartbreaks we could have avoided, and ways in which we chose wisely or unwisely. It is often true that, when we look back every now and then at our lives, we begin to understand our experiences. It is in the rearview mirror of self-reflection that we sometimes discover our blind spots and destructive, ineffective, default behaviors. I also identified my strong need for significance; the strong need to be acknowledged, regarded and accepted.

Having been hurt, neglected, and rejected so often in life, I can now see where that trauma affected every area of my life. I have come to realize that I needed to face the fact that my anger was tied to my pain. I had never looked this pain and anger boldly in the face and acknowledged it. I had never really dealt with the loss of innocence, the loss of opportunities, the loss of connection with my biological family, the loss of my biological parents, the loss of my foster parents, the loss of my "place" in the ministry in the church, or the loss of my marriage to my first wife.

Carol and I often reflect on the response of the leadership and the members of our church who disagreed with our marriage and resisted it, or retaliated against us. Some of our memories still carry a bit of pain but we are now able to laugh and forgive. We also reflect on the concept and value of "Adaptive Leadership".[xi] Adaptive leadership necessitates change, and change is very often viewed as an unwelcomed guest, especially in legalistic and inflexible collectivist environments, where individuals insist on maintaining the status quo at all costs.

My marriage to Carol presented our church with an adaptive challenge. This challenge was perceived as a technical problem. The authorities and some members "pulled out" the church's standard operating manual which stipulates: "This church does not believe in divorce and remarriage, except for the case of sexual immorality or when a non-Christian spouse leaves." In the absence of adaptive leadership, the authorities of the church employed one technical fix after another which only led to social sanction, a high degree of rejection, resentment, gossip about our character and integrity, negative attitudes of members toward each other, disconnection, and a worsening of the conflict.

Adaptive leadership leads to change. That is the problem with adaptive leadership. It points to unchartered waters; it generates uncertainty and can be downright risky. Heiftz (2002: Chapter 1) points to the perils of change: "people cannot see at the beginning of the adaptive process that the new situation will be any better than the current condition. What they see clearly is the potential for loss." The significance of this observation, hit me when I thought about my marriage to Carol. No one in the history of our church ever got divorced and remarried and stayed in the church. Our life change was like a seismic earthquake that signaled a threat to the dogma that the church had already decided was "*so*". It also signaled a loss of certainties and the special regard that they had for us. How should they now respond to us? It appears that, from their perspective, we moved from being faithful and sweet, law-abiding Christians to backsliding adulterers who were bound for hell. How could they still love us?

Understanding the concept of adaptive leadership is helping me to be more empathic, especially toward the leaders of my church.

Both adaptive leadership and power giving leadership involve 'heart-pounding' risks. In a church that has a low tolerance for uncertainty and ambiguity, adaptive challenges are scary. Challenging people to reexamine and change long held beliefs, values, and attitudes is dangerous because individuals can become quite hateful, vindictive, and vicious.

Nevertheless, Carol and I give thanks that our church was able to embark on the risky road of reconciliation with us. I spent 2014 trying to "mend fences" with both leaders and members. In April 2014, our church leaders convened a special mediation retreat. The mediation was moderated by an outside independent person who is both a pastor and a lawyer. The process has been difficult and slow but important work is being done.

Like all other churches, my church has embedded norms and values that are closely guarded. All organized groups or communities operate this way and can feel threatened when these embedded norms and values are disturbed. I believe my church leadership, members, Carol, and I have been tried "by fire" and so far, we have survived. We have all been changed in various ways by the challenge to forgive each other as God has forgiven us. We struggled, but I believe we have learned some important lessons along the way.

My church is not perfect but I love my imperfect church with all its warts and pimples. We have our challenges but we have some wonderful people there. It is a community that is going through metamorphosis, and will one day emerge as a beautiful butterfly.

The Prophet Joel in the Hebrew Scriptures dispenses a very important message to a people who have suffered: *"And I will restore to you the years that the locust hath eaten, the cankerworm, and the caterpillar, and the palmerworm, my great army which I sent among you"* *(Joel 2:25-KJV).* The Book of Joel outlines a very important motif in the Christian Bible – the LORD's message of judgment and the hope of repentance and restoration. This has been my reality, for God continues to establish the theme of restoration in my life. God has brought healing to my emotions and spirit. He has brought health to my body. I have not had a single seizure in over four years. My generalized epilepsy condition is under control! In fact, I have gone from visiting my neurologist monthly, to once a quarter, and now, annually. I have a renewed sense of purpose and self-worth. I enrolled in classes at Bronx Community College and earned credits that I will use toward my pursuit of a degree in history and practical theology. This renewed academic journey has also led me to studies at New York Theological Seminary.

God has given Carol and I an enviable and priceless opportunity to share a deep and enduring love and regard for each other. We are still deeply in love and we find such joy in laughter and helping others. We are able to find humor in experiences that caused us pain. My journey to even greater awareness continues. This time, I am poised and ready for new exploits, new experiences, new and deeper joys, and I intent to work harder to help others in need. As I journey, I find peace and reassurance in the words of the Hebrew Prophet Isaiah (Isaiah 61):

The Year of the LORD's Favor

"The Spirit of the Sovereign Lord is on me,
    because the Lord has anointed me
to proclaim good news to the poor.
He has sent me to bind up the brokenhearted,
    to proclaim freedom for the captives
    and release from darkness for the prisoners,
2   to proclaim the year of the LORD's favor
    and the day of vengeance of our God,
to comfort all who mourn,
3   and provide for those who grieve in Zion—
to bestow on them a crown of beauty
    instead of ashes,
the oil of joy

instead of mourning,
and a garment of praise
instead of a spirit of despair.
They will be called oaks of righteousness,
a planting of the LORD
for the display of his splendor.

4 They will rebuild the ancient ruins
and restore the places long devastated;
they will renew the ruined cities
that have been devastated for generations.
5 Strangers will shepherd your flocks;
foreigners will work your fields and vineyards.
6 And you will be called priests of the LORD,
you will be named ministers of our God.
You will feed on the wealth of nations,
and in their riches you will boast.

7 Instead of your shame
you will receive a double portion,
and instead of disgrace
you will rejoice in your inheritance.
And so you will inherit a double portion in your land,
and everlasting joy will be yours.

8 "For I, the LORD, love justice;
I hate robbery and wrongdoing.
In my faithfulness I will reward my people
and make an everlasting covenant with them.
9 Their descendants will be known among the nations
and their offspring among the peoples.
All who see them will acknowledge
that they are a people the Lord has blessed."

10 I delight greatly in the LORD;
     my soul rejoices in my God.
   For he has clothed me with garments of salvation
     and arrayed me in a robe of his righteousness,
   as a bridegroom adorns his head like a priest,
     and as a bride adorns herself with her jewels.
11 For as the soil makes the sprout come up
     and a garden causes seeds to grow,
   so the Sovereign Lord will make righteousness
     and praise spring up before all nations."

* * *

"The work begins with self-awareness. Self-awareness turned on the switch so I could see where to walk, what to regret, what to embrace, understand the wound and allow myself to heal."
— UnKnown

Sammy and Gregory Long,
President NY Botanical Garden

Mark Cupkovic, Vice President, and Sammy at
the NY Botanical Garden Awards Ceremony

Sammy with his Award gifts for 35 years of
distinguished services to the NY Botanical Garden

Appendix

Finding Purpose in Pain

"For I am about to do something new. See, I have already begun! Do you not see it? I will make a pathway through the wilderness. I will create rivers in the dry wasteland."
— Isaiah 43:19 (New Living Translation)

ROCK is a faith-based, humanitarian public charity that helps children and teens who are affected by poverty and violence. We do so by helping to meet their need for nutrition, shelter, education, healthcare, spiritual formation and leadership development. The mission includes a partnership with the Almighty Arms Children's ministry in Monrovia, Liberia.

Reaching Out to Children with Kindness (Inc.)

ROCK PRESS
"Transformative Words & Deeds"
www.RockReachesOut.org
reachingouttochildren@yahoo.com
www.facebook.com/ROCKreachesout

Returning to my native land was a dream come true. But it was a mixed blessing. Some days, the memory of this trip still floods my mind and causes me to shed tears. Not being able to see my biological parents again sometimes still depresses me. Nevertheless, I've determined that I will work to preserve the memory of their spirit and work. My biological as well as my foster parents – loved and cared for people, especially children.

Carol and I were moved by the desperation we encountered in Liberia. The plight of the majority of the children of Liberia is dire. They are forced to endure the harsh realities of abject poverty – lack of food, poor shelter, little or no education, lack of health care, and they seem destined to remain in the lower class of the society.

Our life's vocation is to minister to and help to meet the needs of children, youths, and their families. We could not erase the images of the many children we saw without shoes, without adequate food, or clothes. Many of these children had lost their parents to civil war or AIDs. We started praying for guidance about how we could become a part of the solution to help those children who are affected by poverty and violence.

Shortly after our return from Liberia in April 2012, we decided to start a nonprofit foundation. Carol got the inspiration to name the organization: *Reaching Out to Children with Kindness – R.O.C.K.* She had recently graduated from the Fordham University Center for Nonprofit Leaders Executive Education Program which trains participants in all aspects of nonprofit leadership, including strategic planning, finance, fundraising, grant writing, public relations, personal communications, and much more. As a part of the program, she was assigned a mentor—Dr. Jeremy Kohomban, President and Chief Executive Officer of The Children's Village and The Institute's Center for Child Welfare Research at the Children's Village Institute in New York. Jeremy provided the valuable guidance and advice we needed.

Carol and I contacted a lawyer to seek advice about incorporating

ROCK so that we could solicit donations independently. ROCK was incorporated in New York State in June 2012. A launching ceremony was held on September 14, 2012, to announce and broadcast its mission and vision. In December 2014, ROCK became recognized by the USA Internal Revenue Service as a tax-exempt public charity organization.

Tax-deductible Donations to the mission of
ROCK can be made as follows:
By check – payable to ROCK, Inc.
986 East Gun Hill Road
Bronx, New York 10469

Or online
Via Paypal at www.rockreachesout.org

Children eating dinner
Dinner-time at the Almighty Arms Children's Orphanage in Monrovia Liberia

Sammy Kamara with children from the
Almighty Arms Children's Orphanage in Monrovia, Liberia

ENDNOTES

Chapter 1

i   Those from the Caribbean are predominantly from the Congo. (source of information on ethnic the population: www.tulane.edu/~internut/Countries/Liberia/liberiaxx.html).

Chapter 8

ii   Executive Mansion, 'Presidential Papers – Documents, Diary and Record of Activities of the Chief Executive', First Year of the Administration of President William R. Tolbert, Jr., July 23, 1971-July 31, 1972 (Monrovia).

iii   Executive Mansion, 'Presidential Papers – Documents, Diary and Record of Activities of the Chief Executive', Second and Third Years of the Administration of President William R. Tolbert, Jr., August 1, 1972-July 31, 1973 and August 1, 1973-July 31, 1974; (Monrovia 1975).

Chapter 11

iv   People's Redemption Council (PRC) - After the coup Doe assumed the rank of general and established a People's Redemption

Council (PRC) composed of himself and 14 other low-ranking officers to rule the country. Doe suspended the nation's constitution until 1984, when a new constitution was approved by referendum. (Britanica.com)

Chapter 15

v   Read more: Charles Taylor Biography (Political Leader/ President of Liberia) | Infoplease.com http://www.infoplease.com/biography/var/charlestaylor.html

Chapter 16

vi   http://wonderland1981.wordpress.com/2012/06/06/the-last-day-on-earth-for-liberian-president-samuel-k-doe/
The Liberian Civil War – Mark Husband Liberia – America's Stepchild. Retrieved from https://youtu.be/94j2DMWCErg on June 25, 2012.
Wikipedia articles on Samuel Doe and Liberia.
Google searches and various photo sites.

Chapter 18

vii   TimeRime.com

Chapter 19

viii   Fadiru B. Koroma, Freetown, Sierra Leone, *War in Liberian Threatens to Destabilize the Region*, Aug. 14, 2002

Chapter 21

ix http://www.youtube.com/watch?v=sOoR1Ta_4Nc

x http://video.pbs.org/video/2155873888/ or purchase the DVD on Amazon.com

Epilogue

xi The Practice of Adaptive Leadership: Tools and Tactics for Changing Your Organization and the World by Ronald Heifetz, Alexander Grashow and Marty Linsky